Virginia Woolf

To the Lighthouse

A CASEBOOK

EDITED BY

MORRIS BEJA

M

MACMILLAN

First published 1970
7th reprint 1990

Published by
MACMILLAN EDUCATION LTD
Houndmills, Basingstoke, Hampshire RG21 2XS
and London
Companies and representatives
throughout the world

Printed in Hong Kong

ISBN 0–333–03689–1

CONTENTS

Acknowledgements   7

General Editor's Preface   9

Introduction   11

Part 1: *Background and First Reviews*

Three Portraits of Leslie Stephen

   F. W. MAITLAND, p. 35 – NOËL ANNAN, p. 36 –
   VIRGINIA WOOLF, p. 50

The Writing and Reception of *To the Lighthouse*

   VIRGINIA WOOLF, p. 56 – LEONARD WOOLF, p. 65 –
   VIRGINIA WOOLF, p. 66 – TIMES LITERARY SUPPLE-
   MENT, p. 73 – CONRAD AIKEN, p. 76 – LEONARD
   WOOLF, p. 80

Part 2: *Studies*

WILLIAM TROY: Virginia Woolf and the Novel of
  Sensibility   85

DAVID DAICHES: The Semi-transparent Envelope   90

ERICH AUERBACH: The Brown Stocking   105

JAMES HAFLEY: The Creative Modulation of
  Perspective   133

NORMAN FRIEDMAN: Double Vision in *To the*
  Lighthouse   149

JOSEPH L. BLOTNER: Mythic Patterns in *To the*
  Lighthouse   169

SHARON KAEHELE and HOWARD GERMAN: *To the Lighthouse*: symbol and vision   189

MORRIS BEJA: Matches Struck in the Dark: Virginia Woolf's moments of vision   210

JEAN GUIGUET: *To the Lighthouse*   231

Select Bibliography   246

Notes on Contributors   249

Index   251

ACKNOWLEDGEMENTS

F. W. Maitland, *The Life and Letters of Leslie Stephen* (Gerald Duckworth & Co. Ltd); Noël Gilroy Annan, *Leslie Stephen: his thought and character in relation to his time* (MacGibbon & Kee and Harvard University Press); Virginia Woolf, 'Leslie Stephen' and 'Modern Fiction' (*Collected Essays*) and extracts from *A Writer's Diary* (copyright 1953, 1954 Leonard Woolf) and Leonard Woolf, *Sowing: an autobiography of the years 1880–1904* and *Downhill All the Way: an autobiography of the years 1919–1939* (copyright © 1967 by Leonard Woolf) (Mr Leonard Woolf, The Hogarth Press Ltd and Harcourt, Brace & World Inc.); *Times Literary Supplement*, 5 May 1927 (Times Newspapers Ltd); Conrad Aiken, 'The Novel as a Work of Art', from *Collected Criticism* (copyright © 1935, 1939, 1940, 1942, 1951, 1958 by Conrad Aiken) (Mr Conrad Aiken and Oxford University Press); William Troy, 'Virginia Woolf and the Novel of Sensibility' (the estate of William E. Troy and Rutgers University Press); David Daiches, *Virginia Woolf* (copyright New Directions, © 1942, 1963) (David Daiches and New Directions); Erich Auerbach, *Mimesis: the representation of reality in Western literature*, translated by Willard R. Trask, pp. 525–41, 546–53 (Princeton University Press); James Hafley, chapter IV of *The Glass Roof: Virginia Woolf as novelist* (University of California Press); Norman Friedman, 'Double Vision in *To the Lighthouse*' from *English Literary History*, XXII, no. 1 (1955) 61–79 (Professor Norman Friedman and The Johns Hopkins University Press); Joseph L. Blotner, 'Mythic Patterns in *To the Lighthouse*', from *PMLA* LXXI (1956) 547–62 (Modern Language Association of America); Sharon Kaehele and Howard German, '*To the Lighthouse*: symbol and vision', from *Bucknell*

Review, x (May 1962) 328–46 (Mrs Sharon Kaehele German and Mr Howard German); Jean Guiguet, *Virginia Woolf and her Works*, translated by Jean Stewart (Mr Leonard Woolf, The Hogarth Press Ltd and Harcourt, Brace & World Inc.).

TO MY OWN PATIENT FAMILY:
MY NANCY, MY ANDREW, AND ELENI, MY YOUNG
'HAPPIER HELEN'

GENERAL EDITOR'S PREFACE

EACH of this series of Casebooks concerns either one well-known and influential work of literature or two or three closely linked works. The main section consists of critical readings, mostly modern, brought together from journals and books. A selection of reviews and comments by the author's contemporaries is also included, and sometimes comments from the author himself. The Editor's Introduction charts the reputation of the work from its first appearance until the present time.

What is the purpose of such a collection? Chiefly, to assist reading. Our first response to literature may be, or seem to be, 'personal'. Certain qualities of vigour, profundity, beauty or 'truth to experience' strike us, and the work gains a foothold in our mind. Later, an isolated phrase or passage may return to haunt or illuminate. Where did we hear that? we wonder – it could scarcely be better put.

In these and similar ways appreciation begins, but major literature prompts to very much more. There are certain facts we need to know if we are to understand properly. Who were the author's original readers, and what assumptions did he share with them? What was his theory of literature? Was he committed to a particular historical situation, or to a set of beliefs? We need historians as well as critics to help us with this. But there are also more purely literary factors to take account of: the work's structure and rhetoric; its symbols and archetypes; its tone, genre and texture; its use of language; the words on the page. In all these matters critics can inform and enrich our individual responses by offering imaginative recreations of their own.

For the life of a book is not, after all, merely 'personal'; it is more like a tripartite dialogue, between a writer living 'then', a reader living 'now', and whatever forces of survival and honour link the two. Criticism is the public manifestation of this dialogue, a witness to the continuing power of literature to arouse and excite. It illuminates the possibilities and rewards of the dialogue, pushing 'interpretation' as far forward as it can go.

And here, indeed, is the rub: how far can it go? Where does 'interpretation' end and nonsense begin? Why is one interpretation superior to another, and why does each age need to interpret for itself? The critic knows that his insights have value only in so far as they serve the text, and that he must take account of views differing sharply from his own. He knows that his own writing will be judged as well as the work he writes about, so that he cannot simply assert inner illumination or a differing taste.

The critical forum is a place of vigorous conflict and disagreement, but there is nothing in this to cause dismay. What is attested is the complexity of human experience and the richness of literature, not any chaos or relativity of taste. A critic is better seen, no doubt, as an explorer than as an 'authority', but explorers ought to be, and usually are, well equipped. The effect of good criticism is to convince us of what C. S. Lewis called 'the enormous extension of our being which we owe to authors'. A Casebook will be justified only if it helps to promote the same end.

A single volume can represent no more than a small selection of critical opinions. Some critics have been excluded for reasons of space, and it is hoped that readers will follow up the further suggestions in the Select Bibliography. Other contributions have been severed from their original context, to which some readers may wish to return. Indeed, if they take a hint from the critics represented here, they certainly will.

A. E. DYSON

INTRODUCTION

. . . Nancy, reluctantly, saw the world spread out beneath her, as if it were Constantinople seen through a mist, and then, however heavy-eyed one might be, one must needs ask, 'Is that Santa Sofia?' 'Is that the Golden Horn?'[1]

As excerpts from her diary reprinted in this volume show, Virginia Woolf wrote the final scene of *To the Lighthouse*, about the aged Mr Ramsay and his children sailing to the Lighthouse, in September 1926. In that same month William Butler Yeats wrote a poem about his quest for an artifice of eternity, his symbolic journey over water when – an old man, a tattered coat upon a stick – he envisioned sailing the seas to the holy city of Byzantium.[2] The two works by such different artistic personalities share a striking number of spiritual and worldly concerns, including a central preoccupation with what is past, or passing, or to come.

Moreover, just as 'Sailing to Byzantium' is often regarded as perhaps Yeats's greatest poem, so *To the Lighthouse* is the most widely admired of all Virginia Woolf's novels, according to the evidence of both critical praise and popular sales. Even among the vocal detractors of all the rest of her work, *To the Lighthouse* is seen as an exception and held in high regard. For many of them the book is – as it is for F. R. Leavis (or, one suspects, because it is for him) – not merely her 'best novel', but her 'only good one'. To Dr Leavis, the reason for its success is clear – its autobiographical basis, the fact that 'the substance of this

[1] Virginia Woolf, *To the Lighthouse* (1960) pp. 116–17.
[2] The 'happy coincidence' of the *publication* dates of *To the Lighthouse* and 'Sailing to Byzantium' has been noticed by William York Tindall, in *The Literary Symbol* (Bloomington, Indiana, 1955) p. 162.

novel was provided directly by life': 'we know enough about Leslie Stephen, the novelist's father, and his family to know that there is a large measure of direct transcription'.[1] One need not have Dr Leavis's contempt for Mrs Woolf's other novels to share a suspicion that there may indeed be 'a clear relation between this fact and the unique success of *To the Lighthouse* . . .'

In any case, the biographical bases behind the fiction are clear enough, despite the need for more authoritative information about Virginia Woolf's life.[2] Although the setting of *To the Lighthouse* is an island (probably no particular one) in the Hebrides, the comparable setting in Virginia Woolf's own child-hood summers had been St Ives, in Cornwall. Her diary and Leonard Woolf's memoirs reveal how important her memories of this spot were to her. She writes that her 'general sense of the poetry of existence' is often 'connected with the sea and St Ives'.[3] Winifred Holtby's remark that *To the Lighthouse* is a 'ghost story' is true in more ways than she probably realized when she made it in 1932; Virginia Woolf herself sought for such works as this a new name 'to supplant "novel". A new —— by Virginia Woolf. But what? Elegy?' (see below, p. 56).

The counterparts to Mr and Mrs Ramsay were Leslie and Julia Stephen, both of whom had been previously married to partners who had died. Sir Leslie Stephen (1832–1904)[4] was a prominent

[1] 'After *To the Lighthouse*', in *Scrutiny*, x (Jan 1942) 297.

[2] The one full-length volume calling itself a biography, Aileen Pippett's *The Moth and the Star* (Boston, Mass., 1953), is awful. The style and prose are cloying, and the approach to the subject senti-mentalized. The few concrete facts not available in other published sources are for the most part contained in quoted correspondence; when Mrs Woolf's letters are published, the little value the book now has will have been reduced even further. Virginia Woolf's 'mental and physical breakdown in 1905', for example, is dismissed in a single sentence (p. 52).

[3] Virginia Woolf, *A Writer's Diary*, ed. Leonard Woolf (1953) p. 56.

[4] I give these dates even though 'the true length of a person's life, whatever the *Dictionary of National Biography* may say, is always a matter of dispute' – Virginia Woolf, *Orlando* (New York, 1928) pp. 305–6.

philosopher, critic and biographer, who had already been a basis
for one character in a famous English novel – Vernon Whitford
in George Meredith's *The Egoist* (1879). His works – including
the *History of English Thought in the Eighteenth Century, An
Agnostic's Apology and Other Essays*, and hundreds of articles
in *The Dictionary of National Biography*, which he edited –
have much more liveliness and contemporary interest than one
fears Mr Ramsay's volumes would have. Nevertheless he shared
some of Mr Ramsay's philosophic concerns. 'Think of a kitchen
table . . . when you're not there,' Andrew Ramsay tells Lily
Briscoe in an attempt to explain his father's interest in 'subject
and object and the nature of reality'. Stephen himself noticed in
An Agnostic's Apology (1893) that ' "This is a table" is a phrase
which in the first place asserts that I have a certain set of organised
sense-impressions'; and then he went on to discuss how we extend
our experience, 'as we do when we say that the fire is still burning
in the room we have left' (p. 137).[1]

Faced with such a formidable monument of intellect in her
father, Virginia Woolf once wondered about her own 'romanti-
cism. How do I catch it? Not from my father.'[2] From her mother,
then? By all accounts, Julia Jackson Duckworth Stephen was a
'happier Helen' indeed, a beautiful, marvellous woman, greatly
loved by her children; she died in 1895, when Virginia was
thirteen. But although there is a good deal of Mrs Stephen in Mrs
Ramsay, there is also something of Virginia Woolf in her, as
there is even more in Lily – and even some in Mr Ramsay.

Thus we come upon the ambiguities inevitable in semi-auto-
biographical fiction, ambiguities centring on the complex
relationships between fact and fiction, art and history. *To the
Lighthouse*, after all, is a novel, not a biography. Although it has
many of its essential origins in the author's family, that family is
not slavishly duplicated in the novel, and the Ramsays cannot
truly be said to *be* the Stephens. Virginia Woolf dealt with the

[1] See N. C. Thakur, *The Symbolism of Virginia Woolf* (Oxford,
1965) p. 86.
[2] Virginia Woolf and Lytton Strachey, *Letters*, ed. Leonard Woolf
and James Strachey (1956) p. 104.

problems suggested here in an essay published the same year as
To the Lighthouse, 'The New Biography'. The aim of the
biographer, she says, 'the truthful transmission of personality',
involves a paradox, for 'on the one hand there is truth; on the
other there is personality'. In 'order that the light of personality
may shine through, facts must be manipulated'. Consequently,
'the life which is increasingly real to us is the fictitious life . . .'
The gist of her argument is expressed in another essay: 'The
novelist is free; the biographer is tied.'[1] The same sort of dicho-
tomy appears within *To the Lighthouse* itself: Mr Ramsay, the
philosopher, is 'incapable of untruth'; he has 'never tampered
with a fact'. In contrast, Lily, the artist, assumes like Virginia
Woolf the freedom to change things as they are for her own
purposes – as when in a moment of inspiration she decides,
regardless of the 'actual' landscape she is painting, to 'put the
tree further in the middle; then I shall avoid that awkward
space'.

Much of the material in the first section of the present collection deals with these autobiographical topics. The first selection
is a brief excerpt from *The Life and Letters of Leslie Stephen*,
published in 1906, only two years after Stephen's death, by his
friend Frederic William Maitland. A more extensive sampling is
then given of Noël Annan's later study, *Leslie Stephen: his
thought and character in relation to his time*. Mr Annan feels it
necessary to defend Stephen against his daughter, by stressing
the important truth that Mr Ramsay is not the whole story of
Leslie Stephen. But in the process one may feel the need to rescue
Mr Ramsay from Mr Annan, whose summary of the presentation
of Mr Ramsay is probably not the whole story of Mr Ramsay,
either. Although he obviously has his faults, Mr Ramsay is by no
means a totally unattractive figure. Mrs Woolf's fear in handling
the final scene in the boat, in fact, was of succumbing to 'sentimentality' (see below, p. 60). Perhaps, one must admit, Mr
Ramsay – and through his image Leslie Stephen – might have
seemed more sympathetic had she been less cautious. Yet when

[1] *Collected Essays*, IV (1967), 'The New Biography', pp. 229, 234;
'The Art of Biography', p. 221.

a few years later her essay 'Leslie Stephen', also reprinted here, presented a much more favourable picture of her father, the result was less convincing and less memorable. 'On the one hand there is truth; on the other there is personality.'

Various comments in Mrs Woolf's *A Writer's Diary* add to our picture of her father; its publication in 1953 affected all subsequent studies of her work, as a chronological reading of the criticism will show. I have included many entries in the present volume, for the diary plays its unique role in the study of *To the Lighthouse* – inevitably, considering that novel's origins and subject-matter. Still further light is shed on Virginia Woolf's relation to that subject-matter in Leonard Woolf's autobiographies, from which I have chosen two brief excerpts.

The rest of the material in the first section, like all the essays in the second, stresses what *To the Lighthouse* is (a novel) rather than what it is not (a memoir). 'Modern Fiction', famous and well-read though it is, nevertheless seemed an inevitable selection, shedding light as it does on Virginia Woolf's artistic aspirations. Yet one should keep in mind that the essay – with its stress on letting 'us record the atoms as they fall upon the mind in the order in which they fall', on tracing 'the pattern, however disconnected and incoherent in appearance, which each sight or incident scores upon the consciousness' (see below, p. 70) – does not give a true reflection of the aesthetic control evident in all her novels. It does, however, provide clues to her possible answers to what William Bankes calls those 'foolish questions, vain questions, questions one never asked if one was occupied. Is human life like this? Is human life like that?'

In retrospect, 'Modern Fiction' seems among the most important and influential critical essays of our century – especially when backed up by Virginia Woolf's own stature as a writer of modern fiction. Within a decade of its appearance in 1919, she became a literary name to conjure with through the publication of a number of novels, notably *Jacob's Room* (1922), *Mrs Dalloway* (1925) and *To the Lighthouse* (1927). Through her criticism and reviews, too, she exerted critical influence – legend anyway says she did – as an arbiter of taste for the Bloomsbury

Group. In those innocent times, people were indeed supposed to be – no doubt unnecessarily – 'afraid of Virginia Woolf'.

By the time *To the Lighthouse* was published in May 1927 any novel by Mrs Woolf was bound to receive widespread and serious attention. It was in fact reviewed more extensively than any of her previous works and had the most successful sales. The first reactions, from her intimates, had been encouraging. Her husband, Leonard Woolf, for whose opinion she was always especially anxious, called it her 'best book and . . . a "masterpiece" '. Her sister, Vanessa Bell, was another whose opinion, given the family bases of the book, would be immensely important: she was 'enthusiastic', so moved that she 'found the rising of the dead almost painful' (see below, pp. 61, 63). Friends were also ardent; even Lytton Strachey, though he had reservations, thought it 'much better than *Mrs Dalloway*'.[1] Mrs Woolf had less cause to be overjoyed by the initial reviews, which were favourable, but often unenthusiastically or politely or obtusely so. Occasionally they were condescending, like the one in the *Saturday Review* ('let us hope . . . that some day she will lay aside her cleverness', etc.);[2] sometimes with ingenuousness they stepped into areas where they ought to have been wary, as when Louis Kronenberger in the New York *Times* distinguished *To the Lighthouse* from such 'autobiographical' works as *Ulysses*: 'neither Clarissa [Dalloway] nor Mrs Ramsay has anything autobiographical about her; both are complete creations...'[3] The *Times Literary Supplement* review, reprinted here, was not imperceptive, but what Mrs Woolf regarded as its predictability put her under a 'damp cloud' (see below, p. 62).

[1] Quoted in Michael Holroyd, *Lytton Strachey: a critical biography* (New York, 1968) II 531.

[2] T. Earle Welby, 'New Fiction', in *Saturday Review*, CXLIII (7 May 1927) 712.

[3] Louis Kronenberger, 'Virginia Woolf Explores an English Country Home', in *New York Times Book Review*, 8 May 1927, p. 2. There were giants in the earth in those days. In the same issue of the *Book Review* other titles reviewed include Edwin Arlington Robinson's *Tristram*, the English translation of Thomas Mann's *The Magic Mountain*, and Howard Carter's *The Tomb of Tut-ankh-Amen*.

Conrad Aiken's review in the American *Dial*, also included in
our volume, was insightful as well as appreciative, but it showed
discomfort with the general drift of Mrs Woolf's novels and
what Aiken feared was 'their odd and delicious air of parochialism' (see below, p. 77).

With the years, Mrs Woolf's stature within modern literature
of course grew, while *To the Lighthouse* became the steadiest
best-seller among her novels. In 1928 it received the Prix
Femina, and it has remained her most persistently praised book,
followed by *The Waves* (1931) and *Mrs Dalloway*. Many of the
authors of full-length books on Virginia Woolf agree it is her
best novel – and almost invariably critics less than enthusiastic
about her work in general regard it as her most significant
achievement.[1] It is not perfectly clear why this should be so;
for although one may feel that *To the Lighthouse* is in fact her
best book, one finds it hard to pin down its appeal for anyone
who cannot stomach the rest of her work. *To the Lighthouse* is,
after all, though not the same old thing, not atypical either;
actually, none of her books is the same old thing, each is in some
measure an experimental departure from her previous efforts.
The reasons her unfavourable critics give for their approval of
this novel are diverse: F. R. Leavis, as we saw, regards the
strength of the novel as its factual basis; William Troy reflects
another common view when he says that '*To the Lighthouse*,
which is probably her finest performance in every respect, owes
its success not least to the completeness with which the symbol
chosen is identified with the will of every one of the characters'.[2]

[1] See those listed in Jean Guiguet's essay below, p. 245, note 68. In
the Introduction to his *Virginia Woolf and Her Works*, M. Guiguet
provides an extensive and useful (because opinionated) survey of
Virginia Woolf criticism up to 1962. In addition, chapter VII ('Reputation, Critics, Achievement') of A. D. Moody's *Virginia Woolf* (Edinburgh, 1963), presents a thoughtful and spirited defence of Mrs Woolf
against many of her detractors.

[2] 'Virginia Woolf: The Novel of Sensibility', in *Selected Essays*, ed.
Stanley Edgar Hyman (New Brunswick, N.J., 1967) p. 73. The quotation comes from a section of his critical attack not in the excerpt
reprinted in this volume.

Perhaps a run-down of the major charges against her work will help, for *To the Lighthouse* has shared these criticisms, though less than any of the other major novels.

Ironically, considering the nature of her discussion of Mr Wells, Mr Bennett, and Mr Galsworthy in 'Modern Fiction', perhaps the most common attack on her fiction is that it fails to confront 'life' – that it does not deal, that is, with what the particular critic regards as 'real life'. Often enough, the real life thus defended by the critic is merely some corner of human experience that does not include the equally genuine life depicted by Mrs Woolf. In part, such critics are simply unwilling to recognize more than one kind of 'reality'; at times, what they actually mean is that they do not *approve* of the kind of real life she writes about. Above all, they do not like her characters and the world they live in. As William Troy puts it:

. . . Mrs Woolf has written almost exclusively about one class of people, almost, one might say one type of individual, and that, a class or type whose experience is largely vicarious, whose contacts with actuality have been for one or another reason incomplete, unsatisfactory, or inhibited. Made up of poets, metaphysicians, botanists, water-colorists, the world of Mrs Woolf is a kind of superior Bohemia . . . [See below, p. 87.]

The class-consciousness evident here – the very trait of which Virginia Woolf herself is obliquely being accused – is unmistakable. In the Troy essay, as often in these attacks, it is allied to a feeling that Mrs Woolf displays an excessive interest in mere 'sensibility', involving a corresponding unwillingness to confront man's physical being. The sense is that her fiction deals with people out of nature, handiworks without the form of any natural thing. Even for Lytton Strachey the problem with *To the Lighthouse* was its 'lack of copulation – either actual or implied'.[1] So friendly a critic as A. D. Moody regrets that in *To the Lighthouse* 'whatever reality is not subjected to the mind's

[1] Quoted in Holroyd, *Strachey*, II 531. Later I shall try to point to elements of the novel that belie this accusation.

processes is not allowed its due weight and effect' (*Virginia
Woolf*, p. 42). From another vantage point, Mrs Woolf's interest
in 'sensibility' is seen as an element of her 'poetic' art – and
'poetry' in turn is seen as for some reason presumptuously out
of place in a novel. As Robert Peel expressed it in 1933, 'prose
fiction is not poetry, and it is possible that Mrs Woolf is trying to
make the novel do something that the novel cannot do without
destroying itself as a form'.[1] Of course, it was against just this
sort of straitening interpretation of what the proper business of
the novel is that Mrs Woolf was fighting all along. She rejected
the insistence that, in contrast to the poet, the novelist 'must
tame his swiftness to sluggardry; keep his eyes on the ground,
not on the sky: suggest by description, not reveal by illumination'.[2] As a matter of fact, many of the attacks on Virginia
Woolf boil down to a disapproval of her presumption in trying
new things with the novel. For all his desire to be open to the
kind of art Mrs Woolf is attempting, William Troy for example
cannot seem to forgive her for presenting experience which is
'something quite different from experience in the sense in which
it is ordinarily understood in referring to people in life or in
books'.[3] Readers expecting what is ordinarily found in ordinary
literature were inevitably turned off by so daring and untradi-
tional a writer as Virginia Woolf. After so many years and so
much more experimental fiction, however, that particular problem has no doubt been alleviated.

The most famous angle of attack on Virginia Woolf – that of
F. R. Leavis, his periodical, *Scrutiny*, and his followers – has
exemplified just about all these attitudes, although the more
gauche extremes are avoided by Dr Leavis himself. He is perfectly willing to hold, for example, that *To the Lighthouse* 'may
be distinguished among her books as substantially justifying her so

[1] 'Virginia Woolf', in *Criterion*, XIII (Oct 1933) 79.
[2] 'Notes on an Elizabethan Play', in *Collected Essays*, I (1966) 58.
[3] See below, p.88. Cf, not reprinted, his remark that 'the use
of poetic symbols in fiction ... seems to be in direct contradiction
to the foundations of our response to that form' (*Selected Essays*,
p. 77).

obviously "poetical" method . . .' Nevertheless, he regards the
novel as a 'decidedly minor affair' – although once he had mentioned it as one of the works 'expressing the finest consciousness
of the age', along with *The Waste Land, Hugh Selwyn Mauberley*
and another surprising inclusion, *Ulysses.*[1] A similar change of
heart is evident in the comments of his wife, Q. D. Leavis. In
1938 she attacked Mrs Woolf for 'not living in the contemporary
world'. In 1932, however, her book *Fiction and the Reading
Public* had been much more respectful and expressed special
admiration for *To the Lighthouse.*[2]

The first issue of *Scrutiny* had come out the same year; in it
appeared the prototype of its many attacks on Virginia Woolf,
and one of the most formidable: M. C. Bradbrook's 'Notes on
the Style of Mrs Woolf'. This essay, which claimed for instance
that 'to demand "thinking" from Mrs Woolf is clearly illegiti-
mate', obviously wounded the novelist.[3] I had planned to
include it in the present volume, but in an interesting development – apparently indicating a reversal of viewpoint in contrast
to those of Dr and Mrs Leavis – I was refused permission to
reprint it because, I was told, Professor Bradbrook no longer
agrees with it.

In the meantime, another Bradbrook – F. W. Bradbrook, in
The Pelican Guide to English Literature – carried on with dis-
maying unoriginality the *Scrutiny* line, including the opinion
that Mrs Woolf's 'lasting contribution to fiction may be reduced
to a single novel, *To the Lighthouse*'. This essay contains a
remark, suggested by Mrs Woolf's membership in the Bloomsbury Group, that 'the danger of the clique spirit in the modern
literary world does not require stressing to anyone who is

[1] *The Great Tradition* (1948) p. 129; *Education and the University*
(1948) p. 164. It is interesting that both the camps about which people
were so excited only a few years ago – that of C. P. Snow as well as
that of F. R. Leavis – share so little sympathy with Virginia Woolf.
Conceivably, the more cynical among her admirers are as grateful as
not.

[2] 'Caterpillars of the Commonwealth Unite!' in *Scrutiny*, VII (Sept
1938) 203; *Fiction and the Reading Public* (1932) pp. 61, 76, 223.

[3] *Scrutiny*, 1 (May 1932) 38. See *A Writer's Diary*, below, p. 64.

sufficiently alert and informed to see what goes on . . .'¹ The irony of the presence of such a warning in an argument itself so parasitic does not require stressing to anyone who is sufficiently alert . . . etc. Here and in other examples of petty adherence to the *Scrutiny* view, criticism becomes reminiscent of the perversity of which the Ramsay children accuse Charles Tansley, who is not satisfied until he has taken 'something interesting' and 'turned the whole thing round and made it somehow reflect himself and disparage them, put them all on edge somehow with his acid way of peeling the flesh and blood off everything . . .'

The essays here collected represent, I hope, healthier elements in Virginia Woolf criticism; there remains no lack of controversy nevertheless. Again and again the critics in this anthology remind us – most often intentionally, either by explicit statement or by careful procedure; occasionally however by default – that there is no single, exclusive way of looking at this multifaceted novel. For there are essential ambiguities within *To the Lighthouse* that have led to many different interpretations of the novel as a whole and of its key scenes, motifs and symbols. In his essay, for example, Norman Friedman summarizes some of the major readings of just the final dual scenes of Mr Ramsay and the children landing at the Lighthouse while Lily completes her picture (see below, pp. 149–50). There have of course been other interpretations as well, just as there are many views as to the meaning of the central symbol of the Lighthouse itself. 'But what is the light?' Mrs Woolf wonders in her diary (p. 141). But what is the Lighthouse? readers of her novel have wondered. James Hafley summarizes for us some of the past answers to this question, but is concerned that critics have been too exclusive, that they have made the mistake, in James Ramsay's terms, 'of finding the lighthouse "simply one thing" ' (see below, p. 135). Just about all the critics in this volume recognize this danger and refrain from limiting too severely their view of this clearly

¹ 'Virginia Woolf: the theory and practice of fiction', in *The Pelican Guide to English Literature*, VII: *The Modern Age*, ed. Boris Ford (Penguin, 1963) pp. 257, 261.

central symbol. In an unguarded moment, Joseph Blotner is an exception.[1]

But if the Lighthouse is clearly central, it is hardly clearly anything else – except perhaps somehow beneficent, benevolent, even as it is 'hoary . . . distant, austere, in the midst . . .', like Yeats's starlit or moonlit dome. Thus it seems probable that the title *To the Lighthouse* is not merely descriptive, of either an actual journey or of aspirations, but also dedicatory: to the force or forces the Lighthouse represents, to the artifice of eternity it comes to suggest.

The first full-length studies of Virginia Woolf appeared in 1932, in the books by Floris Delattre and Winifred Holtby. M. Delattre's *Le Roman psychologique de Virginia Woolf* pursued psychological topics that have continued to fascinate readers interested in the 'stream of consciousness' novel. Miss Holtby's *Virginia Woolf* was the first full study for the English-speaking public. The introductory section of William Troy's attack, originally published in the same year, is reprinted here. Ruth Gruber's *Virginia Woolf: a study* (1935) was published three years later.

The 1940s saw a great increase in the number of important studies, following Mrs Woolf's suicide in 1941. E. M. Forster, her friend, published a small appreciative book in 1942 (*Virginia Woolf*), the same year as David Daiches's *Virginia Woolf*. Mr Daiches's discussion of *To the Lighthouse*, included in our volume, is a fine introduction to what he calls 'the book which marks the perfection of Virginia Woolf's art'. (By 1963, incidentally, he seemed to have changed his mind; in the Preface to a new edition of his study he says that *Mrs Dalloway* now seems to him 'the most central and in a sense the most *fulfilled* of all her

---

[1] 'Its use is simply this: in its stability, its essential constancy despite cyclical change which is not really change at all, this symbol refers to Mrs Ramsay herself' (see below, p. 186). Yet Mr Blotner also observes that while the window is a 'female' symbol, the Lighthouse is 'male'. That surely does not prevent it from being a symbol of Mrs Ramsay as well; but it does indicate that its use is not 'simply' that.

novels', p. xi.) Other books published in the decade of the 1940s
were short volumes by Joan Bennett and R. L. Chambers, and
the most extensive study to its date, Bernard Blackstone's
Virginia Woolf: a commentary.[1] This book is of great value;
it seemed especially useful when it first appeared, though in
retrospect it may seem less so. Mr Blackstone felt it necessary
in 1949 to devote a good deal of space to summary and basic
explanation; moreover, what were fresh insights seem now
many of them critical commonplaces on the one hand (no doubt
largely due to the book's own influence), or, occasionally, misdirected emphases on the other.

During the same decade several valuable articles also appeared.
Philip Toynbee provided a concise and brilliant statement of his
view of Virginia Woolf's stature as that of an important, fascina-
ting writer, if not one in the very highest rank of all. With a
more scholarly approach, John Hawley Roberts studied the
relationship to Mrs Woolf's work of the aesthetics of Bloomsbury.[2] But the most important essay published around this
time was specifically on *To the Lighthouse*. Erich Auerbach's
chapter in *Mimesis* is one of the most enlightening essays on
Virginia Woolf's art ever written, and the most impressive piece
reprinted in this collection. In it Mr Auerbach not only places
Mrs Woolf within the modern tradition, but helps clarify her
position within the entire sweep of Western literature. His
procedure throughout his book, which begins with Homer and
goes through such figures as·Rabelais, Cervantes and Stendhal,
is to quote or refer to particular passages in given texts and to use
these as 'test cases'. Through this method he 'takes the reader
directly into the subject and makes him sense what is at issue
long before he is expected to cope with anything theoretical' (p.

[1] Joan Bennett, *Virginia Woolf: her art as a novelist*, rev. ed.
(Cambridge, 1964), originally published 1945; R. L. Chambers, *The
Novels of Virginia Woolf* (Edinburgh, 1947); Bernard Blackstone,
Virginia Woolf: a commentary (1949).

[2] Philip Toynbee, 'Virginia Woolf: A Study of Three Experimental
Novels', *Horizon*, XIV (Nov 1946) 290–304; John Hawley Roberts,
' "Vision and Design" in Virginia Woolf', in *PMLA* LXI (Sept
1946) 835–47.

556). His aim in all this is the study of what his subtitle calls *The Representation of Reality in Western Literature*. It is interesting, almost paradoxical, that his twentieth-century example should be Virginia Woolf, who in several books, notably *The Waves* and *Orlando,* is far from what is usually considered a 'realist' – indeed who, as we have seen, is frequently accused of shunning 'reality'. But Mr Auerbach turns out to be wise in his choice, recognizing in 'imitation' much vaster possibilities than other 'mimetic' critics seem willing or able to discern.

The 1950s saw several new trends in Virginia Woolf criticism. Above all, the appearance of *A Writer's Diary* in 1953 greatly affected the readings of her novels, for good or ill. At the same time, more and more attention was being paid outside Great Britain to her work. Europe continued its interest (we have already mentioned Delattre and Auerbach), often with a philosophical, epistemological bent: Maxime Chastaing published *La Philosophie de Virginia Woolf* in 1951, the same year that Vittoria Sanna's *Il romanzo di Virginia Woolf* appeared in Italy; Irma Rantavaara published *Virginia Woolf and Bloomsbury* in Helsinki in 1953. (In England, to be sure, J. K. Johnstone's corresponding study, *The Bloomsbury Group: a study of E. M. Forster, Lytton Strachey, Virginia Woolf and their circle* (1954), came out the next year.) In America, too, a great deal of work was being done, especially of the sort involving painstaking *explication de texte,* close readings or elaborate examinations of the various levels and meanings of individual novels and stories. British readers in particular will no doubt notice that of the nine essays included in the second section of this volume, only one is by a British critic. In regard to *To the Lighthouse,* at least, British talents have been largely expended upon general, sweeping discussions of the sort exemplified in the essay by David Daiches. For more detailed exegeses of specific problems, one must frequently turn to others besides her countrymen.

To be sure, extremism in the pursuit of detail may be a vice, while moderation in the defence of common sense is no virtue. Americans, like other people, sometimes forget such truths, and occasionally their imaginative readings merely reflect misdirected ingenuity. To F. L. Overcarsh, for example, *To the Lighthouse* becomes 'an allegory . . . based principally on the Bible'.[1] His associations are nothing if not elaborate: Mr Ramsay is God; Mrs Ramsay is Eve, Mary, and Christ too, as well as the Roman Catholic Church (because 'like the Catholic Church she has great "beauty", of which much is said . . .' p. 112); the Lighthouse too is God, but it is also the Garden and Paradise; the dinner is nothing less than the Last Supper; Lily is St John, and her 'vision' is that of the Book of Revelation. The final landing at the Lighthouse, then, is seen as the Ascension. In regard to such an interpretation, James Ramsay's reflection that Mr Ramsay looks 'as if he were saying, "There is no God" ', produces problems. So Mr Overcarsh completely ignores it. Actually, perhaps one defending this argument could have explained away James's observation; criticism has been known to perform more formidable tasks. But the ingenuity of Mr Overcarsh, at least, seems to have been stumped, so he simply pretends the phrase never occurs.

James Hafley, in *The Glass Roof: Virginia Woolf as novelist* (1954), from which we reprint a section, is primarily interested in 'her ideas as they are given definition by her technique'. The ideational element he pursues is 'Bergsonism', not always with complete convincingness one must admit. But Mr Hafley is ready to acknowledge that 'Virginia Woolf is not to be explained away by one word, "Bergsonism" or any other' (pp. 1, 43), and such freedom of approach enables him to be open to the nuances of her fiction and illuminating when he discusses them. Taking a different tack, our essay by Norman Friedman, 'Double Vision in *To the Lighthouse*', shows how a perceptive critic can concentrate on one area of imagery in order to illumine an entire work. Joseph Blotner's article, 'Mythic Patterns in *To the Lighthouse*', harks back to Mr Overcarsh's only in so far as it too attempts to make associations between *To the Lighthouse* and ancient literature; although not everyone will be fully converted by its argument, it is thought-provoking and raises significant issues about the role of myth in literature and criticism.

[1] 'The Lighthouse, Face to Face', in *Accent*, x (Winter 1950) 108.

Just as critics have sometimes tended to be too harsh on poor Mr Ramsay, so it could be argued that readers have needed a healthy counter to the unquestioning adulation of Mrs Ramsay that has characterized studies of *To the Lighthouse*. In 1958 Glenn Pedersen attempted such a re-evaluation, but when his essay goes so far as to make her a moral monster and the villain of the piece, it seems merely wrong-headed. In this view, Mrs Ramsay 'is revealed as the negative force which usurps the lighthouse and thus prevents the integration of the family while she lives'. As one might expect, supporting such an argument calls for some awkward manœuvring. Since getting to the Lighthouse is so clearly important, and since everything explicit in the novel seems to point to Mrs Ramsay as the primary force urging that journey, both before and after her death, Mr Pedersen is reduced to saying that '*symbolically* she has prevented James from going to the lighthouse'.[1] This dubious reasoning appears throughout the essay, along with questionable value judgements – as in the view that the fact that 'Mrs Ramsay is not a thinking person' and has a negative 'attitude toward the intellect' is to be held against her (p. 586). The intellectual Mr Pedersen may feel that way, but Virginia Woolf for one surely did not.

The 1960s have produced more books and articles than I can do justice to in so brief an outline as this. Books of value, but from which we could not include any samples, are: A. D. Moody, *Virginia Woolf*, a good brief introduction; Josephine Schaefer, *The Three-Fold Nature of Reality in the Novels of Virginia Woolf* (1965), which – perhaps fortunately – is not so restricted in its view as its title might suggest (its discussion of *To the Lighthouse*, incidentally, presents a balanced view of Mrs Ramsay that is a much more cogent corrective to excessive adulation than Mr Pedersen's essay); and N. C. Thakur, *The Symbolism of Virginia Woolf*, another book with a perhaps misleading title – for it is closer to a list of symbols, metaphors and allusions than to a truly systematic discussion of the nature of Mrs Woolf's 'symbolism'.

[1] 'Vision in *To the Lighthouse*', in *PMLA* LXXIII (Dec 1958) 585, 591 (my italics).

While Norman Friedman's article traces a single group of related images, our selection by Sharon Kaehele and Howard German spreads its net more widely and gathers in various types of imagery. My own essay then examines a specific technique and interest (almost obsession) of Virginia Woolf's, with special reference to *Mrs Dalloway* as well as *To the Lighthouse*. The last essay, by Jean Guiguet, comes from his *Virginia Woolf and Her Works*, the most ambitious and scholarly book on her yet attempted. Originally published in French in 1962, M. Guiguet's study tries to cover all the territory: the life, the 'setting', the criticism, the fiction and biographies, and finally the 'Basic Problems' ('Characters and Human Relations', 'Time and Space', etc.). M. Guiguet's work retains most of the advantages of scholarly thoroughness, and only a few of the drawbacks (such as the fact that the 464 pages of text contain 1743 footnotes).

Which brings us to the present. Right now, the view of Virginia Woolf generally held by critics seems to be that she is one of the important novelists of our century, but that she is not among those very few for whom we all, more or less, reserve the term 'great': Conrad, say, or Joyce, or, less certainly, Lawrence. Sometimes critics making such an observation will find themselves using the word 'minor' – but immediately they will become apologetic, for it seems an odd, unsuitable term for a category into which they also tend to place such literary masters as Laurence Sterne, Emily Brontë or E. M. Forster. Such writers, if not of the very highest rank, have attained what we call – in an even more unsatisfactory term – 'immortality'. Virginia Woolf wanted it, and worried about it: Leonard Woolf's description of her concern for the fate of her books after her death, her sense that 'her mortality or immortality was a part of their mortality or immortality',[1] reminds us of similar apprehensions on the part of Mr Ramsay. Some readers, seeing the often deceptively quiet surface of the world of her fiction, claim to perceive a lack of high ambition or daring as well. But as Philip Toynbee recognizes, 'we should not be content to

[1] Leonard Woolf, *Downhill All the Way: an autobiography of the years 1919–1939* (1967), pp. 205–6.

say that she was one of the three or four best English novelists
of the century. It is not as the superior of Huxley or Isherwood
that she should be seen, but as the claimant to be judged by the
standards which we use for Flaubert, for Dostoyevsky or for
Joyce' ('Virginia Woolf', p. 293).

The decisions about what sort of essays to leave out of this
volume have been guided by standards suggested in *To the
Lighthouse* itself: petty arguments have been excluded ('in-
venting differences', after all, seems to Mrs Ramsay 'such
nonsense'), as have extended Tansley-like dissertations on 'the
influence of something upon somebody' (or, as it is also given,
'the influence of somebody upon something'). Obviously, however, even desirable essays have had to be excluded for lack of
space. But with all the room in the world, in one sense any
collection such as this must inevitably be incomplete – for much
of importance remains to be taught us about this novel. There
are without doubt topics that no essay has yet tackled only because
no one has yet realized their true significance; others have been
touched upon, but still await full development – as when several
of our contributors (notably Mr Blotner) deal with the 'Oedipal'
or more broadly 'Freudian' ramifications of the relationships
described in *To the Lighthouse*.[1]
　　Actually, it is surprising that extended attention has not been
paid to the possibilities for enlightenment that a psychoanalytic
interpretation of this novel might provide. After all, its central
relationships include a marriage in which the husband needs
constant mothering, and in which the wife encourages such
emotional dependence not only in her husband but in 'young
men in particular': 'an attitude towards herself which no woman
could fail to feel or to find agreeable, something trustful, childlike, reverential; which an old woman could take from a young
man without loss of dignity . . .' (p. 15). Of course the young

---

[1] See Blotner, pp. 184–6; Leonard Woolf, p. 65. Also, see, for
example: Rantavaara, *Virginia Woolf and Bloomsbury*, pp. 116, 118;
Tindall, *Literary Symbol*, p. 162; Pedersen, 'Vision', passim; Schaefer,
Three-Fold Nature of Reality, p. 132.

male whose dependent love for Mrs Ramsay is most intense is
her son James. Not that this love is in any way 'abnormal'; for
Freudians, anyway, it is perfectly natural, though one may
suspect that the corollary jealousy and resentment against the
father do go pretty far in his case:

> But his son hated him. He hated him for coming up to them
> . . . he hated the twang and twitter of his father's emotion which,
> vibrating round them, disturbed the perfect simplicity and good
> sense of his relations with his mother. . . . [He] hoped to recall
> his mother's attention, which, he knew angrily, wavered in-
> stantly his father stopped. But no. Nothing would make Mr
> Ramsay move on. (p. 61)

Again and again, James's resentment and jealousy are expressed
in unequivocally sexual terms, as when in the third section of the
novel he remembers how years before he had been sitting with
his mother. His father

> had brought his blade down among them on the terrace and she
> had gone stiff all over, and if there had been an axe handy, a
> knife, or anything with a sharp point he would have seized it and
> struck his father through the heart. His mother had gone stiff
> all over, and then, her arm slackening, so that he felt she listened
> to him no longer, she had risen somehow and gone away and
> left him there, impotent, ridiculous, sitting on the floor grasping
> a pair of scissors. (p. 287)

As this passage indicates, James feels fear as well as 'hatred' in
regard to his father – fear that he will be left 'impotent', a word
that appears elsewhere as well (p. 282). In the light of this sense
of threat, James's resentment against his father's forcing him to
go to the phallic Lighthouse may also have psychic origins.

Irma Rantavaara, who has given us one of the few helpful
discussions of some of these topics, suggests that they may provide clues to Virginia Woolf's own 'grudge . . . against her
father, a trait well in keeping with the supposed mother complex,
though not with the Freudian recipe' (*Virginia Woolf and*

Bloomsbury, p. 116). But of course that does less than justice to
Freud's concepts, in which 'ambivalence' played such a key
role. Within the novel itself, Cam's attitudes toward her father
are revealingly ambivalent. Although she unites with her brother
in 'their compact to fight tyranny to the death', she also recognizes about her father the fact that 'no one attracted her more;
his hands were beautiful to her and his feet, and his voice, and
his words, and his haste, and his temper, and his oddity, and his
passion . . .' (pp. 254, 262).

One may also wonder if Mrs Woolf put some of her own
ambivalent sexual feelings into the spinster, Lily Briscoe. At
one point Lily consciously suspects that she is 'in love' with Mrs
Ramsay, but no doubt she is correct in feeling that that is 'not
true' (p. 35), or at least not the whole truth. Lily, critics often
say, is 'sexless'; but that is a curiously meaningless term. Her
thoughts about William Bankes, for instance – 'you have neither
wife nor child (without any sexual feeling, she longed to cherish
that loneliness)' (p. 42) – make us inevitably aware that anyone
so insistently 'without any sexual feeling' is only dubiously
sexless.

We are also reminded of Freudian patterns in Lily's approach
to her art. It 'was in her nature, or in her sex, she did not know
which', we are told, that 'she exchanged the fluidity of life for
the concentration of painting' (p. 245). Without using jargon
like 'sublimation', Lily herself realizes that she has sacrificed a
life like Mrs Ramsay's, with a house full of children, for a life in
which she stands back and paints that house; and she admits that
the latter seems 'so little, so virginal, against the other' (p. 81).
Her realization that she 'would move the tree to the middle, and
need never marry anybody' (p. 271) thus becomes revealing in
still another context.

'There was no helping Mr Ramsay on the journey he was going,'
Lily reflects. Is it altogether too romantic a reading to feel that
the novel belies her feeling? At the end, Lily will sense, 'Whatever she had wanted to give him, when he left her that morning,
she had given him at last.' Our hope is that the essays in the

present volume may help the reader to reach *To the Lighthouse*, our real concern – the book itself, to which our critics should in all humility finally return us. We must not let our journey there be delayed or distracted by the cleverness of these and other critics. Though like any good guides they may provide us with insights about what is to be seen when our goal is reached, the ultimate journey is still, as Lily Briscoe knows, to the thing itself before it has been made anything, still to the Lighthouse.

Morris Beja

PART ONE

Background
and First Reviews

THREE PORTRAITS OF
LESLIE STEPHEN

Frederic William Maitland

HIS house was by no means a hermit's cell. There was a great deal of coming and going. He would growl at being taken to dinner-parties and having to entertain divers 'bores'; still he submitted and was a cheerful host. I will here give a few words that he wrote long afterwards when he was once more lonely, for they say briefly what has to be said. 'My wife's happiness of course was not of the kind which is noisy or brilliant or conspicuous. She had withdrawn entirely from society during her widowhood, and I, too, had become a recluse. We had our little society in later years. We went out, and had our parties at home. When the children grew up she took [her daughter] Stella to balls, concerts, and so forth, as became a good mother, and she had a considerable circle of acquaintance and many very attached friends. Neither of us cared for "society", as it is called, very much; and I take it that our household appeared to people who did care for society, as a secluded little backwater, though to me it was not less delicious. Julia used to be "at home" on Sunday afternoons; and though we did not attempt to set up a literary or artistic "salon", I can see her surrounded on such occasions by a very lively and pleasant group. Especially, I may say, she took the keenest possible interest in young people; she was loved and admired in return by many young friends; she was happy in watching their friendships or love-makings, and her pleasure was in itself a refinement and a charm. Her courtesy was perfect – sometimes a tacit rebuke to me, who find courtesy to bores a very difficult duty.'

'A true picture so far as it goes,' says a friend of ours, 'but not quite adequate. The room would be very full on those Sunday afternoons, and there were poets and painters and novelists there, enough to terrify a shy young man; and there was music, good music, which, if thrown away upon Stephen, was not thrown away upon all his guests. And if it is very true that his wife was the sun and centre of the "lively and pleasant group", it was not a merely reflected light that shone in his face. He also could take an interest in "young people", and "be happy in watching their friendships or love-makings". I can remember seeing his face radiant with delight, so radiant that the blue eyes dazzled me, – they "dwell in my memory as if they had left a phosphorescent line", – and this because two of the young people were happy. If he was discourteous to bores, no doubt they will say so; it is a way they have.'

(from *The Life and Letters of Leslie Stephen*, 1906)

Noël Gilroy Annan

DURING his two years as a widower Stephen had on more than one occasion, as we have seen, relied on Mrs Duckworth for comfort and advice. Once again it was the Hughes family who had in the first instance introduced them, when Tom Hughes's sister had told Leslie before he married Minny that he ought to consider Julia Jackson carefully. She was then a young girl of ethereal beauty and whom Burne-Jones had chosen as the model for his painting of the Annunciation. Her mother had been one of the seven Pattle sisters famous for their good looks and descended from a dashing French nobleman who had settled in India after the Revolution. Stephen used to meet Julia in London at her uncle's, Thoby Prinsep, who patronised the arts and took both Burne-Jones and G. F. Watts at different times into his household. 'The house', wrote Stephen, 'had a character of its own. People used to go there on Sunday afternoons; they had strawberries and cream and played croquet and strolled about the garden, or were allowed to go to Watts' studio and admire his pictures. . . . And there used to be Leighton and Val Prinsep and his friends who looked terribly smart to me.' In a word, Stephen found it not his sort of world and both the Prinseps and he were a little shy of each other. Everyone danced attention upon Julia; she had proposals from Holman Hunt and the sculptor Woolner, and Stephen dared hardly think that she would cast her eyes in his direction. When she became engaged to Herbert Duckworth, he felt 'a sharp pang of jealousy', possibly because Duckworth was only a year younger than himself; and hearing Duckworth described as 'the perfect type of public school man' confirmed Stephen in his self-distrust and convinced him that such beautiful creatures as Julia Jackson were not for crotchety intellectuals like him. But Duckworth died in 1870, leaving his widow with three small children. 'I was only twenty-four,' she told Stephen, 'when life all seemed a shipwreck', and when Stephen found himself in the same predicament they were drawn to each other. She was still strangely and exquisitely beautiful with wide, wise eyes, which had seen suffering, eyebrows that lifted naturally away to the temples, and an expression sad and poetical. He remembered how even when he married Minny he had been keen to make a good impression on Julia. Soon he began to realise how dear she was to him, discovered he was in love, and on the 5th of February, 1877, proposed.* Julia, taken by surprise, refused him but after an exchange of letters agreed to remain friends on the understanding that marriage was out of the question.† But Stephen returned to the attack and, after

---

* Stephen's highly developed topographical sense made him note where and when this occurred. The lunch at the club in a philosophical spirit had encouraged him to propose to Minny, and it was on this day as he was walking into town that he stopped outside Knightsbridge Barracks and 'suddenly said to myself "I love Julia" '. The mood came upon him in singular places.

† Stephen left an account based on their exchange of letters analysing Julia's state of mind. Stephen writes that 'She already loves me tenderly: she dreams of me and thinks of me constantly: and declares that my love is a blessing which lightens the burthen of her life. But this feeling is blended with a fear of the consequences to me. She feels that she is making me more restless; my position is a trying one; she remembers how she has herself thought of women who had men "devoted" to them, who gave nothing and took everything. . . I suggested that we might continue to live as we were living and yet go

further complicated correspondence over a year and with many
doubts, she finally agreed. They were married on the 26th of
March, 1878. . . .

The present trend in biography bears hard on Leslie Stephen.
Biographers concentrate on those aspects of a man's life which
their age considers important. A generation, suspicious of
worldly success and believing that reality was to be found in the
delicate play of personal relations, has dictated to biographers the
standard of values by which a man should be judged; hatred for
those who tyrannise over other people's lives, mistrust of a
powerful will, admiration for humour, integrity and, above all,
sensitivity towards other people's feelings, became the cardinal
virtues. Judged by this standard Leslie Stephen will be found
wanting. So far from practising what he preached about domestic
affection, Stephen was insensitive, egotistical and, in a subtle way,
tyrannical. In the family, which he worshipped as the sacred
entity on which the whole edifice of society and ethics is built,
he revealed ironically enough what was hidden from his friends:
the inner core of his nature. . . .

through a legal form of marriage, which would give me the right to
be with her as much as I desired. She at once pronounced the scheme
to be – as of course it was – impracticable.' Julia found it soon impossible to give him up (as her mother urged she should if she could
not make up her mind to marry him). 'If I could be quite close to you,'
she writes, 'and feel you holding me, I should be content to die.
Knowing what I am, it is no temptation to me to marry you from the
thought that I·should make your life happier or brighter – I don't
think I should. So if you want an answer, I can only say that as I am
now it would be wrong for me to marry. . . . All this sounds cold and
horrid – but you know I do love you with my whole heart – only it
seems such a poor dead heart.' Later she asks Stephen to decide for her.
He refused: 'the worst thing that could happen would be that she
should become my wife and find that she had been mistaken'. He writes
to her, 'there is no hurry. You may think of me as I think of Troy
(my old collie) – a nice kind loving animal who will take what I give
and be thankful. . . .' On the night of the 5th of January, Stephen dined
with her and as he rose to go, she suddenly looked up and said, 'I will
be your wife and will do my best to be a good wife to you.' Ten days
later she wrote, 'My darling one, I feel most commonplace and quiet.
The only thing I can't quite believe is that we are not married. . . .'

The key to Stephen's character is his effort to change himself. He believed his hypersensitivity to be a weakness and determined to conquer it. The very thought of suffering pained him. He refused ever to visit a hospital; he could not bear to hear the word dentist mentioned; during the Boer War he lay awake at night fancying he could hear the guns on the African battlefields and he would go out of his way to avoid seeing newspaper posters carrying news of the slaughter. As a child he could not bear a word of reproof and if reproached burst into tears. As a man he saw the air thick with imaginary rebuffs and determined never to expose himself. Hypersensitivity, he thought, saps a man's will to go out into the world and do his duty. It must be crushed and destroyed. But as he grew older Stephen doubted whether its ghost had been laid and this bred in him a subtler form of self-mistrust; he knew in his heart that his athletic feats, designed to prove to himself that he could succeed, proved nothing, and that though he had trained his body to endure hardship, his mind was as sensitive as in childhood days. The effort to conquer himself in fact had maimed him: the victory he had won over his own nature was Pyrrhic.

The time has come to count the cost of this victory. It can partly be assessed in his writing. Though as a critic he came to conclusions, his dissatisfaction seeps through the pages; in every essay there is a deutero-Stephen who whispers in the ear of Stephen the critic that all is in vain. No sooner has he laid down a critical canon than he is regarding it quizzically, despairingly. It is not that, in Van Wyck Brooks' phrase, he adopts an Indian-giver style of criticism that takes back with one hand what he has granted with the other; but one can hear a sigh of disbelief that anything that he has written is really worth the reader's effort. But the greater part of the cost fell to the account of his private life since the victory blunted his sensibilities yet left his nature as raw and sensitive as ever. Friends dimly apprehended part of the truth, his family saw all. They became the spectators of his calamity. And this is why we find two different conceptions of Stephen when we come to examine his character, the judgment of his friends, who agreed with Lowell that he was 'the most lovable of men', and the impression left upon his family: the portrait of Vernon Whitford in George Meredith's *The Egoist* and the very dissimilar portrait which appears in the pages of his daughter's novel, *To the Lighthouse*.

Virginia Woolf's Mr Ramsay is utterly insensitive to the feelings of those immediately about him. He resents his limitations as a scholar and vents his chagrin upon his children. His damning utilitarian insistence on factual accuracy, that whether they like it or not the weather will change and the expedition to the Lighthouse will be ruined, takes the joy out of every childhood fancy and expectation. He is for ever jawing with equally unimaginative friends about so-and-so who is a 'first-rate man' and so-and-so who is fundamentally unsound: these alphaminded, dreary academic categories are meaningless in the only world that matters – the world of human beings who breathe and suffer and love. 'The crass blindness and tyranny in him', which makes him fling a plate through the window at breakfast because he finds an earwig in the milk, which forbids him ever to praise his youngest son and makes his son hate him, is described with desolating intensity as Mr Ramsay rows Cam and James to the Lighthouse. 'To pursue truth with such astonishing lack of consideration for other people's feelings, to rend the thin veils of civilisation so wantonly, so brutally, was to her so horrible an outrage of human decency. . . .' Can a man find truth, truth of any value, when he has maimed his feelings, the antennae with which he can sense other people's emotions? It is not that Mr Ramsay ignores his family for the company of shuffling, sniffling old savants like Mr Carmichael; he makes unreasonable emotional demands upon them. He considers himself to be pitied, a man whose life has been wrecked by personal misfortune and who is owed affection and sympathy to sustain him in his great loss. He demands to be told that he is genuinely suffering. 'Sitting in the boat he bowed, he crouched himself, acting instantly his part – the part of a desolate man, widowed, bereft; and so called up before him in hosts people sympathising with him; staged for himself as he sat in the boat, a little drama.' The high-minded moralist turns out to be a ruthless egoist determined to exploit his own suffering and force his family, who are unable to escape, to suffer with him.

The accuracy of this portrait is substantiated in the journal which Stephen wrote for his children and which was called by them, the *Mausoleum Book,* in which he gives an account of his private life. In it he writes of his attempts to subdue Annie Ritchie, his money mania and the countless petty tyrannies with which he exasperated Julia and his children. In his relations with Minny and Julia he adopted two of the classical attitudes of people who demand to be loved: 'People do not really like me, so I will retreat from society and secure myself from any rejection which would mortally wound me'; and, 'You ought to love me because I suffer and am helpless.' Admitting his faults, he puts them down with pathetic honesty – and then tries to justify them. Moods of self-recrimination are followed by explanations of his conduct designed to persuade himself that he was mis-understood. Guilt wells from his pen. He has only to write of Julia and he is pursued by 'hideous morbid fancies' which haunt him that he was at times unkind to her, 'fancies which I know to be utterly baseless and which I am yet unable to disperse by an effort of will. I must live them down.' But he cannot, and the memories return to lie with him at night. 'All this comes back to me – trifles and things that are not quite trifles – and prevents me from saying, as I would so gladly have said, that I never gave her anxiety or caused her needless annoyance.' He worshipped Julia, desired to transform her into an apotheosis of motherhood, but treated her in the home as someone who should be at his beck and call, support him in every emotional crisis, order the minutiae of his life and then submit to his criticism in those household matters of which she was mistress. If a child was late for dinner, it must have been maimed or killed in an accident; and that would be her fault. He would sulk if things did not go his way; if it was suggested that he take a hot bath on coming in soaked with rain from a walk, he would consider his manliness impugned and then like a child pout with injured pride and refuse a piece of his favourite cake at tea. Stephen had cause for guilt. His wife was more remarkable than he. Julia Stephen's memorial was carved by her daughter in the characters of Mrs Ambrose, Mrs Hilbery and Mrs Ramsay; and this is fitting for Virginia Woolf inherited from her mother much of her sensibility and and even an echo of her style. Julia's single publication is lost in oblivion yet it reveals her character as surely as Virginia Woolf's portraits. It is about nursing and called *Notes for Sick Rooms*. Imaginative in that it brings to mind all the details unobserved by the sage, it combines an exquisite sensibility towards other people's sufferings with exceedingly practical advice on how to alleviate them. 'The origin of most things', she begins, 'has been decided on, but the origin of crumbs in bed has never excited sufficient attention among the scientific world' – and from there she analyses the almost impossible task of getting rid of them. From the snuffing of candles, the arrangement of candles, and the position of looking-glasses to the technique of bed-baths and of administering enemas, everything is discussed from the point of view of the sufferer with irony, detachment and common sense. She responded to other people's feelings instinctively; she could heal a child's wound before it was given and read thoughts before they were uttered, and her sympathy was like the touch of a butterfly, delicate and remote – for she knew what it was to live an inner life and respected other people's privacy. Leslie thought himself a practical man but beside her he was a ninny. Leslie thought himself a friend in need, but she knew how to translate sympathy into action. Leslie ploughed furrows of ratiocination to reach conclusions, she had intuitively reached them and acted upon them before he arrived. Thus he was for ever trampling upon her feelings, wounding the person who comforted him, half-conscious of his hebetude, unable to constrain it. Men are to be pitied; and so are we ourselves.

Stephen was an old man when his children were in their 'teens and thus understandably enough, they found him difficult. He lacked the ability, that his wife had to such an extraordinary degree, of apprehending their feelings. He was angelic with children when they were tots, drawing animals, telling stories and writing them letters, but he lacked the patience and imagination to understand them as boys and girls. One day he decided to take over all teaching in the schoolroom and made his children's life so unbearable that he had to be advised to stop. Nothing mattered but that his spirit should live on in them; he was impatient of theirs. Writing to Norton about the son whom his wife most adored, he said, 'Adrian is an attractive, simple little fellow but oddly dreamy and apt to take a great interest in things which are impractical.' The boy, then, must be made to be practical. Adrian in revenge taught himself to imitate his father's voice and, safe in the knowledge of his father's deafness, would strike up before all the family at dinner in the hope of making his brother and sisters giggle; the device worked to perfection until the day when he performed in a growler and discovered that among the peculiar properties of that vehicle was a quality which turned it into a gigantic ear-trumpet, so that his father heard every word. Moans issued from the deeply distressed Stephen, 'Oh, my boy, my boy!' With the merciless insight of children they seized on their father's failings; in particular his habit of dramatising the insignificant into the cosmic. Once as he passed their room stumbling upstairs to his study they heard him talking to himself: 'I wish I were dead . . . I wish I were dead . . . I wish my whiskers would grow.' Mr Ramsay, tyrannical and self-torturing, demanding that the family revolve round him is the fiction of fact.

Stephen tortured himself by sentimentalising the past and wishing it to be the present. The *Mausoleum Book* is in part an act of commemoration in which he recalls incidents from his married years, places a wreath upon them and embalms them in an electuary of sentimentality. He luxuriated in grief, noting in the book with mournful misgivings the death of each friend, the narrowing circle, the anniversaries of desolation, the happiness that could be no more. Stephen's sentimentality is all the more striking because he diagnosed the emotion in others unerringly and defined it as a mood in which we make 'a luxury of grief and regard sympathetic emotion as an end rather than a means – a need rightly despised by men of masculine nature'. Can it be that he failed to make himself entirely the manly affectionate fellow that he wished to be? Sentimentalism, the enjoyment of emotion for its own sake, is no more a vice than many other similar moods, such as nostalgia. But it is often a cloak, a perfumed shroud, donned to conceal the stink of vice, of secret and unknown sins, such as cruelty and coarseness. Stephen was neither cruel nor coarse but his sentimentality concealed his fear of the future, his desire to remain in the past, to remember what had been happiness because he could never know happiness again; and this was inflicted upon his wife and children.

No one can be aware of all his faults, still less change the soil of the temperament in which they grow. Stephen, however, impelled by his Evangelical heritage, searched his soul for faults and tried to change himself. He realised that his habits maddened his family. He knew that they had to tell him things more than twice because, sunk in a brown study, he did not bother to listen. He acknowledged that he was fidgety and troublesome, 'and even when alone in my family, I am sometimes as restless as a hyaena'. When taxed he made promises to mend his ways and always failed. But sincerity depends on the relation between our words and our thoughts, not between our beliefs and our actions, and none of Stephen's protestations was in the least hypocritical or pretending to a feeling of sorrow which he never felt and never wanted to feel. He often consciously tried to reform, and in order to thicken his thin skin, dam up the ooze of his sentimentality and face the future, he adopted two remedies. The first was Carlyle's soporific of work. All the Stephens ruined their health through overwork, a symptom of a deep-seated family neurosis. Although Leslie declared that he had never in his life worked hard except when taking his degree, he added, 'The only reason why I ever get anything done is that I do not waste time in the vain effort to make myself agreeable . . .' he too worked to deaden his feelings. The volume of his publications is considerable: five volumes of histories of thought, five books in the English Men of Letters series, three full-length Life and Letters biographies, two short books of reminiscences, well over a hundred and fifty long articles and introductions, most of them reprinted, his contributions to the *DNB*, together with a mass of more ephemeral journalism, show staggering powers of application. And, like

many of his contemporaries, he was an indefatigable corre-
spondent.

Wounded sensibilities can be soothed by work which brings
forgetfulness in fatigue. They can also be soothed by humour.
Humour is one of man's most valuable weapons against the
weariness of the world. Some people use it as a defence against
mental exertion and laugh problems away which they would
rather not face; others expose the weaknesses of their fellow-men
to restore their belief in themselves; a few employ it to enlighten
themselves about their own character and to see themselves in
relation to society. Stephen belonged to the last class. No one
saw himself more clearly in a ridiculous light. As a young man,
he tried to escape acquiring the more ill-favoured of the academic
characteristics, but when he came to London, he considered
himself branded with the mark of the tribe of dons whom he
compared to toads since 'with an unpromising exterior they both
sometimes bear a precious jewel in their heads'. He was even
able to smile at himself on occasions when most men prefer to
romanticise their appearance: he realised that he was an awkward
lover. The comical and touching way in which he described his
courtships is the mark of one who knew that man, or at any rate
himself, often cuts a ludicrous figure in what should be his most
intense experiences. He employed humour, too, in the way he
questioned emotional clichés: he bequeathed the deprecating
glance to his children in Bloomsbury. Above all, his humour
protected him against self-righteousness. Stephen realised that
a moralist who keeps before his eyes a goal of personal perfection is always in danger of being a prig; the number of times he
mentions that word in his essays betrays his own anxiety to
avoid the charge. Humour, in this connection, is the art of
seeing oneself and one's ideals in relation to other human
beings.

Yet though this excellent virtue ministers to the sensibility,
it enfeebles self-confidence in those who doubt their own
abilities. So Stephen lost on the roundabouts what he made on
the swings. His determination never to lie to himself about
himself convinced him that he was a failure and that nothing

he had done would be long remembered. Writing in the *Mausoleum Book* Stephen said, 'Had I – as I often reflect – no pretext
for calling myself a failure, had I succeeded in my most ambitious
dreams and surpassed all my contemporaries in my own line,
what should I have done? I should have written a book or two
which would have been admired by my own and perhaps by the
next generation. They would have survived so long as active
forces, and a little longer in the memory of the more learned,
because they would have expressed a little better than other books
thoughts which were fomenting in the minds of thousands, some
abler and many little less able than myself. But putting aside the
very few great names with whom I could not in my wildest fancy
compare myself, even the best thinkers become obsolete in a
brief time, and turn out to have been superfluous. Putting my
imaginary achievements at the best, they would have made no
perceptible difference to the world.'* If this kind of analysis
betrays Stephen's sad lack of self-confidence, its honesty must
give us pause. Glancing at the career of the greatest of all Victorian dons, Stephen noted that Jowett was always able to
believe in his own achievements. Jowett, as he cryptically put it,
had 'not known the greatest happiness': he had not married and
begot children. But he had acquired a derivative immortality
from his College, and knew that his work would be carried on
by his chosen successors. This enviable frame of mind enabled
him to retain the illusion which the old usually lose that 'anything you did at your best had any real value, or that anything
you can do hereafter will even reach the moderate standard of
the old work'. Stephen would not accept this illusion, and his
honesty is touched with the annihilating ruthlessness of Turgenev's hero Bazarov, 'If you've made up your mind to mow
down everything, don't spare your own legs.'

* Cf *To the Lighthouse*, part I, 'And his fame lasts how long? Is it
permissible even for a dying hero to think before he dies how men will
speak of him hereafter? His fame lasts perhaps two thousand years.
And what are two thousand years? (asked Mr Ramsay, ironically,
staring at the hedge). . . . His own little light would shine, not very
brightly for a year or two, and then would be merged in some bigger
light, and that in a bigger still.'

Nevertheless, it is honest, and their father's honesty and kindliness impressed themselves upon his children. Stephen's defects in the home were certainly grave, not trivial quirks or endearing eccentricities; nor was his the forgivable habit of blazing up in rows which any family worth its salt soon learns how to extinguish. It says much for his daughters and also for him that they did not deny the sweep of his character and his admirable virtues. The portrait of Mr Ramsay was never intended to be the whole story.* On the centenary of her father's birth Virginia Woolf wrote an article for *The Times* in which she gave a very different account. . . .

These were the qualities which made Meredith and his many other friends love him. And how numerous they were! They were not restricted to his contemporaries or to Clifford or Henley or a dozen others whom he helped. He was granted a privilege often denied to the old: young men such as Desmond MacCarthy enjoyed his company and were kind to him, and H. A. L. Fisher and Maitland, who married into the family, were men he could respect as well as like. Meredith spoke of his equability; his friends knew that he valued them for their qualities, not for their abilities, and that once accepted they would not be dissected and discarded. His integrity was beyond question. Revenge or malice were beneath him, he despised personal gain and all devious ways of influence or persuasion; and if this magnanimity took him a pace or two out of the world, it invested his actions with a noble simplicity.

* Q. D. Leavis in *Scrutiny*, VII (March 1939) 405, 'Leslie Stephen – Cambridge Critic', takes it as a final judgment and calls it a 'brilliant study in the Lytton Strachey manner of a slightly ludicrous, slightly bogus, Victorian philosopher, [which] has somehow served to discredit Leslie Stephen's literary work'. It is difficult to see how the agonising description of the state of mind of a daughter in regard to her father could be conceived as in the Lytton Strachey manner; or, indeed, that Virginia Woolf was preoccupied with debunking her father's character. In an attempt to score a point against Bloomsbury, Q. D. Leavis has omitted to mention the complementary portrait of Stephen as Mr Hilbery in *Night and Day*, and is apparently unaware of the article in *The Times*.

Equability and integrity may keep, but never by themselves make, lasting friends. Nor do his entertaining oddities explain the devotion of his friends. Stephen's famous gruffness could irritate as well as delight. Hardy once wrote in his diary: 'Called on Leslie Stephen. He is just the same or worse; as if dying to express sympathy, but suffering under some terrible curse which prevents his saying any but caustic things, and showing antipathy instead.'

What was it then that made Stephen the 'most lovable of men'? Partly the knowledge that beneath the hard shell there was a soft heart. Stephen's sentimentalism expressed itself in endearing devotions. Thomas Hardy liked a man to care about the past. The first time he met Stephen, he asked him why he had chosen to live in a new street in Kensington with the pavements hardly laid and the road not yet rolled. Stephen replied that 'he had played as a child with his nurse in the fields hard by, and he fancied living on the spot, which was dear to him . . . I felt then that I liked him, which I had first doubted. The feeling never changed.' That was why Stephen loved to walk round Kensington Gardens and Hyde Park, where, wrote his daughter, 'as a little boy his brother Fitzjames and he had made beautiful bows to young Queen Victoria and she had swept them a curtsey'. In the Gardens he had as a child recited *Marmion*; now with his daughters he would shout Newbolt's *Admirals All* at the top of his voice to the astonishment of nannies and park-keepers. But men loved him for reasons deeper than these. Stephen's inner nature was so palpably the contradiction of what he taught that their sympathy went out to him. We admire our friends for their qualities, we often love them for their failings; their failings put them on the same level as ourselves. Looking at Watts' portrait of Stephen one feels that the lower lip of that passionate, tender mouth is beginning to tremble and that Stephen is on the verge of tears. He is shamelessly appealing for love and protection. It was this helplessness in face of bills, servants, parties and the paraphernalia of everyday existence which made women love him. Candida sticks by Morell because she pities the strong man whose defences have collapsed.

'I only met him once when he was an old man visiting his sister in Cambridge,' said E. M. Forster. 'He said little. Then he noticed that I was looking at him and he turned away.' He feared that someone who might not sympathise would solve the riddle of his personality. To the man himself there is always a riddle. Why do I behave like this? Why am I disliked? Why do I fail? Stephen dreaded exposure and deplored the publication of private papers which reveal to posterity something of a man's inner life. Yet he need not have feared. Partly because he was palpably defenceless against such an enquiry, partly because he valued self-knowledge and set out to cure himself and partly because his character (as distinct from his personality) was massive and impressive, he earns respect. Those who desire a visual image to catch the perplexity of his personality, the grandeur and hardness of his character, the oddness and difficulty of the man, should imagine him in silhouette against the background of his times alone with Nature. His life resembled his favourite pursuit. It was a long climb up the slopes and rocks of thought, plodding slowly on to scale the Alps that towered above him. For Thomas Hardy Stephen's spirit became immanent with the peaks he surmounted, so that the Schreckhorn appears:

> Aloof, as if a thing of mood and whim,
> Now that its spare and desolate figure gleams
> Upon my nearing vision, less it seems
> A looming Alp-height than a guise of him
> Who scaled its horn with ventured life and limb,
> Drawn on by vague imaginings, may be,
> Of semblance to his personality
> In its quaint glooms, keen lights, and rugged trim.

> – At his last change, when Life's dull coils unwind,
> Will he, in old love, hitherward escape,
> And the eternal essence of his mind
> Enter this silent adamantine shape,
> And his low voicing haunt its slipping snows
> When dawn that calls the climber dyes them rose?

This, then, is how we shall view him—as a peak set in the mountain range of a certain tradition of thought.

(from *Leslie Stephen: his thought and character
in relation to his time*, 1952)

Virginia Woolf

B Y the time that his children were growing up the great days of my father's life were over. His feats on the river and on the mountains had been won before they were born. Relics of them were to be found lying about the house – the silver cup on the study mantelpiece; the rusty alpenstocks that leant against the bookcase in the corner; and to the end of his days he would speak of great climbers and explorers with a peculiar mixture of admiration and envy. But his own years of activity were over, and my father had to content himself with pottering about the Swiss valleys or taking a stroll across the Cornish moors.

That to potter and to stroll meant more on his lips than on other people's is becoming obvious now that some of his friends have given their own version of those expeditions. He would start off after breakfast alone, or with one companion. Shortly before dinner he would return. If the walk had been succcessful, he would have out his great map and commemorate a new short-cut in red ink. And he was quite capable, it appears, of striding all day across the moors without speaking more than a word or two to his companion. By that time, too, he had written the *History of English Thought in the Eighteenth Century*, which is said by some to be his masterpiece; and the *Science of Ethics* – the book which interested him most; and *The Playground of Europe*, in which is to be found 'The Sunset on Mont Blanc' – in his opinion the best thing he ever wrote.

He still wrote daily and methodically, though never for long at a time. In London he wrote in the large room with three long windows at the top of the house. He wrote lying almost recumbent in a low rocking chair which he tipped to and fro as he wrote,

like a cradle, and as he wrote he smoked a short clay pipe, and
he scattered books round him in a circle. The thud of a book
dropped on the floor could be heard in the room beneath. And
often as he mounted the stairs to his study with his firm, regular
tread he would burst, not into song, for he was entirely un-
musical, but into a strange rhythmical chant, for verse of all
kinds, both 'utter trash', as he called it, and the most sublime
words of Milton and Wordsworth, stuck in his memory, and the
act of walking or climbing seemed to inspire him to recite which-
ever it was that came uppermost or suited his mood.

But it was his dexterity with his fingers that delighted his
children before they could potter along the lanes at his heels or
read his books. He would twist a sheet of paper beneath a pair of
scissors and out would drop an elephant, a stag, or a monkey
with trunks, horns, and tails delicately and exactly formed. Or,
taking a pencil, he would draw beast after beast – an art that he
practised almost unconsciously as he read, so that the fly-leaves
of his books swarm with owls and donkeys as if to illustrate the
'Oh, you ass!' or 'Conceited dunce', that he was wont to scribble
impatiently in the margin. Such brief comments, in which one
may find the germ of the more temperate statements of his essays,
recall some of the characteristics of his talk. He could be very
silent, as his friends have testified. But his remarks, made suddenly in a low voice between the puffs of his pipe, were extremely
effective. Sometimes with one word – but his one word was
accompanied by a gesture of the hand – he would dispose of the
tissue of exaggerations which his own sobriety seemed to pro-
voke. 'There are 40,000,000 unmarried women in London alone!'
Lady Ritchie once informed him. 'Oh, Annie, Annie!' my father
exclaimed in tones of horrified but affectionate rebuke. But Lady
Ritchie, as if she enjoyed being rebuked, would pile it up even
higher next time she came.

The stories he told to amuse his children of adventures in
the Alps – but accidents only happened, he would explain, if you
were so foolish as to disobey your guides – or of those long
walks, after one of which, from Cambridge to London on a hot
day, 'I drank, I am sorry to say, rather more than was good for

me', were told very briefly, but with a curious power to impress the scene. The things that he did not say were always there in the background. So, too, though he seldom told anecdotes, and his memory for facts was bad, when he described a person – and he had known many people, both famous and obscure – he would convey exactly what he thought of him in two or three words. And what he thought might be the opposite of what other people thought. He had a way of upsetting established reputations and disregarding conventional values that could be disconcerting, and sometimes perhaps wounding, though no one was more respectful of any feeling that seemed to him genuine. But when, suddenly opening his bright blue eyes, and rousing himself from what had seemed complete abstraction, he gave his opinion, it was difficult to disregard it. It was a habit, especially when deafness made him unaware that his opinion could be heard, that had its inconveniences.

'I am the most easily bored of men', he wrote, truthfully as usual: and when, as was inevitable in a large family, some visitor threatened to stay not merely for tea but also for dinner, my father would express his anguish at first by twisting and untwisting a certain lock of hair. Then he would burst out, half to himself, half to the powers above, but quite audibly, 'Why can't he go? Why can't he go?' Yet such is the charm of simplicity – and did he not say, also truthfully, that 'bores are the salt of the earth'? – that the bores seldom went, or, if they did, forgave him and came again.

Too much, perhaps, has been said of his silence; too much stress has been laid upon his reserve. He loved clear thinking, he hated sentimentality and gush; but this by no means meant that he was cold and unemotional, perpetually critical and condemnatory in daily life. On the contrary, it was his power of feeling strongly and of expressing his feeling with vigour that made him sometimes so alarming as a companion. A lady, for instance, complained of the wet summer that was spoiling her tour in Cornwall. But to my father, though he never called himself a democrat, the rain meant that the corn was being laid; some poor man was being ruined; and the energy with which he expressed his sympathy – not with the lady – left her discomfited. He had something of the same respect for farmers and fishermen that he had for climbers and explorers. So, too, he talked little of patriotism, but during the South African War – and all wars were hateful to him – he lay awake thinking that he heard the guns on the battlefield. Again, neither his reason nor his cold common sense helped to convince him that a child could be late for dinner without having been maimed or killed in an accident. And not all his mathematics together with a bank balance, which he insisted must be ample in the extreme, could persuade him, when it came to signing a cheque, that the whole family was not 'shooting Niagara to ruin', as he put it. The pictures that he would draw of old age and the Bankruptcy Court, of ruined men of letters who have to support large families in small houses at Wimbledon (he owned a very small house at Wimbledon) might have convinced those who complain of his understatements that hyperbole was well within his reach had he chosen.

Yet the unreasonable mood was superficial, as the rapidity with which it vanished would prove. The cheque-book was shut; Wimbledon and the workhouse were forgotten. Some thought of a humorous kind made him chuckle. Taking his hat and his stick, calling for his dog and his daughter, he would stride off into Kensington Gardens, where he had walked as a little boy, where his brother Fitzjames and he had made beautiful bows to young Queen Victoria and she had swept them a curtsy, and so, round the Serpentine, to Hyde Park Corner, where he had once saluted the great Duke himself; and so home. He was not then in the least 'alarming'; he was very simple, very confiding; and his silence, though one might last unbroken from the Round Pond to the Marble Arch, was curiously full of meaning, as if he were thinking half aloud, about poetry and philosophy and people he had known.

He himself was the most abstemious of men. He smoked a pipe perpetually, but never a cigar. He wore his clothes until they were too shabby to be tolerable; and he held old-fashioned and rather Puritanical views as to the vice of luxury and the sin of idleness. The relations between parents and children today have a freedom that would have been impossible with my father. He expected a certain standard of behaviour, even of ceremony, in family life. Yet if freedom means the right to think one's own thoughts and to follow one's own pursuits, then no one respected and indeed insisted upon freedom more completely than he did. His sons, with the exception of the Army and Navy, should follow whatever professions they chose; his daughters, though he cared little enough for the higher education of women, should have the same liberty. If at one moment he rebuked a daughter sharply for smoking a cigarette – smoking was not in his opinion a nice habit in the other sex – she had only to ask him if she might become a painter, and he assured her that so long as she took her work seriously he would give her all the help he could. He had no special love for painting; but he kept his word. Freedom of that sort was worth thousands of cigarettes.

It was the same with the perhaps more difficult problem of literature. Even today there may be parents who would doubt the wisdom of allowing a girl of fifteen the free run of a large and quite unexpurgated library. But my father allowed it. There were certain facts – very briefly, very shyly he referred to them. Yet 'Read what you like,' he said, and all his books, 'mangy and worthless', as he called them, but certainly they were many and various, were to be had without asking. To read what one liked because one liked it, never to pretend to admire what one did not – that was his only lesson in the art of reading. To write in the fewest possible words, as clearly as possible, exactly what one meant – that was his only lesson in the art of writing. All the rest must be learnt for oneself. Yet a child must have been childish in the extreme not to feel that such was the teaching of a man of great learning and wide experience, though he would never impose his own views or parade his own knowledge. For, as his tailor remarked when he saw my father walk past his shop up Bond Street, 'There goes a gentleman that wears good clothes without knowing it.'

In those last years, grown solitary and very deaf, he would some-times call himself a failure as a writer; he had been 'jack of all trades, and master of none'. But whether he failed or succeeded as a writer, it is permissible to believe that he left a distinct impression of himself on the minds of his friends. Meredith saw him as 'Phoebus Apollo turned fasting friar' in his earlier days; Thomas Hardy, years later, looked at the 'spare and desolate figure' of the Schreckhorn and thought of

> him,
> Who scaled its horn with ventured life and limb,
> Drawn on by vague imaginings, may be,
> Of semblance to his personality
> In its quaint glooms, keen lights, and rugged trim.

But the praise he would have valued most, for though he was an agnostic nobody believed more profoundly in the worth of human relationships, was Meredith's tribute after his death: 'He was the one man to my knowledge worthy to have married your mother.' And Lowell, when he called him 'L.S., the most lovable of men', has best described the quality that makes him, after all these years, unforgettable.

('Leslie Stephen', in *The Times*, 28 November 1932)

THE WRITING AND RECEPTION OF
TO THE LIGHTHOUSE

Virginia Woolf

1925

Thursday, 14 May

. . . But the odd thing is this: honestly I am scarcely a shade
nervous about *Mrs D*. Why is this? Really I am a little bored, for
the first time, at thinking how much I shall have to talk about it
this summer. The truth is that writing is the profound pleasure
and being read the superficial. I'm now all on the strain with
desire to stop journalism and get on to *To the Lighthouse*. This is
going to be fairly short; to have father's character done complete
in it; and mother's; and St Ives; and childhood; and all the usual
things I try to put in – life, death, etc. But the centre is father's
character, sitting in a boat, reciting We perished, each alone,
while he crushes a dying mackerel. However, I must refrain. I
must write a few little stories first and let the *Lighthouse* simmer,
adding to it between tea and dinner till it is complete for writing
out.

Saturday, 27 June

. . . The first fruit of the *C.R.* [*Common Reader*, 1925] (a book too
highly praised now) is a request to write for the *Atlantic Monthly*.
So I am getting pushed into criticism. It is a great standby – this
power to make large sums by formulating views on Stendhal and
Swift. (But while I try to write, I am making up *To the Lighthouse* – the sea is to be heard all through it. I have an idea that I
will invent a new name for my books to supplant 'novel'. A
new —— by Virginia Woolf. But what? Elegy?)

Monday, 20 July

Here the door opened and Morgan [E. M. Forster] came in to

ask us out to lunch with him at the Etoile, which we did, though we had a nice veal and ham pie at home (this is in the classic style of journalists). It comes of Swift perhaps, the last words of which I have just written, and so fill up time here. I should consider my work list now. I think a little story, perhaps a review, this fortnight; having a superstitious wish to begin *To the Lighthouse* the first day at Monk's House. I now think I shall finish it in the two months there. The word 'sentimental' sticks in my gizzard (I'll write it out of me in a story – Ann Watkins of New York is coming on Wednesday to enquire about my stories). But this theme may be sentimental; father and mother and child in the garden; the death; the sail to the Lighthouse. I think, though, that when I begin it I shall enrich it in all sorts of ways; thicken it; give it branches – roots which I do not perceive now. It might contain all characters boiled down; and childhood; and then this impersonal thing, which I'm dared to do by my friends, the flight of time and the consequent break of unity in my design. That passage (I conceive the book in 3 parts. 1. at the drawing room window; 2. seven years passed; 3. the voyage) interests me very much. A new problem like that breaks fresh ground in one's mind; prevents the regular ruts.

Thursday, 30 July
I am intolerably sleepy and annulled and so write here. I do want indeed to consider my next book, but I am inclined to wait for a clearer head. The thing is I vacillate between a single and intense character of father; and a far wider slower book – Bob T. [R. C. Trevelyan] telling me that my speed is terrific and distinctive. My summer's wanderings with the pen have I think shown me one or two new dodges for catching my flies. I have sat here, like an improviser with his hands rambling over the piano. The result is perfectly inconclusive and almost illiterate. I want to learn greater quiet and force. But if I set myself that task, don't I run the risk of falling into the flatness of *N. & D.* [*Night and Day*, 1919]? Have I got the power needed if quiet is not to become insipid? These questions I will leave, for the moment, unanswered. So that episode is over. But, dear me, I'm too dull

to write and must go and fetch Mr Dobrée's novel and read it, I think. Yet I have a thousand things to say. I think I might do something in *To the Lighthouse*, to split up emotions more completely. I think I'm working in that direction.

1926

Friday, 30 April

. . . Yesterday I finished the first part of *To the Lighthouse*, and today began the second. I cannot make it out – here is the most difficult abstract piece of writing – I have to give an empty house, no people's characters, the passage of time, all eyeless and featureless with nothing to cling to; well, I rush at it, and at once scatter out two pages. Is it nonsense, is it brilliance? Why am I so flown with words and apparently free to do exactly what I like? When I read a bit it seems spirited too; needs compressing, but not much else. Compare this dashing fluency with *Mrs Dalloway* (save the end). This is not made up; it is the literal fact.

Tuesday, 25 May

I have finished – sketchily I admit – the second part of *To the Lighthouse* – and may, then, have it all written over by the end of July. A record. 7 months, if it so turns out.

RODMELL, 1926

Wandervögeln

of the sparrow tribe. Two resolute, sunburnt, dusty girls in jerseys and short skirts, with packs on their backs, city clerks, or secretaries, tramping along the road in the hot sunshine at Ripe. My instinct at once throws up a screen, which condemns them: I think them in every way angular, awkward and self-assertive. But all this is a great mistake. These screens shut me out. Have no screens, for screens are made out of our own integument; and get at the thing itself, which has nothing whatever in common with a screen. The screen-making habit, though, is so universal that probably it preserves our sanity. If we had not this device for shutting people off from our sympathies we might perhaps dissolve utterly; separateness would be impossible. But the screens are in the excess; not the sympathy.

Friday, 3 September

... For the rest, Charleston, Tilton [the Keyneses' house], *To the Lighthouse*, Vita, expeditions: the summer dominated by a feeling of washing in boundless warm fresh air – such an August not come my way for years; bicycling; no settled work done, but advantage taken of air for going to the river or over the downs. The novel is now easily within sight of the end, but this, mysteriously, comes no nearer. I am doing Lily on the lawn; but whether it's her last lap, I don't know. Nor am I sure of the quality; the only certainty seems to be that after tapping my antennae in the air vaguely for an hour every morning I generally write with heat and ease till 12.30; and thus do my two pages. So it will be done, written over that is, in 3 weeks, I forecast, from today. What emerges? At this moment I'm casting about for an end. The problem is how to bring Lily and Mr R. together and make a combination of interest at the end. I am feathering about with various ideas. The last chapter which I begin tomorrow is In the Boat: I had meant to end with R. climbing on to the rock. If so, what becomes of Lily and her picture? Should there be a final page about her and Carmichael looking at the picture and summing up R.'s character? In that case I lose the intensity of the moment. If this intervenes between R. and the lighthouse, there's too much chop and change, I think. Could I do it in a parenthesis? So that one had the sense of reading the two things at the same time?

I shall solve it somehow, I suppose. Then I must go on to the question of quality. I think it may run too fast and free and so be rather thin. On the other hand, I think it is subtler and more human than *Jacob's Room* and *Mrs Dalloway*. And I am encouraged by my own abundance as I write. It is proved, I think, that what I have to say is to be said in this manner. As usual, side stories are sprouting in great variety as I wind this up: a book of characters; the whole string being pulled out from some simple sentence, like Clara Pater's 'Don't you find that Barker's pins have no points to them?' I think I can spin out all their entrails this way; but it is hopelessly undramatic. It is all in oratio obliqua. Not quite all; for I have a few direct sentences. The lyric portions of *To the Lighthouse* are collected in the 10-year lapse and don't interfere with the text so much as usual. I feel as if it fetched its circle pretty completely this time; and I don't feel sure what the stock criticism will be. Sentimental? Victorian?

Monday, 13 September
The blessed thing is coming to an end I say to myself with a groan. It's like some prolonged rather painful and yet exciting process of nature, which one desires inexpressibly to have over. Oh the relief of waking and thinking it's done – the relief and the disappointment, I suppose. I am talking of *To the Lighthouse*. . . . As for the book – Morgan said he felt 'This is a failure', as he finished the *Passage to India*. I feel – what? A little stale this last week or two from steady writing. But also a little triumphant. If my feeling is correct, this is the greatest stretch I've put my method to, and I think it holds. By this I mean that I have been dredging up more feelings and characters, I imagine. But Lord knows, until I look at my haul. This is only my own feeling in process. Odd how I'm haunted by that damned criticism of Janet Case's 'it's all dressing . . . technique. (*Mrs Dalloway*). *The Common Reader* has substance.' But then in one's strained state any fly has liberty to settle and it's always the gadflies. Muir praising me intelligently has comparatively little power to encourage – when I'm working, that is – when the ideas halt. And this last lap, in the boat, is hard, because the material is not so rich as it was with Lily on the lawn. I am forced to be more direct and more intense. I am making more use of symbolism, I observe; and I go in dread of 'sentimentality'. Is the whole theme open to that charge? But I doubt that any theme is in itself good or bad. It gives a chance to one's peculiar qualities – that's all.

Tuesday, 23 November
I am re-doing six pages of *Lighthouse* daily. This is not, I think,

so quick as *Mrs D.*: but then I find much of it very sketchy and have to improvise on the typewriter. This I find much easier than re-writing in pen and ink. My present opinion is that it is easily the best of my books: fuller than *J.'s R.* and less spasmodic, occupied with more interesting things than *Mrs D.*, and not complicated with all that desperate accompaniment of madness. It is freer and subtler, I think. Yet I have no idea yet of any other to follow it: which may mean that I have made my method perfect and it will now stay like this and serve whatever use I wish to put it to. Before, some development of method brought fresh subjects in view, because I saw the chance of being able to say them. Yet I am now and then haunted by some semi-mystic very profound life of a woman, which shall all be told on one occasion; and time shall be utterly obliterated; future shall somehow blossom out of the past. One incident – say the fall of a flower – might contain it. My theory being that the actual event practically does not exist – nor time either. But I don't want to force this. I must make up my series book.

1927

Friday, 14 January

This is out of order, but I have no new book and so must record here (and it was here I recorded the beginning of the *Lighthouse*) must record here the end. This moment I have finished the final drudgery. It is now complete for Leonard to read on Monday. Thus I have done it some days under the year and feel thankful to be out of it again. Since October 25th I have been revising and retyping (some parts three times over) and no doubt I should work at it again; but I cannot. What I feel is that it is a hard muscular book, which at this age proves that I have something in me. It has not run out and gone flabby: at least such is my feeling before reading it over.

Sunday, 23 January

Well Leonard has read *To the Lighthouse* and says it is much my best book and it is a 'masterpiece'. He said this without my asking. I came back from Knole and sat without asking him. He calls it entirely new, 'a psychological poem' is his name for it. An improvement upon *Dalloway*; more interesting. Having won this great relief, my mind dismisses the whole thing, as usual, and I forget it and shall only wake up and be worried again over proofs and then when it appears.

Monday, 21 March
My brain is ferociously active. I want to have at my books as if I were conscious of the lapse of time; age and death. Dear me, how lovely some parts of the *Lighthouse* are! Soft and pliable, and I think deep, and never a word wrong for a page at a time. This I feel about the dinner party and the children in the boat; but not of Lily on the lawn. That I do not much like. But I like the end.

Sunday, 1 May
And then I remember how my book is coming out. People will say I am irreverent – people will say a thousand things. But I think, honestly, I care very little this time – even for the opinion of my friends. I am not sure if it is good; I was disappointed when I read it through the first time. Later I liked it. Anyhow it is the best I can do. But would it be a good thing to read my things when they are printed, critically? It is encouraging that in spite of obscurity, affectation and so on my sales rise steadily. We have sold, already, 1220 before publication, and I think it will be about 1500, which for a writer like I am is not bad. Yet, to show I am genuine, I find myself thinking of other things with absorption and forgetting that it will be out on Thursday.

Thursday, 5 May
Book out. We have sold (I think) 1690 before publication – twice *Dalloway*. I write however in the shadow of the damp cloud of *The Times Lit. Sup.* review, which is an exact copy of the *J.'s R.*, *Mrs Dalloway* review, gentlemanly, kindly, timid, praising beauty, doubting character, and leaving me moderately depressed. I am anxious about 'Time Passes'. Think the whole thing may be pronounced soft, shallow, insipid, senti-

mental. Yet, honestly, I don't much care; want to be let alone to
ruminate.

Monday, 16 May
The book. Now on its feet so far as praise is concerned. It has
been out 10 days: Thursday a week ago. Nessa [Vanessa Bell, her
sister] enthusiastic – a sublime, almost upsetting spectacle. She
says it is an amazing portrait of mother; a supreme portrait
painter; has lived in it; found the rising of the dead almost painful. Then Ottoline, then Vita, then Charlie, then Lord Olivier,
then Tommie, then Clive.

1928

Wednesday, 7 November
... Again, one reviewer [of *Orlando*, 1928] says that I have come
to a crisis in the matter of style: it is now so fluent and fluid that
it runs through the mind like water.

That disease began in the *Lighthouse*. The first part came
fluid – how I wrote and wrote!

Shall I now check and consolidate, more in the *Dalloway* and
Jacob's Room style?

Wednesday, 28 November
Father's birthday. He would have been 96, 96, yes, today; and
could have been 96, like other people one has known: but mercifully was not. His life would have entirely ended mine. What
would have happened? No writing, no books; – inconceivable.

I used to think of him and mother daily; but writing the
Lighthouse laid them in my mind. And now he comes back sometimes, but differently. (I believe this to be true – that I was
obsessed by them both, unhealthily; and writing of them was a
necessary act.) He comes back now more as a contemporary. I
must read him some day. I wonder if I can feel again, I hear his
voice, I know this by heart?

So the days pass and I ask myself sometimes whether one is
not hypnotised, as a child by a silver globe, by life; and whether
this is living. It's very quick, bright, exciting. But superficial

perhaps. I should like to take the globe in my hands and feel it quietly, round, smooth, heavy, and so hold it, day after day. I will read Proust I think. I will go backwards and forwards.

1932

Tuesday, 17 May

What is the right attitude towards criticism? What ought I to feel and say when Miss B. [M. C. Bradbrook] devotes an article in *Scrutiny* [vol. 1, May 1932] to attacking me? She is young, Cambridge, ardent. And she says I'm a very bad writer. Now I think the thing to do is to note the pith of what is said – that I don't think – then to use the little kick of energy which opposition supplies to be more vigorously oneself. It is perhaps true that my reputation will now decline. I shall be laughed at and pointed at. What should be my attitude – clearly Arnold Bennett and Wells took the criticism of their youngers in the wrong way. The right way is not to resent; not to be longsuffering and Christian and submissive either. Of course, with my odd mixture of extreme rashness and modesty (to analyse roughly) I very soon recover from praise and blame. But I want to find out an attitude. The most important thing is not to think very much about oneself. To investigate candidly the charge; but not fussily, not very anxiously. On no account to retaliate by going to the other extreme – thinking too much. And now that thorn is out – perhaps too easily.

1934

Tuesday, 16 October

... I am so sleepy. Is this age? I can't shake it off. And so gloomy. That's the end of the book. I looked up past diaries – a reason for keeping them, and found the same misery after *Waves* – after *Lighthouse* I was, I remember, nearer suicide, seriously, than since 1913.

1940

Sunday, 22 December

How beautiful they were, those old people – I mean father and mother – how simple, how clear, how untroubled. I have been dipping into old letters and father's memoirs. He loved her: oh and was so candid and reasonable and transparent – and had such a fastidious delicate mind, educated, and transparent. How serene and gay even, their life reads to me: no mud; no whirlpools. And so human – with the children and the little hum and song of the nursery. But if I read as a contemporary I shall lose my child's vision and so must stop. Nothing turbulent; nothing involved; no introspection.

(from *A Writer's Diary*, 1953)

Leonard Woolf

THE basis of Mr Ramsay's character in *To the Lighthouse*, was, no doubt, taken by Virginia from her father's character; it is, I think, successfully sublimated by the novelist and is not the photograph of a real person stuck into a work of fiction; it is integrated into a work of art. But there are points about it which are both artistically and psychologically of some interest. Having known Leslie Stephen in the flesh and having heard an enormous deal about him from his children, I feel pretty sure that, subject to what I have said above about the artistic sublimation, Mr Ramsay is a pretty good fictional portrait of Leslie Stephen – and yet there are traces of unfairness to Stephen in Ramsay. Leslie Stephen must have been in many ways an exasperating man within the family and he exasperated his daughters, particularly Vanessa. But I think that they exaggerated his exactingness and sentimentality and, in memory, were habitually rather unfair to him owing to a complicated variety of the Oedipus complex. It is interesting to observe a faint streak of this in the drawing and handling of Mr Ramsay.

(from *Sowing: an autobiography of
the years 1880–1904*, 1960)

Virginia Woolf

IN making any survey, even the freest and loosest, of modern fiction, it is difficult not to take it for granted that the modern practice of the art is somehow an improvement upon the old. With their simple tools and primitive materials, it might be said, Fielding did well and Jane Austen even better, but compare their opportunities with ours! Their masterpieces certainly have a strange air of simplicity. And yet the analogy between literature and the process, to choose an example, of making motor cars scarcely holds good beyond the first glance. It is doubtful whether in the course of the centuries, though we have learnt much about making machines, we have learnt anything about making literature. We do not come to write better; all that we can be said to do is to keep moving, now a little in this direction, now in that, but with a circular tendency should the whole course of the track be viewed from a sufficiently lofty pinnacle. It need scarcely be said that we make no claim to stand, even momentarily, upon that vantage-ground. On the flat, in the crowd, half blind with dust, we look back with envy to those happier warriors, whose battle is won and whose achievements wear so serene an air of accomplishment that we can scarcely refrain from whispering that the fight was not so fierce for them as for us. It is for the historian of literature to decide; for him to say if we are now beginning or ending or standing in the middle of a great period of prose fiction, for down in the plain little is visible. We only know that certain gratitudes and hostilities inspire us; that certain paths seem to lead to fertile land, others to the dust and the desert; and of this perhaps it may be worth while to attempt some account.

Our quarrel, then, is not with the classics, and if we speak of quarrelling with Mr Wells, Mr Bennett, and Mr Galsworthy, it is partly that by the mere fact of their existence in the flesh their work has a living, breathing, everyday imperfection which bids us take what liberties with it we choose. But it is also true that, while we thank them for a thousand gifts, we reserve our unconditional gratitude for Mr Hardy, for Mr Conrad, and in much lesser degree for the Mr Hudson of *The Purple Land, Green Mansions,* and *Far Away and Long Ago.* Mr Wells, Mr Bennett, and Mr Galsworthy have excited so many hopes and disappointed them so persistently that our gratitude largely takes the form of thanking them for having shown us what they might have done but have not done; what we certainly could not do, but as certainly, perhaps, do not wish to do. No single phrase will sum up the charge or grievance which we have to bring against a mass of work so large in its volume and embodying so many qualities, both admirable and the reverse. If we tried to formulate our meaning in one word we should say that these three writers are materialists. It is because they are concerned not with the spirit but with the body that they have disappointed us, and left us with the feeling that the sooner English fiction turns its back upon them, as politely as may be, and marches, if only into the desert, the better for its soul. Naturally, no single word reaches the centre of three separate targets. In the case of Mr Wells it falls notably wide of the mark. And yet even with him it indicates to our thinking the fatal alloy in his genius, the great clod of clay that has got itself mixed up with the purity of his inspiration. But Mr Bennett is perhaps the worst culprit of the three, inasmuch as he is by far the best workman. He can make a book so well constructed and solid in its craftsmanship that it is difficult for the most exacting of critics to see through what chink or crevice decay can creep in. There is not so much as a draught between the frames of the windows, or a crack in the boards. And yet – if life should refuse to live there? That is a risk which the creator of *The Old Wives' Tale,* George Cannon, Edwin Clayhanger, and hosts of other figures, may well claim to have surmounted. His characters live abundantly, even unexpectedly, but it remains to ask how do they live, and what do they live for? More and more they seem to us, deserting even the well-built villa in the Five Towns, to spend their time in some softly padded first-class railway carriage, pressing bells and buttons innumerable; and the destiny to which they travel so luxuriously becomes more and more unquestionably an eternity of bliss spent in the very best hotel in Brighton. It can scarcely be said of Mr Wells that he is a materialist in the sense that he takes too much delight in the solidity of his fabric. His mind is too generous in its sympathies to allow him to spend much time in making things shipshape and substantial. He is a materialist from sheer goodness of heart, taking upon his shoulders the work that ought to have been discharged by Government officials, and in the plethora of his ideas and facts scarcely having leisure to realize, or forgetting to think important, the crudity and coarseness of his human beings. Yet what more damaging criticism can there be both of his earth and of his Heaven than that they are to be inhabited here and hereafter by his Joans and his Peters? Does not the inferiority of their natures tarnish whatever institutions and ideals may be provided for them by the generosity of their creator? Nor, profoundly though we respect the integrity and humanity of Mr Galsworthy, shall we find what we seek in his pages.

If we fasten, then, one label on all these books, on which is one word, materialists, we mean by it that they write of unimportant things; that they spend immense skill and immense industry making the trivial and the transitory appear the true and the enduring.

We have to admit that we are exacting, and, further, that we find it difficult to justify our discontent by explaining what it is that we exact. We frame our question differently at different times. But it reappears most persistently as we drop the finished novel on the crest of a sigh – Is it worth while? What is the point of it all? Can it be that, owing to one of those little deviations which the human spirit seems to make from time to time, Mr Bennett has come down with his magnificent apparatus for catching life just an inch or two on the wrong side? Life escapes; and perhaps without life nothing else is worth while. It is a confession of vagueness to have to make use of such a figure as this, but we scarcely better the matter by speaking, as critics are prone to do, of reality. Admitting the vagueness which afflicts all criticism of novels, let us hazard the opinion that for us at this moment the form of fiction most in vogue more often misses than secures the thing we seek. Whether we call it life or spirit, truth or reality, this, the essential thing, has moved off, or on, and refuses to be contained any longer in such ill-fitting vestments as we provide. Nevertheless, we go on perseveringly, conscientiously, constructing our two and thirty chapters after a design which more and more ceases to resemble the vision in our minds. So much of the enormous labour of proving the solidity, the likeness to life, of the story is not merely labour thrown away but labour misplaced to the extent of obscuring and blotting out the light of the conception. The writer seems constrained, not by his own free will but by some powerful and unscrupulous tyrant who has him in thrall, to provide a plot, to provide comedy, tragedy, love interest, and an air of probability embalming the whole so impeccable that if all his figures were to come to life they would find themselves dressed down to the last button of their coats in the fashion of the hour. The tyrant is obeyed; the novel is done to a turn. But sometimes, more and more often as time goes by, we suspect a momentary doubt, a spasm of rebellion, as the pages fill themselves in the customary way. Is life like this? Must novels be like this?

Look within and life, it seems, is very far from being 'like this'. Examine for a moment an ordinary mind on an ordinary day. The mind receives a myriad impressions – trivial, fantastic, evanescent or engraved with the sharpness of steel. From all sides they come, an incessant shower of innumerable atoms; and as they fall, as they shape themselves into the life of Monday or Tuesday, the accent falls differently from of old; the moment of importance came not here but there; so that, if a writer were a free man and not a slave, if he could write what he chose, not what he must, if he could base his work upon his own feeling and not upon convention, there would be no plot, no comedy, no tragedy, no love interest or catastrophe in the accepted style, and perhaps not a single button sewn on as the Bond Street tailors would have it. Life is not a series of gig-lamps symmetrically arranged; life is a luminous halo, a semi-transparent envelope surrounding us from the beginning of consciousness to the end. Is it not the task of the novelist to convey this varying, this unknown and uncircumscribed spirit, whatever aberration or complexity it may display, with as little mixture of the alien and external as possible? We are not pleading merely for courage and sincerity: we are suggesting that the proper stuff of fiction is a little other than custom would have us believe it.

It is, at any rate, in some such fashion as this that we seek to define the quality which distinguishes the work of several young writers, among whom Mr James Joyce is the most notable, from that of their predecessors. They attempt to come closer to life, and to preserve more sincerely and exactly what interests and moves them, even if to do so they must discard most of the conventions which are commonly observed by the novelist. Let us record the atoms as they fall upon the mind in the order in which they fall, let us trace the pattern, however disconnected and incoherent in appearance, which each sight or incident scores upon the consciousness. Let us not take it for granted that life exists more fully in what is commonly thought big than in what is commonly thought small. Anyone who has read *A Portrait of the Artist as a Young Man* or, what promises to be a far more interesting work, *Ulysses*, now [written April 1919] appearing in the *Little Review*, will have hazarded some theory of this nature as to Mr Joyce's intention. On our part, with such a fragment before us, it is hazarded rather than affirmed; but whatever the intention of the whole, there can be no question but that it is of the utmost sincerity and that the result, difficult or unpleasant as we may judge it, is undeniably important. In contrast with those whom we have called materialists, Mr Joyce is spiritual; he is concerned at all costs to reveal the flickerings of that innermost flame which flashes its messages through the brain, and in order to preserve it he disregards with complete courage whatever seems to him adventitious, whether it be probability, or coherence, or any other of these signposts which for generations have served to support the imagination of a reader when called upon to imagine what he can neither touch nor see. The scene in the cemetery, for instance, with its brilliancy, its sordidity, its incoherence, its sudden lightning flashes of significance, does undoubtedly come so close to the quick of the mind that, on a first reading at any rate, it is difficult not to acclaim a masterpiece. If we want life itself, here surely we have it. Indeed, we find ourselves fumbling rather awkwardly if we try to say what else we wish, and for what reason a work of such originality yet fails to compare, for we must take high examples, with *Youth* or *The Mayor of Caster-bridge*. It fails because of the comparative poverty of the writer's mind, we might say simply and have done with it. But it is possible to press a little further and wonder whether we may not refer our sense of being in a bright yet narrow room, confined and shut in, rather than enlarged and set free, to some limitation imposed by the method as well as by the mind. Is it the method that inhibits the creative power? Is it due to the method that we feel neither jovial nor magnanimous, but centred in a self which, in spite of its tremor of susceptibility, never embraces or creates what is outside itself and beyond? Does the emphasis laid, perhaps didactically, upon indecency contribute to the effect of something angular and isolated? Or is it merely that in any effort of such originality it is much easier, for contemporaries especially, to feel what it lacks than to name what it gives? In any case it is a mistake to stand outside examining 'methods'. Any method is right, every method is right, that expresses what we wish to express, if we are writers; that brings us closer to the novelist's intention if we are readers. This method has the merit of bringing us closer to what we were prepared to call life itself; did not the reading of *Ulysses* suggest how much of life is excluded or ignored, and did it not come with a shock to open *Tristram Shandy* or even *Pendennis* and be by them convinced that there are not only other aspects of life, but more important ones into the bargain.

However this may be, the problem before the novelist at present, as we suppose it to have been in the past, is to contrive means of being free to set down what he chooses. He has to have the courage to say that what interests him is no longer 'this' but 'that': out of 'that' alone must he construct his work. For the moderns 'that', the point of interest, lies very likely in the dark places of psychology. At once, therefore, the accent falls a little differently; the emphasis is upon something hitherto ignored; at once a different outline of form becomes necessary, difficult for us to grasp, incomprehensible to our predecessors. No one but a modern, no one perhaps but a Russian, would have felt the interest of the situation which Tchekov has made into the short story which he calls 'Gusev'. Some Russian soldiers lie ill on board a ship which is taking them back to Russia. We are given a few scraps of their talk and some of their thoughts; then one of them dies and is carried away; the talk goes on among the others for a time, until Gusev himself dies, and looking 'like a carrot or a radish' is thrown overboard. The emphasis is laid upon such unexpected places that at first it seems as if there were no emphasis at all; and then, as the eyes accustom themselves to twilight and discern the shapes of things in a room we see how complete the story is, how profound, and how truly in obedience to his vision Tchekov has chosen this, that, and the other, and placed them together to compose something new. But it is impossible to say 'this is comic', or 'that is tragic', nor are we certain, since short stories, we have been taught, should be brief and conclusive, whether this, which is vague and inconclusive, should be called a short story at all.

The most elementary remarks upon modern English fiction can hardly avoid some mention of the Russian influence, and if the Russians are mentioned one runs the risk of feeling that to write of any fiction save theirs is waste of time. If we want understanding of the soul and heart where else shall we find it of comparable profundity? If we are sick of our own materialism the least considerable of their novelists has by right of birth a natural reverence for the human spirit. 'Learn to make yourself akin to people. . . . But let this sympathy be not with the mind – for it is easy with the mind – but with the heart, with love towards them.' In every great Russian writer we seem to discern the features of a saint, if sympathy for the sufferings of others, love towards them, endeavour to reach some goal worthy of the most exacting demands of the spirit constitute saintliness. It is the saint in them which confounds us with a feeling of our own irreligious triviality, and turns so many of our famous novels to tinsel and trickery. The conclusions of the Russian mind, thus comprehensive and compassionate, are inevitably, perhaps, of the utmost sadness. More accurately indeed we might speak of the inconclusiveness of the Russian mind. It is the sense that there is no answer, that if honestly examined life presents question after question which must be left to sound on and on after the story is over in hopeless interrogation that fills us with a deep, and finally it may be with a resentful, despair. They are right perhaps; unquestionably they see further than we do and without our gross impediments of vision. But perhaps we see something that escapes them, or why should this voice of protest mix itself with our gloom? The voice of protest is the voice of another and an ancient civilization which seems to have bred in us the instinct to enjoy and fight rather than to suffer and understand. English fiction from Sterne to Meredith bears witness to our natural delight in humour and comedy, in the beauty of earth, in the activities of the intellect, and in the splendour of the body. But any deductions that we may draw from the comparison of two fictions so immeasurably far apart are futile save indeed as they flood us with a view of the infinite possibilities of the art and remind us that there is no limit to the horizon, and that nothing – no 'method', no experiment, even of the wildest – is forbidden, but only falsity and pretence. 'The proper stuff of fiction' does not exist; everything is the proper stuff of fiction, every feeling, every thought; every quality of brain and spirit is drawn upon; no perception comes amiss. And if we can imagine the art of fiction come alive and standing in our midst, she would un-doubtedly bid us break her and bully her, as well as honour and love her, for so her youth is renewed and her sovereignty assured.

(first published as 'Modern Novels' in *Times Literary Supplement*, 10 April 1919; revised as 'Modern Fiction' for *The Common Reader*, 1925)

Times Literary Supplement

EACH of Mrs Woolf's novels has inspired a lively curiosity as to the next. One wondered what would follow *Mrs Dalloway*; and its successor, with certain points of likeness, is yet a different thing. It is still more different from most other stories. A case like Mrs Woolf's makes one feel the difficulty of getting a common measure to estimate fiction; for her work, so adventurous and intellectually imaginative, really invites a higher test than is applied to most novels.

In form *To the Lighthouse* is as elastic as a novel can be. It has no plot, though it has a scheme and a motive; it shows characters in outline rather than in the round; and while it depends almost entirely on the passing of time, it expands or contracts the time-sense very freely. The first and longest part of the book is almost stationary, and describes a party of people gathered in the summer at a house on the Scottish coast. James, the youngest of the Ramsay children, is thwarted of a visit to the lighthouse. In the next part, much briefer, sea-winds and caretakers are having their way with the house while one year follows another; Mrs Ramsay and her eldest daughter have died, a son is killed in the war, and the place is forsaken. In the last part the house is alive again with the surviving Ramsays and two of the former guests. Mr Ramsay, the philosopher, grimly magnificent, heads an expedition to the lighthouse; and James, now sixteen, accomplishes his dream, though all the family have a sense of paternal tyranny.

Such are the bare bones of the framework; but one feels they are no more like the whole story than the skeleton carved in a medieval tomb is to the robed and comely effigy above it. For the book has its own motion: a soft stir and light of perceptions, meeting or crossing, of the gestures and attitudes, the feelings and thoughts of people: of instants in which these are radiant or absurd, have the burden of sadness or of the inexplicable. It is a reflective book, with an ironical or wistful questioning of life and reality. Somehow this steals into the pages, whether there is a sunny peace in the garden, or Mrs Ramsay is interrupted in a fairy-tale, or a couple is late for dinner, so that one is inclined to say that this question of the meaning of things, however masked, is not only the essence but the real protagonist in the story. One is hardly surprised when it emerges openly now and again towards the end:

What was it then? What did it mean? Could things thrust their hands up and grip one; could the blade cut; the fist grasp? Was there no safety? No learning by heart of the ways of the world? No guide, no shelter, but all was miracle, and leaping from the pinnacle of a tower into the air? Could it be, even for elderly people, that this was life? – startling, unexpected, unknown? For one moment she felt that if they both got up, here, now on the lawn, and demanded an explanation, why it was so short, why it was so inexplicable, said it with violence, as two fully-equipped human beings from whom nothing should be hid might speak, then, beauty would roll itself up; the space would fill; those empty flourishes would form into shape; if they said it loud enough Mrs Ramsay would return. 'Mrs Ramsay!' she said aloud, 'Mrs Ramsay!' The tears ran down her face.

Perhaps this is one reason why you are less conscious of Mrs Woolf's characters than they are of each other. They have an acute consciousness which reminds you of the people in Henry James, but with a difference. The characters of Henry James are so absorbed in each other that they have no problem beyond the truth, or otherwise, of their relations; and they are so intensely seen as persons that they are real. But the people in Mrs Woolf's book seem to be looking through each other at some farther question; and, although they interact vividly, they are not completely real. No doubt, as Lily Briscoe the painter thinks in the novel, to know people in outline is one way of knowing them. And they are seen here in the way they are meant to be seen. But the result is that, while you know quite well the kind of people represented in the story, they lack something as individuals. Mr Ramsay, certainly – masterful and helpless, egotist and hero – does leave a deep mark by the end. His wife, with her calm beauty, her sympathy and swift decided actions, is more of a type, though her personality is subtly pervasive even when she has ceased to live. But there is a significant curtness in the parenthesis which (surely with a slip in punctuation) announces her death: 'Mr Ramsay stumbling along a passage stretched his arms out one dark morning, but Mrs Ramsay having died rather suddenly the night before he stretched his arms out. They remained empty.' Here Mrs Woolf's detachment seems a little strained, and, in fact, this transitional part of the book is not its strongest part.

One comes back, however, to the charm and pleasure of her design. It is carried through with a rare subtlety. Every little thread in it – Mr Ramsay writing a book, Lily Briscoe struggling with her picture, the lights in the bay, the pathos and the absurdity – is woven in one texture, which has piquancy and poetry by turns. A sad book in the main, with all its entertainment, it is one to return to; for it has that power of leaving a vision which is less often found, perhaps, in novels than in a short story. This springs from a real emotion, best described in words of Mrs Woolf's own:

There might be lovers whose gift it was to choose out the elements of things and place them together and so, giving them a wholeness not theirs in life, make of some scene, or meeting of people (all now gone and separate), one of those globed compacted things over which thought lingers, and love plays.

(5 May 1927)

Conrad Aiken

AMONG contemporary writers of fiction, Mrs Woolf is a curious and anomalous figure. In some respects, she is as 'modern', as radical, as Mr Joyce or Miss Richardson or M. Jules Romains; she is a highly self-conscious examiner of consciousness, a bold and original experimenter with the technique of novel-writing; but she is also, and just as strikingly, in other respects 'old-fashioned'. This anomaly does not defy analysis. The aroma of 'old-fashionedness' that rises from these highly original and modern novels – from the pages of *Jacob's Room*, *Mrs Dalloway*, and now again from those of *To the Lighthouse* – is a quality of attitude; a quality, to use a word which is itself nowadays old-fashioned, but none the less fragrant, of spirit. For in this regard, Mrs Woolf is no more modern than Jane Austen: she breathes the

same air of gentility, of sequestration, of tradition; of life and
people and things all brought, by the slow polish of centuries of
tradition and use, to a pervasive refinement in which discrimination, on every conceivable plane, has become as instinctive and
easy as the beat of a wing. Her people are 'gentle' people; her
houses are the houses of gentlefolk; and the consciousness that
informs both is a consciousness of well-being and culture, of the
richness and lustre and dignity of tradition; a disciplined consciousness, in which emotions and feelings find their appropriate
attitudes as easily and naturally – as *habitually*, one is tempted to
say – as a skilled writer finds words.

It is this tightly circumscribed choice of scene – to use 'scene'
in a social sense – that gives to Mrs Woolf's novels, despite her
modernity of technique and insight, their odd and delicious air of
parochialism, as of some small village-world, as bright and vivid
and perfect in its tininess as a miniature: a small complete world
which time has somehow missed. Going into these houses, one
would almost expect to find antimacassars on the chair-backs and
daguerreotype albums on the tables. For these people – these
Clarissa Dalloways and Mrs Ramsays and Lily Briscoes – are all
vibrantly and saturatedly conscious of background. And they all
have the curious innocence that accompanies that sort of awareness. They are the creatures of seclusion, the creatures of shelter;
they are exquisite beings, so perfectly and elaborately adapted to
their environment that they have taken on something of the
roundness and perfection of works of art. Their life, in a sense, is
a sea-pool life: unruffled and secret: almost, if we can share the
cool illusion of the sea-pool's occupants, inviolable. They hear
rumours of the sea itself, that vast and terrifying force that lies
somewhere beyond them, or around them, but they cherish a
sublime faith that it will not disturb them; and if it does, at last,
break in upon them with cataclysmic force, a chaos of disorder
and undisciplined violence, they can find no language for the
disaster: they are simply bewildered.

But if, choosing such people, and such a *mise en scène*, for her
material, Mrs Woolf inevitably makes her readers think of *Pride
and Prejudice* and *Mansfield Park*, she compels us just as sharply,

by her method of evoking them, to think of *Pilgrimage* and
Ulysses and *The Death of a Nobody*. Mrs Woolf is an excellent
critic, an extremely conscious and brilliant craftsman in prose; she
is intensely interested in the technique of fiction; and one has at
times wondered, so vividly from her prose has arisen a kind of
self-consciousness of adroitness, whether she might not lose her
way and give us a mere series of virtuosities or *tours de force*. It
is easy to understand why Katherine Mansfield distrusted 'Mr
Bennett and Mrs Brown'. She felt a kind of sterility in this
dexterous holding of the raw stuff of life at arm's length, this
playing with it as if it were a toy. Why not be more immediate –
why not surrender to it? And one did indeed feel a rather baffling
aloofness in this attitude: it was as if Mrs Woolf were a little afraid
to come to grips with anything so coarse, preferred to see it
through a safe thickness of plate-glass. It was as if she could not
be quite at ease with life until she had stilled it, reduced it to the
mobile immobility of art – reduced it, even, to such comfortable
proportions and orderliness as would not disturb the drawing-
room. In *Jacob's Room*, however, and *Mrs Dalloway*, Mrs Woolf
began to make it clear that this tendency to sterile dexterity,
though pronounced, might not be fatal; and now, in her new
novel, *To the Lighthouse*, she relieves one's doubts, on this score,
almost entirely.

For, if one still feels, during the first part of this novel almost
depressingly, and intermittently thereafter, Mrs Woolf's irritating
air as of carrying an enormous technical burden: her air of saying
'See how easily I do this!' or 'This is incomparably complex and
difficult, but I have the brains for it': nevertheless, one's irritation
is soon lost in the growing sense that Mrs Woolf has at last found
a complexity and force of theme which is commensurate with the
elaborateness and self-consciousness of her technical 'pattern'.
By degrees, one forgets the manner in the matter. One resists the
manner, petulantly objects to it, in vain: the moment comes when
at last one ceases to be aware of something persistently artificial
in this highly feminine style, and finds oneself simply immersed
in the vividness and actuality of this world of Mrs Woolf's – believing in it, in fact, with the utmost intensity, and feeling it with

that completeness of surrender with which one feels the most moving of poetry. It is not easy to say whether this abdication of 'distance' on the reader's part indicates that Mrs Woolf has now achieved a depth of poetic understanding, a vitality, which was somehow just lacking in the earlier novels, or whether it merely indicates a final triumph of technique. Can one profitably try to make a distinction between work that is manufactured, bitterly and strenuously, by sheer *will* to imagination, and work that is born of imagination all complete – assuming that the former is, in the upshot, just as convincing as the latter? Certainly one feels everywhere in Mrs Woolf's work this will to imagine, this canvassing of possibilities by a restless and searching and brilliant mind: one feels this mind at work, matching and selecting, rejecting this colour and accepting that, saying, 'It is this that the heroine would say, it is this that she would think'; and nevertheless Mrs Woolf's step is so sure, her choice is so nearly invariably right, and her imagination, even if deliberately willed, is so imaginative, that in the end she makes a beautiful success of it. She makes her Mrs Ramsay – by giving us her stream of consciousness – amazingly alive; and she supplements this just sufficiently, from *outside*, as it were, by giving us also, intermittently, the streams of consciousness of her husband, of her friend Lily Briscoe, of her children: so that we are documented, as to Mrs Ramsay, from every quarter and arrive at a solid vision of her by a process of triangulation. The richness and copiousness and ease, with which this is done, are a delight. These people are astoundingly real: they belong to a special 'class', as Mrs Woolf's characters nearly always do, and exhale a Jane-Austenish aroma of smallness and lostness and incompleteness: but they are magnificently real. We live in that delicious house with them – we feel the minute textures of their lives with their own vivid senses – we imagine with their extraordinary imaginations, are self-conscious with their self-consciousness – and ultimately we know them as well, as terribly, as we know ourselves.

Thus, curiously, Mrs Woolf has rounded the circle. Apparently, at the outset of her work, avoiding any attempt to present life 'immediately', as Chekhov and Katherine Mansfield preferred to do; and choosing instead a medium more sophisticated and conscious, as if she never for a moment wished us to forget the *frame* of the picture, and the fact that the picture *was* a picture; she has finally brought this method to such perfection, or so perfectly allowed it to flower of itself, that the artificial has become natural, the mediate has become immediate. The technical brilliance glows, melts, falls away; and there remains a poetic apprehension of life of extraordinary loveliness. Nothing happens, in this houseful of odd nice people, and yet all of life happens. The tragic futility, the absurdity, the pathetic beauty of life – we experience all of this in our sharing of seven hours of Mrs Ramsay's wasted or not wasted existence. We have seen, through her, the world.

('The Novel as Work of Art',
from *Dial*, July 1927)

Leonard Woolf

ALTHOUGH her day-to-day mental health in general became stronger and more stable through the 1920s and 1930s, the crises of exhaustion and black despair when she had finished a book seemed each time to become deeper and more dangerous. We had a terrifying time with *The Years* in 1936; she was much nearer a complete breakdown than she had ever been since 1913. . . . But at the beginning of May she was in such a state that I insisted that she should break off and take a complete holiday for a fortnight. We drove down into the west country by slow stages, stopping in Weymouth, Lyme Regis, and Beckey Falls on Dartmoor, until we reached Budock Vean in that strange primordial somnolent Cornish peninsula between Falmouth and Helford Passage, where the names of the villages soothe one by their strangeness – Gweek and Constantine and Mawnan Smith. As a child Virginia had spent summer after summer in Leslie Stephen's house at St Ives in Cornwall – the scene of *To the Lighthouse* is St Ives and the lighthouse in the book is the Godrevy light which she saw night by night shine across the bay into the windows of Talland House. No casements are so magic, no faery lands so forlorn as those which all our lives we treasure in our memory of the summer holidays of our childhood. Cornwall never failed to fill Virginia with this delicious feeling of nostalgia and romance.

I thought that for Virginia's jangled nerves I might find in Cornwall the balm which the unfortunate Jeremiah thought – mistakenly – he might find in Gilead to salve the 'hurt of the daughter of my people'. That was why I drove west and stayed in Budock Vean, and revisited Coverack and the Lizard and Penzance, and went on to stay with Will and Ka Arnold-Forster in that strange house, Eagle's Nest, perched high up on the rock at Zennor a few miles from St Ives. As the final cure, we wandered round St Ives and crept into the garden of Talland House and in the dusk Virginia peered through the ground-floor windows to see the ghosts of her childhood. I do not know whether, like Heine, she saw the Doppelgänger and heard the mournful echo of Schubert's song: 'Heart, do you remember that empty house? Do you remember who used to live there? Ah, someone comes! Wringing her hands! Terrible! It is myself. I can see my own face. Hi, Ghost! What does it mean? What are you doing, mocking what I went through here all those years ago.'

(from *Downhill All the Way: an autobiography of the years 1919–1939*, 1967)

PART TWO

Studies

William Troy

VIRGINIA WOOLF AND THE NOVEL OF SENSIBILITY (1932)

Life is not a series of gig-lamps symmetrically arranged; but a *luminous halo, a semi-transparent envelope* surrounding us from the beginning of consciousness to the end.

NOT only in rhythm and tone but also in the imponderable vagueness of its diction this statement has a familiar ring to the modern ear. The phrases in italics alone are sufficient to suggest its proper order and place in contemporary thought. For if this is not the exact voice of Henri Bergson, it is at least a very successful imitation. Dropped so casually by Mrs Woolf in the course of a dissertation on the art of fiction, such a statement really implies an acceptance of a whole theory of metaphysics. Behind it lies all that resistance to the naturalistic formula, all that enthusiastic surrender to the world of flux and individual intuition, which has constituted the influence of Bergson on the art and literature of the past thirty years. Whether Mrs Woolf was affected by this influence directly, or through the medium of Proust or some other secondary source, is not very important. The evidence is clear enough in her work that the fundamental view of reality on which it is based derives from what was the most popular ideology of her generation. What is so often regarded as unique in her fiction is actually less the result of an individual attitude than of the dominant metaphysical bias of a whole generation.

For members of that generation concerned with fiction the philosophy of flux and intuition offered a relief from the cumbersome technique and mechanical pattern of naturalism. (Against even such mild adherents to the doctrine as Wells and Bennett Mrs Woolf raised the attack in *Mr Bennett and Mrs Brown.*) Moreover, the new philosophy opened up sources of interest for the novel which allowed it to dispense with whatever values such writers as George Eliot and Henry James had depended on in a still remoter period. Like naturalism, it brought with it its own version of an esthetic; it supplied a medium which involved no values other than the primary one of self-expression. Of course one cannot wholly ignore the helpful co-operation of psycho-analysis. But to distinguish between the metaphysical and the psychological origins of the new techniques is not a profitable task. It is not difficult to understand how the subjective novel could have derived its assumptions from the one field, its method from the other. And the fusion between them had been completed by the time Mrs Woolf published her little pamphlet. Everybody, in Rebecca West's phrase, was 'doing' a novel in the period immediately following the World War. Everybody, that is to say, was writing a quasi-poetic rendition of his sensibility in a form which it was agreed should be called the novel.

Possessing a mind schooled in abstract theory, especially alert to the intellectual novelties of her own time, Mrs Woolf was naturally attracted by a method which in addition to being contemporary offered so much to the speculative mind. But the deeper causes of the attraction, it is now evident, were embedded in Mrs Woolf's own temperament or sensibility. The subjective mode is the only mode especially designed for temperaments immersed in their own sensibility, obsessed with its movements and vacillations, fascinated by its instability. It was the only mode possible for someone like Proust; it was alone capable of projecting the sensibility which, because it has remained so uniform throughout her work, we may be permitted to call Mrs Woolf's own. Here it happens to be Bernard, in *The Waves*, speaking:

A space was cleared in my mind. I saw through the thick leaves of habit. Leaning over the gate I regretted so much litter, so much unaccomplishment and separation, for one cannot cross London to see a friend, life being so full of engagements; nor take ship to India and see a naked man spearing fish in blue water. I said life had been imperfect, an unfinished phrase. It had been impossible for me, taking snuff as I do from my bagman met in a train, to keep coherency – that sense of the generations, of women carrying red pitchers to the Nile, of the nightingale who sings among conquests and migrations . . .

But this might be almost any one of Mrs Woolf's characters; and from such a passage we can appreciate how perfectly the subjective or 'confessional' method is adapted to the particular sensibility reflected throughout her work.

And if we require in turn some explanation for this hieratic cultivation of the sensibility, we need only examine for a moment the nature and quality of the experience represented by most of her characters. From *The Voyage Out* to *The Waves* Mrs Woolf has written almost exclusively about one class of people, almost, one might say, one type of individual, and that, a class or type whose experience is largely vicarious, whose contacts with actuality have been for one or another reason incomplete, unsatisfactory, or inhibited. Made up of poets, metaphysicians, botanists, water-colorists, the world of Mrs Woolf is a kind of superior Bohemia, as acutely refined and aristocratic in its way as the world of Henry James, except that its inhabitants concentrate on their sensations and impressions rather than on their problems of conduct. (Such problems, of course, do not exist for them since they rarely allow themselves even the possibility of action.) Life for these people, therefore, is painful less for what it has done to them than for what their excessive sensitivity causes them to make of it. Almost every one of them is the victim of some vast and inarticulate fixation: Mrs Dalloway on Peter Walsh, Lily Briscoe in *To the Lighthouse* on Mrs Ramsay, everyone in *The Waves* on Percival. All of them, like Neville in the last-named book, are listening for 'that wild hunting-song, Percival's music'. For all of them what Percival represents is something lost or denied, something which must remain for ever outside the intense circle of their own renunciation. No consolation is left them but solitude, a timeless solitude in which to descend to a kind of self-induced nirvana. 'Heaven be praised for solitude!' cries Bernard toward the close of *The Waves*. 'Heaven be praised for solitude that has removed the pressure of the eye, the solicitation of the body, and all need of lies and phrases.' Through

solitude these people are able to relieve themselves with finality
from the responsibilities of living, they are able to complete their
divorce from reality even to the extent of escaping the burden
of personality. Nothing in Mrs Woolf's work serves as a better
revelation of her characters as a whole than these ruminations of
Mrs Ramsay in *To the Lighthouse*:

To be silent; to be alone. All the being and the doing, expansive,
glittering, vocal, evaporated; and one shrunk, with a sense of
solemnity, to being oneself, a wedge-shaped core of darkness
. . . When life sank down for a moment, *the range of experience
seemed limitless*. . . . Losing personality, one lost the fret, the
hurry, the stir; and there rose to her lips always some exclamation of triumph over life when things came together in this
peace, this rest, this eternity . . .

What Mrs Ramsay really means to say is that when life sinks
down in this manner the range of *implicit* experience is limitless.
Once one has abandoned the effort to act upon reality, either
with the will or the intellect, the mind is permitted to wander in
freedom through the stored treasures of its memories and impressions, following no course but that of fancy or simple association, murmuring Pillicock sat on Pillicock's Hill or Come away,
come away, Death, 'mingling poetry and nonsense, floating in
the stream'. But experience in this sense is something quite different from experience in the sense in which it is ordinarily understood in referring to people in life or in books. It does not involve
that active impact of character upon reality which provides the
objective materials of experience in both literature and life. And
if it leads to its own peculiar triumphs, it does so only through a
dread of being and doing, an abdication of personality and a
shrinking into the solitary darkness.

Because of this self-imposed limitation of their experience,
therefore, the characters of Mrs Woolf are unable to *function*
anywhere but on the single plane of the sensibility. On this plane
alone is enacted whatever movement, drama, or tragedy occurs
in her works. The movement of course is centrifugal, the drama
unrealized, the tragedy hushed. The only truly dramatic moments

in these novels are, significantly enough, precisely those in which the characters seem now and again to catch a single, brief glimpse of that imposing world of fact which they have forsworn. The scenes we remember best are those like the one in *Mrs Dalloway* in which the heroine, bright, excited, and happy among the guests at her party, is brought suddenly face to face with the fact of death. Or like the extremely moving one at the end of *To the Lighthouse* in which Lily Briscoe at last breaks into tears and cries aloud the hallowed name of Mrs Ramsay. In such scenes Mrs Woolf is excellent; no living novelist can translate these nuances of perception in quite the same way; and their effect in her work is of an occasional transitory rift in that diaphanous 'envelope' with which she surrounds her characters from beginning to end.

SOURCE: *Symposium*, III (1932); reprinted in *Selected Essays* (1967).

David Daiches

THE SEMI-TRANSPARENT ENVELOPE (1942)

Two years after *Mrs Dalloway* there appeared the book which marks the perfection of Virginia Woolf's art: *To the Lighthouse*. Here, instead of taking a group of characters in upper middle-class London society and wringing some rarefied meaning out of their states of mind, she keeps her characters throughout the novel on an island in the Hebrides, an island unparticularized and remote, which, by its setting and associations, helps her to break down the apparent concreteness of character and events into that 'luminous halo' which for her was the most adequate symbol of life. The basic plot framework is simple enough. The book is divided into three sections: the first, 'The Window', deals with Mr and Mrs Ramsay, their children and their guests on holiday on the island one late September day a few years before the First World War; the second, 'Time Passes', gives an impressionist rendering of the change and decay which their house on the island suffers in the years following: the war prevents the family from revisiting the place, Mrs Ramsay dies, Andrew Ramsay is killed in the war, Prue Ramsay dies in childbirth – all this is suggested parenthetically in the course of the account of the decay of the house; in the third and final section, 'The Lighthouse', we see the remnant of the Ramsay family revisiting their house on the island some ten years later, with some of the same guests, and the book closes with Lily Briscoe, a guest on both visits, completing a picture she had begun on the first visit – completing it in the light of the vision which finally comes to her and enables her to see for a moment in their proper relation the true significance of the dead Mrs Ramsay, of the whole Ramsay family, and of the physical scene in front of her. A further tie-up is effected in the actual visit to the lighthouse made by Mr Ramsay and two of the children in the last section: this visit had been planned in the first section, but had been put off owing to bad weather, much to the disappointment of young James Ramsay and his mother, and so the visit, when it actually takes place years after Mrs Ramsay's death, with James no longer a small boy but an adolescent, has a certain symbolic meaning. The arrival of the Ramsays at the lighthouse, and Lily Briscoe's achievement of her vision as she sits in front of the Ramsays' house painting and meditating, occur contemporaneously, and this conjunction possesses further symbolic significance.

Upon this framework Virginia Woolf weaves a delicate pattern of symbolic thoughts and situations. The book opens with a certain deliberate abruptness: ' "Yes, of course, if it's fine tomorrow," said Mrs Ramsay. "But you'll have to be up with the lark," she added.'

She is referring to the expedition to the lighthouse, on which young James, aged six, had set his heart. The planning and eventual accomplishment of this expedition constitute the main principle of integration employed by Virginia Woolf to unify the story. Following the opening remark of Mrs Ramsay come James's reactions:

To her son these words conveyed an extraordinary joy, as if it were settled, the expedition were bound to take place, and the wonder to which he had looked forward, for years and years it seemed, was, after a night's darkness and a day's sail, within touch. Since he belonged, even at the age of six, to that great clan which cannot keep this feeling separate from that, but must let future prospects, with their joys and sorrows, cloud what is actually at hand, since to such people even in earliest childhood any turn in the wheel of sensation has the power to crystallise and transfix the moment upon which its gloom or radiance rests, James Ramsay, sitting on the floor cutting out pictures from the illustrated catalogue of the Army and Navy Stores, endowed the picture of a refrigerator, as his mother spoke, with heavenly bliss. It was fringed with joy. The wheelbarrow, the lawnmower, the sound of poplar trees, leaves whitening before rain, rooks cawing, brooms knocking, dresses rustling – all these were so

coloured and distinguished in his mind that he had already his
private code, his secret language, though he appeared the image
of stark and uncompromising severity, with his high forehead
and his fierce blue eyes, impeccably candid and pure, frowning
slightly at the sight of human frailty, so that his mother, watching
him guide his scissors neatly round the refrigerator, imagined
him all red and ermine on the Bench or directing a stern and
momentous enterprise in some crisis of public affairs.

Here is a careful weaving together of character's consciousness,
author's comment, and one character's view of another. On
James's happy expectation crashes his father's ruthless remarks:
'"But," said his father, stopping in front of the drawing-room
window, "it won't be fine."'

This remark arouses in James a fierce, frustrated anger. 'Had
there been an axe handy, or a poker, any weapon that would have
gashed a hole in his father's breast and killed him, there and
then, James would have seized it.' Mr Ramsay was always right,
and James knew that his prophecy could not be laughed off.
But his anger at his father's deliberate dashing of his hopes was
increased rather than modified by this knowledge, and the
grudge entered into his subconscious to be finally exorcized
only when, ten years later, they arrive at the lighthouse and
Mr Ramsay turns and compliments James on his steering of the
boat.

Virginia Woolf's handling of this point is, however, much
subtler than this bald summary would suggest. For the theme is
symbolic in its implications, and in her elaboration of it Virginia
Woolf not only brings out the full character of James and his
father, establishes their complex relation to each other, indicates
the relation of Mr Ramsay to the other characters and their
relation to him, and illuminates some general problems concerning the relation of parents to children, husband to wife, and
people to each other, but also endeavours to suggest indirectly
certain profound ideas about experience and its dependence on
time and personality. What is the most significant quality in
experience? This is the question which *To the Lighthouse* seems
designed to answer. In what sense can one personality ever

'know' another? What relation do our various memories of a single object bear to the 'real' object? What remains when a personality has been 'spilt on air' and exists only as a group of contradictory impressions in others, who are also moving towards death? In what way does time condition human experience and its values? Out of that complex of retrospect and anticipation which is consciousness, what knowledge can emerge, what vision can be achieved? These are further problems which the book's form and content are designed to illuminate.

And so, with this limited collection of characters – the Ramsays and their guests – Virginia Woolf passes from one consciousness to another, from one group to another, exploring the significance of their reactions, following the course of their meditations, carefully arranging and patterning the images that rise up in their minds, bringing together, with care and economy, a select number of symbolic incidents, until a design has been achieved, the solidity of objective things breaks down, and experience is seen as something fluid though with definite shape, inexpressible yet significant.

In *Mrs Dalloway* Virginia Woolf set the scene of her action with precision. We know at any given moment what part of London we are in. Streets and buildings are given their real names, and carefully particularized. But in *To the Lighthouse* for the first time in a full-length novel Virginia Woolf reduces the particularizing details of the setting to a minimum. We know from one fleeting reference, that we are on an island in the Hebrides[1] but that is all the information we get. For the rest, we learn that the Ramsays' house is within walking distance of the 'town' and situated on a bay. It is clear that Virginia Woolf is here more concerned with conveying a general impression of sea, sand and rocks than with describing any particular place. It is a symbolic setting: this group of people temporarily isolated from the rest of society on this remote island represents a microcosm of society, while the background of natural scenery provides images and suggestions that can be used as interpretative symbols. Throughout the book the characters are presented and re-presented until they are finally seen as symbolic. We are

shown now their own minds, now their reactions on the minds
of others, now the memory they leave when they are gone, now
their relation to the landscape, till eventually all this adds up to
something barely expressible (indeed not directly expressible at
all) yet significant. For a split second everything falls into a pattern, and then the meaning is lost again, as (to employ a simile
that keeps recurring in *To the Lighthouse*) we look out of the
windows of a speeding train and see for one brief moment a
group of figures that conveys some strange new meaning.
With the temporary attainment of maximum pattern the book
ends. Lily Briscoe, the painter, the spinster who will not marry
and keeps looking for the proper significance of characters and
scenes, is deputy for the author: when she, thinking of the now
dead Mrs Ramsay and of Mr Ramsay off in the boat to the lighthouse, and endeavouring at the same time to find the proper way
of finishing her picture, finally has her 'vision', the pattern is
complete, she finishes her painting, and the book ends. The
Ramsays have at last landed at the lighthouse. Lily Briscoe,
thinking of them as she paints, recognizes their landing as somehow significant. So does old Mr Carmichael, who has been dozing
in a chair on the lawn not far from her. And the final threads
come together:

'He has landed,' she said aloud. 'It is finished.' Then, surging
up, puffing slightly, old Mr Carmichael stood beside her, looking
like an old pagan god, shaggy, with weeds in his hair and the
trident (it was only a French novel) in his hand. He stood by her
on the edge of the lawn, swaying a little in his bulk, and said,
shading his eyes with his hand: 'They will have landed,' and she
felt that she had been right. They had not needed to speak. They
had been thinking the same things and he had answered her without her asking him anything. He stood there as if he were spreading his hands over all the weakness and suffering of mankind;
she thought he was surveying, tolerantly and compassionately,
their final destiny. Now he has crowned the occasion, she
thought, when his hand slowly fell, as if she had seen him let fall
from his great height a wreath of violets and asphodels which,
fluttering slowly, lay at length upon the earth.

Quickly, as if she were recalled by something over there, she turned to her canvas. There it was – her picture. Yes, with all its greens and blues, its lines running up and across, its attempt at something. It would be hung in the attics, she thought; it would be destroyed. But what did that matter? she asked herself, taking up her brush again. She looked at the steps; they were empty; she looked at her canvas; it was blurred. With a sudden intensity, as if she saw it clear for a second, she drew a line there, in the centre. It was done; it was finished. Yes, she thought, laying down her brush in extreme fatigue, I have had my vision.

The characters in *To the Lighthouse* are carefully arranged in their relation to each other, so that a definite symbolic pattern emerges. Mr Ramsay, the professor of philosophy, who made one original contribution to thought in his youth and has since been repeating and elaborating it without being able to see through to the ultimate implications of his system; his wife, who knows more of life in an unsystematic and intuitive way, who has no illusions ('There was no treachery too base for the world to commit; she knew that. No happiness lasted; she knew that') yet presides over her family with a calm and competent efficiency; Lily Briscoe, who refuses to get married and tries to express her sense of reality in terms of colour and form; Charles Tansley, the aggressive young philosopher with an inferiority complex; old Mr Carmichael, who dozes unsocially in the sun and eventually turns out to be a lyric poet; Minta Doyle and Paul Rayley, the undistinguished couple whom Mrs Ramsay gently urges into a not too successful marriage – each character has a very precise function in this carefully organized story. The lighthouse itself, standing lonely in the midst of the sea, is a symbol of the individual who is at once a unique being and a part of the flux of history. To reach the lighthouse is, in a sense, to make contact with a truth outside oneself, to surrender the uniqueness of one's ego to an impersonal reality. Mr Ramsay, who is an egotist constantly seeking applause and encourage-ment from others, resents his young son's enthusiasm for visiting the lighthouse, and only years later, when his wife has died and his own life is almost worn out, does he win this freedom from

self – and it is significant that Virginia Woolf makes Mr Ramsay
escape from his egotistic preoccupations for the first time just
before the boat finally reaches the lighthouse. Indeed, the personal grudges nourished by each of the characters fall away just
as they arrive; Mr Ramsay ceases to pose with his book and
breaks out with an exclamation of admiration for James's steering; James and his sister Cam lose their resentment at their
father's way of bullying them into this expedition and cease
hugging their grievances: 'What do you want? they both wanted
to ask. They both wanted to say, Ask us anything and we will
give it you. But he did not ask them anything.' And at the
moment when they land, Lily Briscoe and old Mr Carmichael,
who had not joined the expedition, suddenly develop a mood of
tolerance and compassion for mankind, and Lily has the vision
which enables her to complete her picture.

There is a colour symbolism running right through the book.
When Lily Briscoe is wrestling unsuccessfully with her painting,
in the first part of the book, she sees the colours as 'bright violet
and staring white', but just as she achieves her final vision at the
book's conclusion, and is thus able to complete her picture, she
notices that the lighthouse 'had melted away into a blue haze';
and though she sees the canvas clearly for a second before
drawing the final line, the implication remains that this blurring
of colours is bound up with her vision. Mr Ramsay, who
visualizes the last, unattainable, step in his philosophy as glimmer-
ing *red* in the distance, is contrasted with the less egotistical Lily,
who works with blues and greens, and with Mrs Ramsay, who
is indicated on Lily's canvas as 'a triangular purple shape'. Red
and brown appear to be the colours of individuality and egotism,
while blue and green are the colours of impersonality. Mr
Ramsay, until the very end of the book, is represented as an
egotist, and his colour is red or brown; Lily is the impersonal
artist, and her colour is blue; Mrs Ramsay stands somewhere
between, and her colour is purple.[2] The journey to the lighthouse
is the journey from egotism to impersonality.

But it is much more than that. The story opens with Mrs
Ramsay promising young James that if it is fine they will go to

the lighthouse tomorrow, whereupon Mr Ramsay points out
that it won't be fine, and arouses James's long lived resentment.
It concludes, ten years later when Mrs Ramsay is dead and
James is sixteen, with the arrival of Mr Ramsay, James and Cam
at the lighthouse and the shedding at that moment of all their
personal grudges and resentments – all of which synchronize
with Lily's achievement of her vision. The story is obviously
more than the contrast between the initial and the final situation,
for between these two points there is an abundance of detail –
description of character and of characters' thought processes –
and a number of symbolic situations which widen the implications of the book as it proceeds and prevent the reader from
identifying its meaning with any single 'moral'.

The theme of the relation of the individual to existence as a
whole is treated in a variety of ways. It recurs as a constantly
shifting thought pattern in character after character. Lily Briscoe,
the artist, is observing Mr Ramsay, philosopher and egotist:

Lily Briscoe went on putting away her brushes, looking up,
looking down. Looking up, there he was – Mr Ramsay – advan-
cing towards them, swinging, careless, oblivious, remote. A bit of
a hypocrite? she repeated. Oh, no – the most sincere of men, the
truest (here he was), the best; but, looking down, she thought,
he is absorbed in himself, he is tyrannical, he is unjust; and kept
looking down, purposely, for only so could she keep steady,
staying with the Ramsays. Directly one looked up and saw them,
what she called 'being in love' flooded them. They became part of
that unreal but penetrating and exciting universe which is the
world seen through the eyes of love. The sky stuck to them; the
birds sang through them. And, what was even more exciting,
she felt, too, as she saw Mr Ramsay bearing down and retreating,
and Mrs Ramsay sitting with James in the window and the cloud
moving and the tree bending, how life, from being made up of
little separate incidents which one lived one by one, became
curled and whole like a wave which bore one up with it and threw
one down with it, there, with a dash on the beach.

Speculations of this kind are constantly juxtaposed to specific incidents, which take on a symbolic quality in the light of the juxtaposition:

Standing now, apparently transfixed, by the pear tree, impressions poured in upon her of those two men, and to follow her thought was like following a voice which speaks too quickly to be taken down by one's pencil, and the voice was her own voice saying without prompting undeniable, everlasting, contradictory things, so that even the fissures and humps on the bark of the pear tree were irrevocably fixed there for eternity. You have greatness, she continued, but Mr Ramsay has none of it. He is petty, selfish, vain, egotistical; he is spoilt; he is a tyrant; he wears Mrs Ramsay to death; but he has what you (she addressed Mr Bankes) have not; a fiery unworldliness; he knows nothing about trifles; he loves dogs and his children. He has eight. Mr Bankes has none. Did he not come down in two coats the other night and let Mrs Ramsay trim his hair into a pudding basin? All of this danced up and down, like a company of gnats, each separate, but all marvellously controlled in an invisible elastic net – danced up and down in Lily's mind, in and about the branches of the pear tree, where still hung in effigy the scrubbed kitchen table, symbol of her profound respect for Mr Ramsay's mind, until her thought which had spun quicker and quicker exploded of its own intensity; she felt released; a shot went off close at hand, and there came, flying from its fragments, frightened, effusive, tumultuous, a flock of starlings.

'Jasper!' said Mr Bankes. They turned the way the starlings flew, over the terrace. Following the scatter of swift-flying birds in the sky they stepped through the gap in the high hedge straight into Mr Ramsay, who boomed tragically at them, 'Some one had blundered!'

The stream of consciousness of one character enables us to see individual actions of other characters in their proper symbolic meaning. It is a subtle and effective device.

It would take too much space to discuss the minor devices employed by Virginia Woolf in order to help expand the meaning into something profounder yet vaguer than any specific thesis. The main theme concerns the relation of personality, death, and time to each other; the relation of the individual to the sum of experience in general. Many devices are used to suggest this problem – presented less as a problem than as a situation, a quality in life on which the significance of living depends. Minor points such as the characteristic gesture of Mr Ramsay (raising his hand as if to avert something), symbolic images such as the hand cleaving the blue sea, specific ideas suggested in the thought process of one or other of the characters (each of whom can be made at any time to speak for the author by any one of a number of devices which present that character as having momentarily transcended the limitations of his personality and glimpsed some kind of eternal truth) – all help to enrich the implications of the story. Here, for example, is Lily Briscoe, symbol of the artist and his relation to experience:

She wanted to go straight up to him and say, 'Mr Carmichael!' Then he would look up benevolently as always, from his smoky vague green eyes. But one only woke people if one knew what one wanted to say to them. And she wanted to say not one thing, but everything. Little words that broke up the thought and dis-membered it said nothing. 'About life, about death; about Mrs Ramsay' – no, she thought, one could say nothing to nobody. The urgency of the moment always missed its mark. Words fluttered sideways and struck the object inches too low. Then one gave it up; then the idea sunk back again; then one became like most middle-aged people, cautious, furtive, with wrinkles between the eyes and a look of perpetual apprehension. For how could one express in words these emotions of the body? express that emptiness there? (She was looking at the drawing-room steps; they looked extraordinarily empty.) It was one's body feeling, not one's mind. The physical sensations that went with the bare look of the steps had become suddenly extremely un-pleasant. . . . Oh, Mrs Ramsay! she called out silently, to that essence which sat by the boat, that abstract one made of her, that woman in grey, as if to abuse her for having gone, and then having gone, come back again. It had seemed so safe, thinking of her. Ghost, air, nothingness, a thing you could play with easily and safely at any time of day or night, she had been that, and then suddenly she put her hand out and wrung the heart thus. . . .

'What does it mean? How do you explain it all?' she wanted to say, turning to Mr Carmichael again. For the whole world seemed to have dissolved in this early morning hour into a pool of thought, a deep basin of reality, and one could almost fancy that had Mr Carmichael spoken, for instance, a little tear would have rent the surface pool. And then? Something would emerge. A hand would be shoved up, a blade would be flashed. It was nonsense of course.

Here the thoughts and images contained in a character's reverie reflect back and forth on other aspects of the story and enrich the meaning of the whole.

Finally, the reader might ponder on the symbolism of the window in the first section. Mr Ramsay paces up and down in the growing darkness outside, while Mrs Ramsay and James sit by the window, watching him pass back and forth. There is a detailed symbolism here, as deliberate, though not so obvious, as that of Maeterlinck's *Interior*.

Virginia Woolf's characteristic concern with the relation of personality to time, change and death is manifested in her treatment of the character of Mrs Ramsay, who is alive in the first section and whose death is recorded parenthetically in the 'Time Passes' interlude. Yet her personality dominates the book: she lives, in section three, in the memory of the others; her character has become part of history, including and determining the present. As she is about to finish her painting Lily Briscoe thinks of Mrs Ramsay as still influential after death:

Mrs Ramsay, she thought, stepping back and screwing up her eyes. (It must have altered the design a good deal when she was sitting on the step with James. There must have been a shadow.) When she thought of herself and Charles throwing ducks and drakes and of the whole scene on the beach, it seemed to depend somehow upon Mrs Ramsay sitting under the rock, with a pad on her knee, writing letters. (She wrote innumerable letters, and sometimes the wind took them and she and Charles just saved a page from the sea.) But what a power was in the human soul! she thought. That woman sitting there writing under the rock resolved everything into simplicity; made these angers, irritations fall off like old rags; she brought together this and that and then this, and so made out of that miserable silliness and spite (she and Charles squabbling, sparring, had been silly and spiteful) something – this scene on the beach for example, this moment of friendship and liking – which survived, after all these years complete, so that she dipped into it to re-fashion her memory of him, and there it stayed in the mind affecting one almost like a work of art.

And she goes on to speculate on the present significance of the woman who had been dead now for five years:

What is the meaning of life? That was all – a simple question; one that tended to close in on one with years. The great revelation had never come. The great revelation perhaps never did come. Instead there were little daily miracles, illuminations, matches struck unexpectedly in the dark; here was one. This, that, and the other; herself and Charles Tansley and the breaking wave; Mrs Ramsay bringing them together; Mrs Ramsay saying, 'Life stand still here'; Mrs Ramsay making of the moment something permanent (as in another sphere Lily herself tried to make of the moment something permanent) – this was of the nature of a revelation. In the midst of chaos there was shape; this eternal passing and flowing (she looked at the clouds going and the leaves shaking) was struck into stability. Life stand still here, Mrs Ramsay said. 'Mrs Ramsay! Mrs Ramsay!' she repeated. She owed it all to her.

One can compare this with the reverie of Mrs Dalloway on learning of the death of Septimus Warren Smith; the way of relating one character to another is not dissimilar. And just as, at the end of the former book, Mrs Dalloway suddenly has her final illumination after she has watched the old woman opposite go into her bedroom and pull down the blind, so Lily, sitting painting outside the Ramsays' house, sees, just before her final vision, somebody come into the room behind the window:

Suddenly the window at which she was looking was whitened by some light stuff behind it. At last then somebody had come

into the drawing-room; somebody was sitting in the chair. For
Heaven's sake, she prayed, let them sit still there and not come
floundering out to talk to her. Mercifully, whoever it was stayed
still inside; had settled by some stroke of luck so as to throw an
odd-shaped triangular shadow over the step. It altered the composition of the picture a little. It was interesting. It might be
useful. Her mood was coming back to her. One must keep on
looking without for a second relaxing the intensity of emotion,
the determination not to be put off, not to be bamboozled. One
must hold the scene – so – in a vise and let nothing come in and
spoil it. One wanted, she thought, dipping her brush deliberately, to be on a level with ordinary experience, to feel simply
that's a chair, that's a table, and yet at the same time, It's a
miracle, it's an ecstasy. The problem might be solved after all.
Ah, but what had happened? Some wave of white went over the
window pane. The air must have stirred some flounce in the
room. Her heart leapt at her and seized her and tortured her.

'Mrs Ramsay! Mrs Ramsay!' she cried, feeling the old horror
come back – to want and want and not to have. Could she inflict
that still? And then, quietly, as if she refrained, that too became
part of ordinary experience, was on a level with the chair, with
the table. Mrs Ramsay – it was part of her perfect goodness –
sat there quite simply, in the chair, flicked her needles to and fro,
knitted her reddish-brown stocking, cast her shadow on the step.
There she sat.

Symbolically, the past returns and shapes the present. Mrs
Ramsay comes back into Lily Briscoe's picture, as she had been
part of the original design ten years before, and out of this
meeting of two very different personalities across the years
the final insight results. Across the water at the same moment
Mr Ramsay, by his praise of James's handling of the boat, is
exorcising the ghost of James's early resentment, also ten years
old, and all the threads of the story are finally coming together.
It is a masterly piece of construction.

To the Lighthouse is a work in which plot, locale, and treatment are so carefully bound up with each other that the resulting
whole is more finely organized and more effective than anything
else Virginia Woolf wrote. The setting in an indefinite island

off the north-west coast of Scotland enables her to indulge in her characteristic symbolic rarefications with maximum effect, for here form and content fit perfectly and inevitably. Middle-class London is not, perhaps, the best scene for a tenuous meditative work of this kind, and *Mrs Dalloway* might be said to suffer from a certain incompatibility between the content and the method of treatment. A misty island is more effective than a London dinner party as the setting for a novel of indirect philosophic suggestion, and as a result qualities of Virginia Woolf's writing which in her other works tend to appear if not as faults at least as of doubtful appropriateness, are seen in this work to their fullest advantage. In *To the Lighthouse* Virginia Woolf found a subject that enabled her to do full justice to her technique.

SOURCE: *Virginia Woolf* (1942; rev. ed. 1963).

NOTES

1. There are precisely three indications of the locality of the setting in *To the Lighthouse*. 'Scotland' is mentioned on page 44 (Harcourt, Brace edition): 'and no lockmaker in the whole of Scotland can mend a bolt'. A map of the Hebrides is referred to on page 170. And when Minta loses her brooch, Paul resolves that if he could not find it 'he would slip out of the house at dawn when they were all asleep and if he could not find it he would go to Edinburgh and buy her another'. Glasgow, however, and not Edinburgh would be the obvious city to go to if they were anywhere in the Hebrides, so this reference is misleading. The present writer, who knows the west coast of Scotland, has amused himself by trying to pin down the island, but has found that it is impossible to do so. The details given by Virginia Woolf are at once too general to be identified with any particular place and too specific (position of the beach, distance from the lighthouse, relation to 'the town', type of vegetation, etc.) to be made to fit in with any spot chosen at random. What island in the Hebrides is there, large enough to contain a 'town' (p. 18, etc.), yet small enough to appear 'very small', 'like a thin leaf', when one had sailed only a few miles away; possessing both cliffs, 'park-like prospects', trees, sandy beach, sand dunes (p. 105), accommodating at walking distance from the 'town' a large house with lawn, cultivated garden, tennis court, and other

amenities, and with local inhabitants named McNab (the charwoman) and Macalister (the boatman). Neither Macalister nor McNab is an Island name. Virginia Woolf's scene is either a composite one (with perhaps some suggestions from Cornwall) or largely imaginary.

2. There is a beautiful example of this colour symbolism on p. 270 (Harcourt, Brace edition): 'Wherever she happened to be, painting, here, in the country or in London, the vision would come to her, and her eyes, half closing, sought something to base her vision on. She looked down the railway carriage, the omnibus; took a line from shoulder or cheek; looked at the windows opposite; at Piccadilly, lamp-strung in the evening. All had been part of the fields of death. But always something – it might be a face, a voice, a paper boy crying *Standard, News* – thrust through, snubbed her, waked her, required and got in the end an effort of attention, so that the vision must be perpetually remade. Now again, moved as she was by some instinctive need of distance and blue, she looked at the bay beneath her, making hillocks of the blue bars of the waves, and stony fields of the purpler spaces, again she was roused as usual by something incongruous. There was a brown spot in the middle of the bay. It was a boat. Yes, she realised that after a second. But whose boat? Mr Ramsay's boat, she replied. Mr Ramsay; the man who had marched past her, with his hand raised, aloof, at the head of a procession, in his beautiful boots, asking her for sympathy, which she had refused. The boat was now half way across the bay.'

This passage, while taking its place naturally in the development of the story, at the same time throws an important light on the earlier and later parts of the book, clarifying symbolism and enriching significance. The artist, having an 'instinctive need of . . . blue', sees Mr Ramsay's boat as a *brown* spot on a *blue* sea. Brown is the personal colour, the egotistic colour; blue belongs to the impersonality of the artist.

Erich Auerbach

THE BROWN STOCKING (1946)

'And even if it isn't fine to-morrow,' said Mrs Ramsay, raising her eyes to glance at William Bankes and Lily Briscoe as they passed, 'it will be another day. And now,' she said, thinking that Lily's charm was her Chinese eyes, aslant in her white, puckered little face, but it would take a clever man to see it, 'and now stand up, and let me measure your leg,' for they might go to the Lighthouse after all, and she must see if the stocking did not need to be an inch or two longer in the leg.

Smiling, for an admirable idea had flashed upon her this very second – William and Lily should marry – she took the heather mixture stocking, with its criss-cross of steel needles at the mouth of it, and measured it against James's leg.

'My dear, stand still,' she said, for in his jealousy, not liking to serve as measuring-block for the Lighthouse keeper's little boy, James fidgeted purposely; and if he did that, how could she see, was it too long, was it too short? she asked.

She looked up – what demon possessed him, her youngest, her cherished? – and saw the room, saw the chairs, thought them fearfully shabby. Their entrails, as Andrew said the other day, were all over the floor; but then what was the point, she asked herself, of buying good chairs to let them spoil up here all through the winter when the house, with only one old woman to see to it, positively dripped with wet? Never mind: the rent was precisely twopence halfpenny; the children loved it; it did her husband good to be three thousand, or if she must be accurate, three hundred miles from his library and his lectures and his disciples; and there was room for visitors. Mats, camp beds, crazy ghosts of chairs and tables whose London life of service was done – they did well enough here; and a photograph or two, and books. Books, she thought, grew of themselves. She never had time to read them. Alas! even the books that had been given her, and

inscribed by the hand of the poet himself: 'For her whose wishes
must be obeyed . . .' 'The happier Helen of our days . . .' dis-
graceful to say, she had never read them. And Croom on the
Mind and Bates on the Savage Customs of Polynesia ('My dear,
stand still,' she said) – neither of those could one send to the
Lighthouse. At a certain moment, she supposed, the house
would become so shabby that something must be done. If they
could be taught to wipe their feet and not bring the beach in with
them – that would be something. Crabs, she had to allow, if
Andrew really wished to dissect them, or if Jasper believed that
one could make soup from seaweed, one could not prevent it;
or Rose's objects – shells, reeds, stones; for they were gifted,
her children, but all in quite different ways. And the result of it
was, she sighed, taking in the whole room from floor to ceiling,
as she held the stocking against James's leg, that things got
shabbier and got shabbier summer after summer. The mat was
fading; the wall-paper was flapping. You couldn't tell any more
that those were roses on it. Still, if every door in a house is left
perpetually open, and no lockmaker in the whole of Scotland
can mend a bolt, things must spoil. What was the use of flinging a
green Cashmere shawl over the edge of a picture frame? In two
weeks it would be the colour of pea soup. But it was the doors
that annoyed her; every door was left open. She listened. The
drawing-room door was open; the hall door was open; it sounded
as if the bedroom doors were open; and certainly the window on
the landing was open, for that she had opened herself. That
windows should be open, and doors shut – simple as it was,
could none of them remember it? She would go into the maids'
bedrooms at night and find them sealed like ovens, except for
Marie's, the Swiss girl, who would rather go without a bath than
without fresh air, but then at home, she had said, 'the mountains
are so beautiful.' She had said that last night looking out of the
window with tears in her eyes. 'The mountains are so beautiful.'
Her father was dying there, Mrs Ramsay knew. He was leaving
them fatherless. Scolding and demonstrating (how to make a bed,
how to open a window, with hands that shut and spread like a
Frenchwoman's) all had folded itself quietly about her, when the
girl spoke, as, after a flight through the sunshine the wings of a
bird fold themselves quietly and the blue of its plumage changes
from bright steel to soft purple. She had stood there silent for

there was nothing to be said. He had cancer of the throat. At the recollection – how she had stood there, how the girl had said 'At home the mountains are so beautiful,' and there was no hope, no hope whatever, she had a spasm of irritation, and speaking sharply, said to James:

'Stand still. Don't be tiresome,' so that he knew instantly that her severity was real, and straightened his leg and she measured it.

The stocking was too short by half an inch at least, making allowance for the fact that Sorley's little boy would be less well grown than James.

'It's too short,' she said, 'ever so much too short.'

Never did anybody look so sad. Bitter and black, half-way down, in the darkness, in the shaft which ran from the sunlight to the depths, perhaps a tear formed; a tear fell; the waters swayed this way and that, received it, and were at rest. Never did anybody look so sad.

But was it nothing but looks? people said. What was there behind it – her beauty, her splendour? Had he blown his brains out, they asked, had he died the week before they were married – some other, earlier lover, of whom rumours reached one? Or was there nothing? nothing, but an incomparable beauty which she lived behind, and could do nothing to disturb? For easily though she might have said at some moment of intimacy when stories of great passion, of love foiled, of ambition thwarted came her way how she too had known or felt or been through it herself, she never spoke. She was silent always. She knew then – she knew without having learnt. Her simplicity fathomed what clever people falsified. Her singleness of mind made her drop plumb like a stone, alight exact as a bird, gave her, naturally, this swoop and fall of the spirit upon truth which delighted, eased, sustained – falsely perhaps.

('Nature has but little clay,' said Mr Bankes once, hearing her voice on the telephone, and much moved by it though she was only telling him a fact about a train, 'like that of which she moulded you.' He saw her at the end of the line, Greek, blue-eyed, straight-nosed. How incongruous it seemed to be telephoning to a woman like that. The Graces assembling seemed to have joined hands in meadows of asphodel to compose that face. Yes, he would catch the 10:30 at Euston.

'But she's no more aware of her beauty than a child,' said Mr Bankes, replacing the receiver and crossing the room to see what progress the workmen were making with an hotel which they were building at the back of his house. And he thought of Mrs Ramsay as he looked at that stir among the unfinished walls. For always, he thought, there was something incongruous to be worked into the harmony of her face. She clapped a deerstalker's hat on her head; she ran across the lawn in goloshes to snatch a child from mischief. So that if it was her beauty merely that one thought of, one must remember the quivering thing, the living thing (they were carrying bricks up a little plank as he watched them), and work it into the picture; or if one thought of her simply as a woman, one must endow her with some freak of idiosyncrasy; or suppose some latent desire to doff her royalty of form as if her beauty bored her and all that men say of beauty, and she wanted only to be like other people, insignificant. He did not know. He did not know. He must go to his work.)

Knitting her reddish-brown hairy stocking, with her head outlined absurdly by the gilt frame, the green shawl which she had tossed over the edge of the frame, and the authenticated masterpiece by Michael Angelo, Mrs Ramsay smoothed out what had been harsh in her manner a moment before, raised his head, and kissed her little boy on the forehead. 'Let's find another picture to cut out,' she said.

THIS piece of narrative prose is the fifth section of part 1 in Virginia Woolf's novel, *To the Lighthouse*, which was first published in 1927. The situation in which the characters find themselves can be almost completely deduced from the text itself. Nowhere in the novel is it set forth systematically, by way of introduction or exposition, or in any other way than as it is here. I shall, however, briefly summarize what the situation is at the beginning of our passage. This will make it easier for the reader to understand the following analysis; it will also serve to bring out more clearly a number of important motifs from earlier sections which are here only alluded to.

Mrs Ramsay is the wife of an eminent London professor of philosophy; she is very beautiful but definitely no longer young. With her youngest son, James – he is six years old – she is sitting

by the window in a good-sized summer house on one of the
Hebrides islands. The professor has rented it for many years. In
addition to the Ramsays, their eight children, and the servants,
there are a number of guests in the house, friends on longer or
shorter visits. Among them is a well-known botanist, William
Bankes, an elderly widower, and Lily Briscoe, who is a painter.
These two are just passing by the window. James is sitting on
the floor busily cutting pictures from an illustrated catalogue.
Shortly before, his mother had told him that, if the weather
should be fine, they would sail to the lighthouse the next day.
This is an expedition James has been looking forward to for a
long time. The people at the lighthouse are to receive various
presents; among these are stockings for the lighthouse-keeper's
boy. The violent joy which James had felt when the trip was
announced had been as violently cut short by his father's acid
observation that the weather would not be fine the next day.
One of the guests, with malicious emphasis, has added some
corroborative meteorological details. After all the others have
left the room, Mrs Ramsay, to console James, speaks the words
with which our passage opens.

The continuity of the section is established through an exterior
occurrence involving Mrs Ramsay and James: the measuring
of the stocking. Immediately after her consoling words (if it isn't
fine tomorrow, we'll go some other day), Mrs Ramsay makes
James stand up so that she can measure the stocking for the
lighthouse-keeper's son against his leg. A little further on she
rather absent-mindedly tells him to stand still – the boy is
fidgeting because his jealousy makes him a little stubborn and
perhaps also because he is still under the impression of the
disappointment of a few moments ago. Many lines later, the
warning to stand still is repeated more sharply. James obeys,
the measuring takes place, and it is found that the stocking is
still considerably too short. After another long interval the scene
concludes with Mrs Ramsay kissing the boy on the forehead
(she thus makes up for the sharp tone of her second order to
him to stand still) and her proposing to help him look for another
picture to cut out. Here the section ends.

This entirely insignificant occurrence is constantly interspersed with other elements which, although they do not interrupt its progress, take up far more time in the narration than the whole scene can possibly have lasted. Most of these elements are inner processes, that is, movements within the consciousness of individual personages, and not necessarily of personages involved in the exterior occurrence but also of others who are not even present at the time: 'people', or 'Mr Bankes'. In addition other exterior occurrences which might be called secondary and which pertain to quite different times and places (the telephone conversation, the construction of the building, for example) are worked in and made to serve as the frame for what goes on in the consciousness of third persons. Let us examine this in detail.

Mrs Ramsay's very first remark is twice interrupted: first by the visual impression she receives of William Bankes and Lily Briscoe passing by together, and then, after a few intervening words serving the progress of the exterior occurrence, by the impression which the two persons passing by have left in her: the charm of Lily's Chinese eyes, which it is not for every man to see – whereupon she finishes her sentence and also allows her consciousness to dwell for a moment on the measuring of the stocking: we may yet go to the lighthouse, and so I must make sure the stocking is long enough. At this point there flashes into her mind the idea which has been prepared by her reflection on Lily's Chinese eyes (William and Lily ought to marry) – an admirable idea, she loves making matches. Smiling, she begins measuring the stocking. But the boy, in his stubborn and jealous love of her, refuses to stand still. How can she see whether the stocking is the right length if the boy keeps fidgeting about? What is the matter with James, her youngest, her darling? She looks up. Her eye falls on the room – and a long parenthesis begins. From the shabby chairs of which Andrew, her eldest son, said the other day that their entrails were all over the floor, her thoughts wander on, probing the objects and the people of her environment. The shabby furniture . . . but still good enough for up here; the advantages of the summer place; so cheap, so good for the children, for her husband; easily fitted up with a few old pieces of furniture, some pictures and books. Books – it is ages since she has had time to read books, even the books which have been dedicated to her (here the lighthouse flashes in for a second, as a place where one can't send such erudite volumes as some of those lying about the room). Then the house again: if the family would only be a little more careful. But, of course, Andrew brings in crabs he wants to dissect; the other children gather seaweed, shells, stones; and she has to let them. All the children are gifted, each in a different way. But naturally, the house gets shabbier as a result (here the parenthesis is interrupted for a moment; she holds the stocking against James's leg); everything goes to ruin. If only the doors weren't always left open. See, everything is getting spoiled, even that Cashmere shawl on the picture frame. The doors are always left open; they are open again now. She listens: Yes, they are all open. The window on the landing is open too; she opened it herself. Windows must be open, doors closed. Why is it that no one can get that into his head? If you go to the maids' rooms at night, you will find all the windows closed. Only the Swiss maid always keeps her window open. She needs fresh air. Yesterday she looked out of the window with tears in her eyes and said: At home the mountains are so beautiful. Mrs Ramsay knew that 'at home' the girl's father was dying. Mrs Ramsay had just been trying to teach her how to make beds, how to open windows. She had been talking away and had scolded the girl too. But then she had stopped talking (comparison with a bird folding its wings after flying in sunlight). She had stopped talking, for there was nothing one could say; he has cancer of the throat. At this point, remembering how she had stood there, how the girl had said at home the mountains were so beautiful – and there was no hope left – a sudden tense exasperation arises in her (exasperation with the cruel meaninglessness of a life whose continuance she is nevertheless striving with all her powers to abet, support, and secure). Her exasperation flows out into the exterior action. The parenthesis suddenly closes (it cannot have taken up more than a few seconds; just now she was still smiling over the thought of a marriage between Mr Bankes and Lily Briscoe), and she says sharply to James: Stand still. Don't be so tiresome.

This is the first major parenthesis. The second starts a little later, after the stocking has been measured and found to be still much too short. It starts with the paragraph which begins and ends with the motif, 'never did anybody look so sad'.

Who is speaking in this paragraph? Who is looking at Mrs Ramsay here, who concludes that never did anybody look so sad? Who is expressing these doubtful, obscure suppositions? – about the tear which – perhaps – forms and falls in the dark, about the water swaying this way and that, receiving it, and then returning to rest? There is no one near the window in the room but Mrs Ramsay and James. It cannot be either of them, nor the 'people' who begin to speak in the next paragraph. Perhaps it is the author. However, if that be so, the author certainly does not speak like one who has a knowledge of his characters – in this case, of Mrs Ramsay – and who, out of his knowledge, can describe their personality and momentary state of mind objectively and with certainty. Virginia Woolf wrote this paragraph. She did not identify it through grammatical and typographical devices as the speech or thought of a third person. One is obliged to assume that it contains direct statements of her own. But she does not seem to bear in mind that she is the author and hence ought to know how matters stand with her characters. The person speaking here, whoever it is, acts the part of one who has only an impression of Mrs Ramsay, who looks at her face and renders the impression received, but is doubtful of its proper interpretation. 'Never did anybody look so sad' is not an objective statement. In rendering the shock received by one looking at Mrs Ramsay's face, it verges upon a realm beyond reality. And in the ensuing passage the speakers no longer seem to be human beings at all but spirits between heaven and earth, nameless spirits capable of penetrating the depths of the human soul, capable too of knowing something about it, but not of attaining clarity as to what is in process there, with the result that what they report has a doubtful ring, comparable in a way to those 'certain airs, detached from the body of the wind', which in a later passage (2, 2) move about the house at night, 'questioning and wondering'. However that may be, here too we are not dealing with objective utterances on the part of the author in respect to one of the characters. No one is certain of anything here: it is all mere supposition, glances cast by one person upon another whose enigma he cannot solve.

This continues in the following paragraph. Suppositions as to the meaning of Mrs Ramsay's expression are made and discussed. But the level of tone descends slightly, from the poetic and non-real to the practical and earthly; and now a speaker is introduced: 'People said.' People wonder whether some recollection of an unhappy occurrence in her earlier life is hidden behind her radiant beauty. There have been rumors to that effect. But perhaps the rumors are wrong: nothing of this is to be learned directly from her; she is silent when such things come up in conversation. But supposing she has never experienced anything of the sort herself, she yet knows everything even without experience. The simplicity and genuineness of her being unfailingly light upon the truth of things, and, falsely perhaps, delight, ease, sustain.

Is it still 'people' who are speaking here? We might almost be tempted to doubt it, for the last words sound almost too personal and thoughtful for the gossip of 'people'. And immediately afterward, suddenly and unexpectedly, an entirely new speaker, a new scene, and a new time are introduced. We find Mr Bankes at the telephone talking to Mrs Ramsay, who has called him to tell him about a train connection, evidently with reference to a journey they are planning to make together. The paragraph about the tear had already taken us out of the room where Mrs Ramsay and James are sitting by the window; it had transported us to an undefinable scene beyond the realm of reality. The paragraph in which the rumors are discussed has a concretely earthly but not clearly identified scene. Now we find ourselves in a precisely determined place, but far away from the summer house – in London, in Mr Bankes's house. The time is not stated ('once'), but apparently the telephone conversation took

place long (perhaps as much as several years) before this particular sojourn in the house on the island. But what Mr Bankes
says over the telephone is in perfect continuity with the preceding paragraph. Again not objectively but in the form of the
impression received by a specific person at a specific moment, it
as it were sums up all that precedes – the scene with the Swiss
maid, the hidden sadness in Mrs Ramsay's beautiful face, what
people think about her, and the impression she makes: Nature
has but little clay like that of which she molded her. Did Mr
Bankes really say that to her over the telephone? Or did he only
want to say it when he heard her voice, which moved him
deeply, and it came into his mind how strange it was to be
talking over the telephone with this wonderful woman, so like
a Greek goddess? The sentence is enclosed in quotation marks, so
one would suppose that he really spoke it. But this is not certain,
for the first words of his soliloquy, which follows, are likewise
enclosed in quotation marks. In any case, he quickly gets hold of
himself, for he answers in a matter-of-fact way that he will
catch the 10:30 at Euston.

But his emotion does not die away so quickly. As he puts
down the receiver and walks across the room to the window in
order to watch the work on a new building across the way –
apparently his usual and characteristic procedure when he wants
to relax and let his thoughts wander freely – he continues to be
preoccupied with Mrs Ramsay. There is always something
strange about her, something that does not quite go with her
beauty (as for instance telephoning); she has no awareness of her
beauty, or at most only a childish awareness; her dress and her
actions show that at times. She is constantly getting involved
in everyday realities which are hard to reconcile with the harmony
of her face. In his methodical way he tries to explain her in-
congruities to himself. He puts forward some conjectures but
cannot make up his mind. Meanwhile his momentary impressions
of the work on the new building keep crowding in. Finally he
gives it up. With the somewhat impatient, determined matter-of-
factness of a methodical and scientific worker (which he is) he
shakes off the insoluble problem 'Mrs Ramsay'. He knows no

solution (the repetition of 'he did not know' symbolizes his impatient shaking it off). He has to get back to his work.

Here the second long interruption comes to an end and we are taken back to the room where Mrs Ramsay and James are. The exterior occurrence is brought to a close with the kiss on James's forehead and the resumption of the cutting out of pictures. But here too we have only an exterior change. A scene previously abandoned reappears, suddenly and with as little transition as if it had never been left, as though the long interruption were only a glance which someone (who?) has cast from it into the depths of time. But the theme (Mrs Ramsay, her beauty, the enigma of her character, her absoluteness, which nevertheless always exercises itself in the relativity and ambiguity of life, in what does not become her beauty) carries over directly from the last phase of the interruption (that is, Mr Bankes's fruitless reflections) into the situation in which we now find Mrs Ramsay: 'with her head outlined absurdly by the gilt frame' etc. – for once again what is around her is not suited to her, is 'something incongruous'. And the kiss she gives her little boy, the words she speaks to him, although they are a genuine gift of life, which James accepts as the most natural and simple truth, are yet heavy with unsolved mystery.

Our analysis of the passage yields a number of distinguishing stylistic characteristics, which we shall now attempt to formulate.

The writer as narrator of objective facts has almost completely vanished; almost everything stated appears by way of reflection in the consciousness of the dramatis personae. When it is a question of the house, for example, or of the Swiss maid, we are not given the objective information which Virginia Woolf possesses regarding these objects of her creative imagination but what Mrs Ramsay thinks or feels about them at a particular moment. Similarly we are not taken into Virginia Woolf's confidence and allowed to share her knowledge of Mrs Ramsay's character; we are given her character as it is reflected in and as it affects various figures in the novel: the nameless spirits which assume certain things about a tear, the people who wonder about

her, and Mr Bankes. In our passage this goes so far that there
actually seems to be no viewpoint at all outside the novel from
which the people and events within it are observed, any more
than there seems to be an objective reality apart from what is in
the consciousness of the characters. Remnants of such a reality
survive at best in brief references to the exterior frame of the
action, such as 'said Mrs Ramsay, raising her eyes . . .' or 'said
Mr Bankes once, hearing her voice'. The last paragraph ('Knitting
her reddish-brown hairy stocking . . .') might perhaps also be
mentioned in this connection. But this is already somewhat
doubtful. The occurrence is described objectively, but as for its
interpretation, the tone indicates that the author looks at Mrs
Ramsay not with knowing but with doubting and questioning
eyes – even as some character in the novel would see her in the
situation in which she is described, would hear her speak the
words given.

The devices employed in this instance (and by a number of
contemporary writers as well) to express the contents of the
consciousness of the dramatis personae have been analyzed and
described syntactically. Some of them have been named (*erlebte
Rede*, stream of consciousness, *monologue intérieur* are examples).
Yet these stylistic forms, especially the *erlebte Rede*, were used in
literature much earlier too, but not for the same aesthetic purpose.
And in addition to them there are other possibilities – hardly
definable in terms of syntax – of obscuring and even obliterating
the impression of an objective reality completely known to the
author; possibilities, that is, dependent not on form but on
intonation and context. A case in point is the passage under discussion, where the author at times achieves the intended effect by
representing herself to be someone who doubts, wonders, hesi-
tates, as though the truth about her characters were not better
known to her than it is to them or to the reader. It is all, then, a
matter of the author's attitude toward the reality of the world he
represents. And this attitude differs entirely from that of authors
who interpret the actions, situations, and characters of their
personages with objective assurance, as was the general practice
in earlier times. Goethe or Keller, Dickens or Meredith, Balzac

or Zola told us out of their certain knowledge what their characters did, what they felt and thought while doing it, and how their actions and thoughts were to be interpreted. They knew everything about their characters. To be sure, in past periods too we were frequently told about the subjective reactions of the characters in a novel or story; at times even in the form of *erlebte Rede*, although more frequently as a monologue, and of course in most instances with an introductory phrase something like 'it seemed to him that . . .' or 'at this moment he felt that . . .' or the like. Yet in such cases there was hardly ever any attempt to render the flow and the play of consciousness adrift in the current of changing impressions (as is done in our text both for Mrs Ramsay and for Mr Bankes); instead, the content of the individual's consciousness was rationally limited to things connected with the particular incident being related or the particular situation being described. . . . And what is still more important: the author, with his knowledge of an objective truth, never abdicated his position as the final and governing authority. Again, earlier writers, especially from the end of the nineteenth century on, had produced narrative works which on the whole undertook to give us an extremely subjective, individualistic, and often eccentrically aberrant impression of reality, and which neither sought nor were able to ascertain anything objective or generally valid in regard to it. Sometimes such works took the form of first-person novels; sometimes they did not. As an example of the latter case I mention Huysmans's novel *A rebours*. But all that too is basically different from the modern procedure here described on the basis of Virginia Woolf's text, although the latter, it is true, evolved from the former. The essential characteristic of the technique represented by Virginia Woolf is that we are given not merely one person whose consciousness (that is, the impressions it receives) is rendered, but many persons, with frequent shifts from one to the other – in our text, Mrs Ramsay, 'people', Mr Bankes, in brief interludes James, the Swiss maid in a flash-back, and the nameless ones who speculate over a tear. The multiplicity of persons suggests that we are here after all confronted with an endeavor to investigate an objective reality, that is,

specifically, the 'real' Mrs Ramsay. She is, to be sure, an enigma
and such she basically remains, but she is as it were encircled by
the content of all the various consciousnesses directed upon her
(including her own); there is an attempt to approach her from
many sides as closely as human possibilities of perception and
expression can succeed in doing. The design of a close approach
to objective reality by means of numerous subjective impressions
received by various individuals (and at various times) is important in the modern technique which we are here examining.
It basically differentiates it from the unipersonal subjectivism
which allows only a single and generally a very unusual person
to make himself heard and admits only that one person's way
of looking at reality. In terms of literary history, to be sure, there
are close connections between the two methods of representing
consciousness – the unipersonal subjective method and the
multipersonal method with synthesis as its aim. The latter
developed from the former, and there are works in which the
two overlap, so that we can watch the development. This is
especially the case in Marcel Proust's great novel. . . .

Another stylistic peculiarity to be observed in our text –
though one that is closely and necessarily connected with the
'multipersonal representation of consciousness' just discussed –
has to do with the treatment of time. That there is something
peculiar about the treatment of time in modern narrative literature is nothing new; several studies have been published on the
subject. These were primarily attempts to establish a connection
between the pertinent phenomena and contemporary philosophical doctrines or trends – undoubtedly a justifiable under-
taking and useful for an appreciation of the community of
interests and inner purposes shown in the activity of many of our
contemporaries. We shall begin by describing the procedure
with reference to our present example. We remarked earlier that
the act of measuring the length of the stocking and the speaking
of the words related to it must have taken much less time than an
attentive reader who tries not to miss anything will require to
read the passage – even if we assume that a brief pause inter-
vened between the measuring and the kiss of reconciliation on

James's forehead. However, the time the narration takes is not devoted to the occurrence itself (which is rendered rather tersely) but to interludes. Two long excursuses are inserted, whose relations in time to the occurrence which frames them seem to be entirely different. The first excursus, a representation of what goes on in Mrs Ramsay's mind while she measures the stocking (more precisely, between the first absent-minded and the second sharp order to James to hold his leg still) belongs in time to the framing occurrence, and it is only the representation of it which takes a greater number of seconds and even minutes than the measuring – the reason being that the road taken by consciousness is sometimes traversed far more quickly than language is able to render it, if we want to make ourselves intelligible to a third person, and that is the intention here. What goes on in Mrs Ramsay's mind in itself contains nothing enigmatic; these are ideas which arise from her daily life and may well be called normal – her secret lies deeper, and it is only when the switch from the open windows to the Swiss maid's words comes, that something happens which lifts the veil a little. On the whole, however, the mirroring of Mrs Ramsay's consciousness is much more easily comprehensible than the sort of thing we get in such cases from other authors (James Joyce, for example). But simple and trivial as are the ideas which arise one after the other in Mrs Ramsay's consciousness, they are at the same time essential and significant. They amount to a synthesis of the intricacies of life in which her incomparable beauty has been caught, in which it at once manifests and conceals itself. Of course, writers of earlier periods too occasionally devoted some time and a few sentences to telling the reader what at a specific moment passed through their characters' minds – but for such a purpose they would hardly have chosen so accidental an occasion as Mrs Ramsay's looking up, so that, quite involuntarily, her eyes fall on the furniture. Nor would it have occurred to them to render the continuous rumination of consciousness in its natural and purposeless freedom. And finally they would not have inserted the entire process between two exterior occurrences so close together in time as the two warnings to James to keep still (both of which,

after all, take place while she is on the point of holding the unfinished stocking to his leg); so that, in a surprising fashion unknown to earlier periods, a sharp contrast results between the
brief span of time occupied by the exterior event and the dream-
like wealth of a process of consciousness which traverses a whole
subjective universe. These are the characteristic and distinctively
new features of the technique: a chance occasion releasing processes of consciousness; a natural and even, if you will, a naturalistic rendering of those processes in their peculiar freedom, which
is neither restrained by a purpose nor directed by a specific subject of thought; elaboration of the contrast between 'exterior'
and 'interior' time. The three have in common what they reveal
of the author's attitude: he submits, much more than was done
in earlier realistic works, to the random contingency of real
phenomena; and even though he winnows and stylizes the
material of the real world – as of course he cannot help doing –
he does not proceed rationalistically, nor with a view to bringing
a continuity of exterior events to a planned conclusion. In
Virginia Woolf's case the exterior events have actually lost their
hegemony, they serve to release and interpret inner events,
whereas before her time (and still today in many instances)
inner movements preponderantly function to prepare and moti-
vate significant exterior happenings. This too is apparent in the
randomness and contingency of the exterior occasion (looking
up because James does not keep his foot still), which releases
the much more significant inner process.

The temporal relation between the second excursus and the
framing occurrence is of a different sort: its content (the passage
on the tear, the things people think about Mrs Ramsay, the
telephone conversation with Mr Bankes and his reflections while
watching the building of the new hotel) is not a part of the
framing occurrence either in terms of time or of place. Other
times and places are in question; it is an excursus of the same
type as the story of the origin of Odysseus' scar. . . .[1] Even from
that, however, it is different in structure. In the Homer passage
the excursus was linked to the scar which Euryclea touches with
her hands, and although the moment at which the touching of

the scar occurs is one of high and dramatic tension, the scene nevertheless immediately shifts to another clear and luminous present, and this present seems actually designed to cut off the dramatic tension and cause the entire footwashing scene to be temporarily forgotten. In Virginia Woolf's passage, there is no question of any tension. Nothing of importance in a dramatic sense takes place; the problem is the length of the stocking. The point of departure for the excursus is Mrs Ramsay's facial expression: 'never did anybody look so sad'. In fact several excursuses start from here; three, to be exact. And all three differ in time and place, differ too in definiteness of time and place, the first being situated quite vaguely, the second somewhat more definitely, and the third with comparative precision. Yet none of them is so exactly situated in time as the successive episodes of the story of Odysseus' youth, for even in the case of the telephone scene we have only an inexact indication of when it occurred. As a result it becomes possible to accomplish the shifting of the scene away from the window-nook much more unnoticeably and smoothly than the changing of scene and time in the episode of the scar. In the passage on the tear the reader may still be in doubt as to whether there has been any shift at all. The nameless speakers may have entered the room and be looking at Mrs Ramsay. In the second paragraph this interpretation is no longer possible, but the 'people' whose gossip is reproduced are still looking at Mrs Ramsay's face – not here and now, at the summer-house window, but it is still the same face and has the same expression. And even in the third part, where the face is no longer physically seen (for Mr Bankes is talking to Mrs Ramsay over the telephone), it is nonetheless present to his inner vision; so that not for an instant does the theme (the solution of the enigma Mrs Ramsay), and even the moment when the problem is formulated (the expression of her face while she measures the length of the stocking), vanish from the reader's memory. In terms of the exterior event the three parts of the excursus have nothing to do with one another. They have no common and externally coherent development, as have the episodes of Odysseus' youth which are related with reference to the origin of the scar; they are connected only by the one thing they have in common – looking at Mrs Ramsay, and more specifically at the Mrs Ramsay who, with an unfathomable expression of sadness behind her radiant beauty, concludes that the stocking is still much too short. It is only this common focus which connects the otherwise totally different parts of the excursus; but the connection is strong enough to deprive them of the independent 'present' which the episode of the scar possesses. They are nothing but attempts to interpret 'never did anybody look so sad'; they carry on this theme, which itself carries on after they conclude: there has been no change of theme at all. In contrast, the scene in which Euryclea recognizes Odysseus is interrupted and divided into two parts by the excursus on the origin of the scar. In our passage, there is no such clear distinction between two exterior occurrences and between two presents. However insignificant as an exterior event the framing occurrence (the measuring of the stocking) may be, the picture of Mrs Ramsay's face which arises from it remains present throughout the excursus; the excursus itself is nothing but a background for that picture, which seems as it were to open into the depths of time – just as the first excursus, released by Mrs Ramsay's unintentional glance at the furniture, was an opening of the picture into the depths of consciousness.

The two excursuses, then, are not as different as they at first appeared. It is not so very important that the first, so far as time is concerned (and place too), runs its course within the framing occurrence, while the second conjures up other times and places. The times and places of the second are not independent; they serve only the polyphonic treatment of the image which releases it; as a matter of fact, they impress us (as does the interior time of the first excursus) like an occurrence in the consciousness of some observer (to be sure, he is not identified) who might see Mrs Ramsay at the described moment and whose meditation upon the unsolved enigma of her personality might contain memories of what others (people, Mr Bankes) say and think about her. In both excursuses we are dealing with attempts to fathom a more genuine, a deeper, and indeed a more real reality;

in both cases the incident which releases the excursus appears accidental and is poor in content; in both cases it makes little difference whether the excursuses employ only the consciousness-content, and hence only interior time, or whether they also employ exterior shifts of time. After all, the process of consciousness in the first excursus likewise includes shifts of time and scene, especially the episode with the Swiss maid. The important point is that an insignificant exterior occurrence releases ideas and chains of ideas which cut loose from the present of the exterior occurrence and range freely through the depths of time. It is as though an apparently simple text revealed its proper content only in the commentary on it, a simple musical theme only in the development-section. This enables us also to understand the close relation between the treatment of time and the 'multipersonal representation of consciousness' discussed earlier. The ideas arising in consciousness are not tied to the present of the exterior occurrence which releases them. Virginia Woolf's peculiar technique, as exemplified in our text, consists in the fact that the exterior objective reality of the momentary present which the author directly reports and which appears as established fact – in our instance the measuring of the stocking – is nothing but an occasion (although perhaps not an entirely accidental one). The stress is placed entirely on what the occasion releases, things which are not seen directly but by reflection, which are not tied to the present of the framing occurrence which releases them. . . .

The distinctive characteristics of the realistic novel of the era between the two great wars . . . – multipersonal representation of consciousness, time strata, disintegration of the continuity of exterior events, shifting of the narrative viewpoint (all of which are interrelated and difficult to separate) – seem to us indicative of a striving for certain objectives, of certain tendencies and needs on the part of both authors and public. These objectives, tendencies, and needs are numerous; they seem in part to be mutually contradictory; yet they form so much one whole that when we undertake to describe them analytically, we are in constant danger of unwittingly passing from one to another.

Let us begin with a tendency which is particularly striking in
our text from Virginia Woolf. She holds to minor, unimpressive,
random events: measuring the stocking, a fragment of a conversation with the maid, a telephone call. Great changes, exterior
turning points, let alone catastrophes, do not occur; and though
elsewhere in *To the Lighthouse* such things are mentioned, it is
hastily, without preparation or context, incidentally, and as it
were only for the sake of information. The same tendency is to be
observed in other and very different writers, such as Proust or
Hamsun. In Thomas Mann's *Buddenbrooks* we still have a novel
structure consisting of the chronological sequence of important
exterior events which affect the Buddenbrook family; and if
Flaubert – in many respects a precursor – lingers as a matter of
principle over insignificant events and everyday circumstances
which hardly advance the action, there is nevertheless to be
sensed throughout *Madame Bovary* (though we may wonder
how this would have worked out in *Bouvard et Pécuchet*) a
constant slow-moving chronological approach first to partial
crises and finally to the concluding catastrophe, and it is this
approach which dominates the plan of the work as a whole.
But a shift in emphasis followed; and now many writers present
minor happenings, which are insignificant as exterior factors in a
person's destiny, for their own sake or rather as points of departure for the development of motifs, for a penetration which
opens up new perspectives into a milieu or a consciousness or
the given historical setting. They have discarded presenting the
story of their characters with any claim to exterior completeness,
in chronological order, and with the emphasis on important
exterior turning points of destiny. James Joyce's tremendous
novel – an encyclopedic work, a mirror of Dublin, of Ireland, a
mirror too of Europe and its millennia – has for its frame the
externally insignificant course of a day in the lives of a school-
teacher and an advertising broker. It takes up less than twenty-
four hours in their lives – just as *To the Lighthouse* describes
portions of two days widely separated in time. (There is here
also, as we must not fail to observe, a similarity to Dante's
Comedy.) Proust presents individual days and hours from

different periods, but the exterior events which are the determining factors in the destinies of the novel's characters during the intervening lapses of time are mentioned only incidentally, in retrospect or anticipation. The ends the narrator has in mind are not to be seen in them; often the reader has to supplement them. The way in which the father's death is brought up . . . – incidentally, allusively, and in anticipation – offers a good example. This shift of emphasis expresses something that we might call a transfer of confidence: the great exterior turning points and blows of fate are granted less importance; they are credited with less power of yielding decisive information concerning the subject; on the other hand there is confidence that in any random fragment plucked from the course of a life at any time the totality of its fate is contained and can be portrayed. There is greater confidence in syntheses gained through full exploitation of an everyday occurrence than in a chronologically well-ordered total treatment which accompanies the subject from beginning to end, attempts not to omit anything externally important, and emphasizes the great turning points of destiny. It is possible to compare this technique of modern writers with that of certain modern philologists who hold that the interpretation of a few passages from *Hamlet, Phèdre,* or *Faust* can be made to yield more, and more decisive, information about Shakespeare, Racine, or Goethe and their times than would a systematic and chronological treatment of their lives and works. Indeed, the present book [*Mimesis*] may be cited as an illustration. I could never have written anything in the nature of a history of European realism; the material would have swamped me; I should have had to enter into hopeless discussions concerning the delimitation of the various periods and the allocation of the various writers to them, and above all concerning the definition of the concept realism. Furthermore, for the sake of completeness, I should have had to deal with some things of which I am but casually informed, and hence to become acquainted with them *ad hoc* by reading up on them (which, in my opinion, is a poor way of acquiring and using knowledge); and the motifs which direct my investigation, and for the sake of which it is written, would have been completely buried under a mass of factual information which has long been known and can easily be looked up in reference books. As opposed to this I see the possibility of success and profit in a method which consists in letting myself be guided by a few motifs which I have worked out gradually and without a specific purpose, and in trying them out on a series of texts which have become familiar and vital to me in the course of my philological activity; for I am convinced that these basic motifs in the history of the representation of reality – provided I have seen them correctly – must be demonstrable in any random realistic text. But to return to those modern writers who prefer the exploitation of random everyday events, contained within a few hours and days, to the complete and chronological representation of a total exterior continuum – they too (more or less consciously) are guided by the consideration that it is a hopeless venture to try to be really complete within the total exterior continuum and yet to make what is essential stand out. Then too they hesitate to impose upon life, which is their subject, an order which it does not possess in itself. He who represents the course of a human life, or a sequence of events extending over a prolonged period of time, and represents it from beginning to end, must prune and isolate arbitrarily. Life has always long since begun, and it is always still going on. And the people whose story the author is telling experience much more than he can ever hope to tell. But the things that happen to a few individuals in the course of a few minutes, hours, or possibly even days – these one can hope to report with reasonable completeness. And here, furthermore, one comes upon the order and the interpretation of life which arise from life itself: that is, those which grow up in the individuals themselves, which are to be discerned in their thoughts, their consciousness, and in a more concealed form in their words and actions. For there is always going on within us a process of formulation and interpretation whose subject-matter is our own self. We are constantly endeavoring to give meaning and order to our lives in the past, the present, and the future, to our surroundings, the world in which we live; with the result that our lives appear in our own conception as total entities – which to be sure are always changing, more or less radically, more or less rapidly, depending on the extent to which we are obliged, inclined, and able to assimilate the onrush of new experience. These are the forms of order and interpretation which the modern writers here under discussion attempt to grasp in the random moment – not one order and one interpretation, but many, which may either be those of different persons or of the same person at different times; so that overlapping, complementing, and contradiction yield something that we might call a synthesized cosmic view or at least a challenge to the reader's will to interpretive synthesis.

Here we have returned once again to the reflection of multiple consciousnesses. It is easy to understand that such a technique had to develop gradually and that it did so precisely during the decades of the First World War period and after. The widening of man's horizon, and the increase of his experiences, knowledge, ideas, and possible forms of existence, which began in the sixteenth century, continued through the nineteenth at an ever faster tempo – with such a tremendous acceleration since the beginning of the twentieth that synthetic and objective attempts at interpretation are produced and demolished every instant. The tremendous tempo of the changes proved the more confusing because they could not be surveyed as a whole. They occurred simultaneously in many separate departments of science, technology, and economics, with the result that no one – not even those who were leaders in the separate departments – could foresee or evaluate the resulting overall situations. Furthermore, the changes did not produce the same effects in all places, so that the differences of attainment between the various social strata of one and the same people and between different peoples came to be – if not greater – at least more noticeable. The spread of publicity and the crowding of mankind on a shrinking globe sharpened awareness of the differences in ways of life and attitudes, and mobilized the interests and forms of existence which the new changes either furthered or threatened. In all parts of the world crises of adjustment arose; they increased in number and coalesced. They led to the upheavals which we have not weathered yet. In Europe this violent clash of the most heterogeneous ways of life and kinds of endeavor undermined not only those religious, philosophical, ethical, and economic principles which were part of the traditional heritage and which, despite many earlier shocks, had maintained their position of authority through slow adaptation and transformation; nor yet only the ideas of the Enlightenment, the ideas of democracy and liberalism which had been revolutionary in the eighteenth century and were still so during the first half of the nineteenth; it undermined even the new revolutionary forces of socialism, whose origins did not go back beyond the heyday of the capitalist system. These forces threatened to split up and disintegrate. They lost their unity and clear definition through the formation of numerous mutually hostile groups, through strange alliances which some of these groups effected with non-socialist ideologies, through the capitulation of most of them during the First World War, and finally through the propensity on the part of many of their most radical advocates for changing over into the camp of their most extreme enemies. Otherwise too there was an increasingly strong factionalism — at times crystallizing around important poets, philosophers, and scholars, but in the majority of cases pseudo-scientific, syncretistic, and primitive. The temptation to entrust oneself to a sect which solved all problems with a single formula, whose power of suggestion imposed solidarity, and which ostracized everything which would not fit in and submit — this temptation was so great that, with many people, fascism hardly had to employ force when the time came for it to spread through the countries of old European culture, absorbing the smaller sects.

As recently as the nineteenth century, and even at the beginning of the twentieth, so much clearly formulable and recognized community of thought and feeling remained in those countries that a writer engaged in representing reality had reliable criteria at hand by which to organize it. At least, within the range of contemporary movements, he could discern certain specific trends; he could delimit opposing attitudes and ways of life with a certain degree of clarity. To be sure, this had long since begun to grow increasingly difficult. Flaubert (to confine ourselves to realistic writers) already suffered from the lack of valid foundations for his work; and the subsequent increasing predilection for ruthlessly subjectivistic perspectives is another symptom. At the time of the First World War and after – in a Europe unsure of itself, overflowing with unsettled ideologies and ways of life, and pregnant with disaster – certain writers distinguished by instinct and insight find a method which dissolves reality into multiple and multivalent reflections of consciousness. That this method should have been developed at this time is not hard to understand.

But the method is not only a symptom of the confusion and helplessness, not only a mirror of the decline of our world. There is, to be sure, a good deal to be said for such a view. There is in all these works a certain atmosphere of universal doom: especially in *Ulysses*, with its mocking *odi-et-amo* hodgepodge of the European tradition, with its blatant and painful cynicism, and its uninterpretable symbolism – for even the most painstaking analysis can hardly emerge with anything more than an appreciation of the multiple enmeshment of the motifs but with nothing of the purpose and meaning of the work itself. And most of the other novels which employ multiple reflection of consciousness also leave the reader with an impression of hopelessness. There is often something confusing, something hazy about them, something hostile to the reality which they represent. We not infrequently find a turning away from the practical will to live, or delight in portraying it under its most brutal forms. There is hatred of culture and civilization, brought out by means of the subtlest stylistic devices which culture and civilization have developed, and often a radical and fanatical urge to destroy. Common to almost all of these novels is haziness, vague indefinability of meaning: precisely the kind of uninterpretable symbolism which is also to be encountered in other forms of art of the same period.

But something entirely different takes place here too. Let us turn again to the text which was our starting-point. It breathes an air of vague and hopeless sadness. We never come to learn what Mrs Ramsay's situation really is. Only the sadness, the vanity of her beauty and vital force emerge from the depths of secrecy. Even when we have read the whole novel, the meaning of the relationship between the planned trip to the lighthouse and the actual trip many years later remains unexpressed, enigmatic, only dimly to be conjectured, as does the content of Lily Briscoe's concluding vision which enables her to finish her painting with one stroke of the brush. It is one of the few books of this type which are filled with good and genuine love but also, in its feminine way, with irony, amorphous sadness, and doubt of life. Yet what realistic depth is achieved in every individual occurrence, for example the measuring of the stocking! Aspects of the occurrence come to the fore, and links to other occurrences, which, before this time, had hardly been sensed, which had never been clearly seen and attended to, and yet they are determining factors in our real lives. What takes place here in Virginia Woolf's novel is precisely what was attempted everywhere in works of this kind (although not everywhere with the same insight and mastery) – that is, to put the emphasis on the random occurrence, to exploit it not in the service of a planned continuity of action but in itself. And in the process something new and elemental appeared: nothing less than the wealth of reality and depth of life in every moment to which we surrender ourselves without prejudice. To be sure, what happens in that moment – be it outer or inner processes – concerns in a very personal way the individuals who live in it, but it also (and for that very reason) concerns the elementary things which men in general have in common. It is precisely the random moment which is comparatively independent of the controversial and unstable orders over which men fight and despair; it passes unaffected by them, as daily life. The more it is exploited, the more the elementary things which our lives have in common come to light. The more numerous, varied, and simple the people are who appear as subjects of such random moments, the more effectively must what they have in common shine forth. In this unprejudiced and exploratory type of representation we cannot but see to what an extent – below the surface conflicts – the differences between men's ways of life and forms of thought have already lessened. The strata of societies and their different ways of life have become inextricably mingled. There are no longer even exotic peoples. A century ago (in Mérimée for example), Corsicans or Spaniards were still exotic; today the term would be quite unsuitable for Pearl Buck's Chinese peasants. Beneath the conflicts, and also through them, an economic and cultural leveling process is taking place. It is still a long way to a common life of mankind on earth, but the goal begins to be visible. And it is most concretely visible now in the unprejudiced, precise, interior and exterior representation of the random moment in the lives of different people. So the complicated process of dissolution which led to fragmentation of the exterior action, to reflection of consciousness, and to stratification of time seems to be tending toward a very simple solution. Perhaps it will be too simple to please those who, despite all its dangers and catastrophes, admire and love our epoch for the sake of its abundance of life and the incomparable historical vantage point which it affords. But they are few in number, and probably they will not live to see much more than the first forewarnings of the approaching unification and simplification.

SOURCE: *Mimesis: the representation of reality in Western literature* (1946; translation, by Willard R. Trask, 1953).

NOTE

1. [*Editor's note.*] The following is the first paragraph of 'Odysseus' Scar', chapter 1 of Auerbach's *Mimesis*, of which the present essay is chapter 20: 'Readers of the *Odyssey* will remember the well-prepared and touching scene in book 19, when Odysseus has at last come home, the scene in which the old housekeeper Euryclea, who had been his nurse, recognizes him by a scar on his thigh. The stranger has won Penelope's good will; at his request she tells the housekeeper to wash his feet, which, in all old stories, is the first duty of hospitality toward a tired traveler. Euryclea busies herself fetching water and mixing cold with hot, meanwhile speaking sadly of her absent master, who is probably of the same age as the guest, and who perhaps, like the guest,

is even now wandering somewhere, a stranger; and she remarks how
astonishingly like him the guest looks. Meanwhile Odysseus, remembering his scar, moves back out of the light; he knows that, despite his
efforts to hide his identity, Euryclea will now recognize him, but he
wants at least to keep Penelope in ignorance. No sooner has the old
woman touched the scar than, in her joyous surprise, she lets Odysseus'
foot drop into the basin; the water spills over, she is about to cry out
her joy; Odysseus restrains her with whispered threats and endear-
ments; she recovers herself and conceals her emotion. Penelope,
whose attention Athena's foresight had diverted from the incident, has
observed nothing.'

James Hafley

THE CREATIVE MODULATION
OF PERSPECTIVE (1954)

True life exists where the living being is conscious of itself as an indivisible 'I', in whom all impressions, feelings, etc., become one. So long as the 'I' struggles, as nearly the whole animal world does, merely to crush the other creatures known to him, in order to attain his own temporary advantage, true spiritual life which is without time and space remains unexpressed and imprisoned. True spiritual life is liberated when a man neither rejoices in his own happiness, nor suffers from his own suffering, but suffers and rejoices with the worries and pleasures of others and is fused with them into a common life. . . .

There are two consciousnesses in us: one – the animal; the other – the spiritual. The spiritual is not always shown in us, but it is this that makes our true spiritual life, which is not subject to time . . . there are times in my long life which are clearly preserved in my memory, and other times which have completely disappeared, they no longer exist. The moments which remain are most frequently the moments when the spirit in me awoke. . . . Spiritual life is a recollection. A recollection is not the past, it is always the present. It is our spirit, which shows itself more or less clearly, that contains the progress of man's temporary existence. There can be no progress for the spirit, for it is not in time. What the life in time is for, we do not know; it is only a transitory phenomenon. Speaking metaphorically, I see this manifestation of the spirit in us as the breathing of God.[1]

EVEN if it were not known that Virginia Woolf herself translated these remarks of Tolstoi, their affinity to *Mrs Dalloway* would be obvious. But there is a shift in emphasis between the first and second paragraphs of this passage – a shift from spiritual life to spirit itself, from definition to illustration. A shift similar to this constitutes the first step in what can be understood as

Virginia Woolf's creative modulation of her perspective. Having given artistic definition to her vision of experience, having realized a total *donnée*, Virginia Woolf was now able to manipulate that formal perspective in various ways; and thus she was modulating the philosophical perspective as well, discovering new angles, new emphases, new modes, with each new construct. *Mrs Dalloway* defines – but *To the Lighthouse* illustrates – her own concept of reality.

To the Lighthouse was published in 1927, twelve years after *The Voyage Out*. It is divided into three main parts: 'The Window', 'Time Passes', and 'The Lighthouse'. The first part is concerned with the events of one evening and night in mid-September of about 1910, and the third part with the events of one morning ten years later. Unity of place is preserved throughout, and the setting is at once precise and vague. It is a house at Finlay in the Skye Islands; but when Paul Rayley thinks of slipping out of the house early in the morning to go all the way to Edinburgh and replace a brooch that Minta Doyle has lost, the reader may begin to think – although Paul's state of mind might account for his resolve – of the notorious seacoast of Bohemia in *The Winter's Tale*; however, Virginia Woolf too was notorious for her lack of attention to factual accuracy,[2] and the exact scene of the action is unimportant.

Indeed, the action itself might be considered equally unimportant. In the first part of the book James Ramsay wishes to go to the lighthouse, but cannot because of bad weather; in the third part he finally makes the journey, but against his will. This is the central action of the novel. Parallel to it runs the progress of Lily Briscoe's painting. At first she cannot formalize her vision upon canvas; finally she succeeds in completing the picture, but not at all to her satisfaction. The climax of the novel – Mrs Ramsay's death – is mentioned very casually in a parenthetical sentence; the catastrophe – Mr Ramsay's arrival at the lighthouse and Lily's completion of her painting – comes as an exhausted afterthought. No act, no event can be pinned down: even Mrs Ramsay's dinner party, by far the longest scene in the book, is not self-contained, for it concludes with her own realization that the party had begun to end some time ago. Not an act or a series of acts, but action itself – movement rather than movements – is described by this novel.

The characters themselves are for the most part seen in action: Mr Ramsay pacing up and down the terrace, Cam running wildly and stopping only at her mother's call. In this movement three things alone remain fixed: Mrs Ramsay, the lighthouse, and Lily's painting. Even these must not be labeled, for 'nothing was simply one thing'. So, for example, even the lighthouse is both stark and misty. Arriving at the lighthouse, James remembers it as he had seen it when he was a child of six:

The Lighthouse was then a silvery, misty-looking tower with a yellow eye, that opened suddenly, and softly in the evening. Now –
James looked at the Lighthouse. He could see the white-washed rocks; the tower, stark and straight; he could see that it was barred with black and white; he could see windows in it; he could even see washing spread on the rocks to dry. So that was the Lighthouse, was it?
No, the other was also the Lighthouse. For nothing was simply one thing. The other Lighthouse was true too.

This very important passage serves to comment upon the numerous interpretations of the lighthouse symbol. Almost every critic explains the lighthouse differently – and almost every critic makes what would seem to be the mistake of finding the lighthouse 'simply one thing'. H. K. Russell declares that the lighthouse is the feminine creative principle; that Mrs Ramsay equals Bergson's 'intuition' equals Joyce's 'Anna Livia Plurabelle'.[3] Joan Bennett calls the alternate light and shadow of the lighthouse the rhythm of joy and sorrow, understanding and misunderstanding.[4] Daiches says: 'The Lighthouse . . . standing lonely in the midst of the sea, is a symbol of the individual who is at once a unique being and a part of the flux of history. To reach the Lighthouse is, in a sense, to make contact with a truth outside oneself, to surrender the uniqueness of one's ego to an impersonal reality'[5] – surely a worthwhile comment. F. L.

Overcarsh, in a detailed interpretation of the novel, avoids calling the lighthouse simply one thing. He finds the novel as a whole an allegory of the Old and New Testaments; Mrs Ramsay is Eve, the Blessed Virgin, and Christ; Mr Ramsay is, among other things, God the Father; the lighthouse is Eden and Heaven; the strokes of the lighthouse are the Persons of the Trinity, the third of them, long and steady, representing the Holy Ghost.[6] Perhaps more precise than any of these interpretations is John Graham's statement that the lighthouse as symbol has no one meaning, that it is 'a vital synthesis of time and eternity: an objective correlative for Mrs Ramsay's vision, after whose death it is her meaning.'[7]

Mrs Ramsay is of course the central character, and one of Virginia Woolf's most successful creations. She is projected more as a symbol than as an individual: she is never called by a first name, for example, and she wears gray clothes during the day and black at night, so that the reader is given the odd impression of looking at once upon and through her whenever she appears. Despite this intentional indefiniteness, Mrs Ramsay emerges as a human being of great appeal, though the facts about her are symbolical as well as literal. She is an extremely beautiful woman of fifty, an inveterate matchmaker, and the mother of eight children; she is very nearsighted; she exaggerates everything; she is a practical nurse, and much concerned with the improvement of social conditions. Like Clarissa Dalloway (and Terence Hewet), Mrs Ramsay can create moments of unity that remain intact in the memory, 'affecting one almost like a work of art'.

Mr Ramsay, her husband, has been generally looked upon as something of a villain. He is eleven years older than his wife, and a teacher of philosophy possessed of a superb intellect. He is long-sighted, precisely factual, and pessimistic. Certainly he is Mrs Ramsay's opposite, but he 'is not a figure of fun',[8] as many critics have thought him. He is, to be sure, suggestive of Leslie Stephen, notably in his habit of shouting out poetry to himself and his detestation of the long dinner parties at which his wife is so good a hostess. Q. D. Leavis says: 'Everyone has read *To the Lighthouse,* and the portrait-piece of Mr Ramsay by Leslie Stephen's gifted daughter elicited immediate recognition from the oldest generation. Yes, that's Leslie Stephen, the word went round; and that brilliant study in the Lytton Strachey manner of a slightly ludicrous, slightly bogus, Victorian philosopher somehow served to discredit Leslie Stephen's literary work. But it is obvious to any student of it that the work could not have been produced by Mr Ramsay.'[9] Then it should also be obvious that Virginia Woolf had no intention of ridiculing her father or Mr Ramsay, whose eccentricities are no more meant to be belittling than are those of his wife. Mr Ramsay is admirable, if not always correct; he is human, but not evil.[10]

The essential difference between Mr and Mrs Ramsay is that whereas he identifies himself with the land and thinks the sea a destroyer, she – like Lily Briscoe – believes that life is the sea and not the land. Thus Mrs Ramsay 'felt . . . that community of feeling with other people which emotion gives as if the walls of partition had become so still that practically (the feeling was one of relief and happiness) it was all one stream, and chairs, tables, maps, were hers, were theirs, it did not matter whose, and [they] would carry it on when she was dead'. Lily, the artist, sees 'how life, from being made up of little separate incidents which one lives one by one, became curled and whole like a wave which bore one up with it and threw one down with it, there, with a dash on the beach'. Mr Ramsay thinks of 'the dark of human ignorance, how we know nothing and the sea eats away the ground we stand on'. For him, and for James, 'loneliness . . . was . . . the truth about things'. In the same way, Mr Ramsay is afraid that he will be forgot, that time will destroy his work; Mrs Ramsay, however, since she does not draw a line around her individuality, does not fear time; and Lily finishes her painting, even though she knows that it will never be displayed, because 'one might say, even of this scrawl, not of that actual picture, perhaps, but of what it attempted, that it "remained for ever" '.

To the Lighthouse is really the story of a contest between two kinds of truth – Mr Ramsay's and Mrs Ramsay's. For him, truth is factual truth; for her, truth is the movement toward truth: since truth is always *being* made, and never *is* made, the struggle for truth is the truth itself. The form of this novel at once expresses and verifies Mrs Ramsay's truth. According to Bergson, certainty can follow only from factual extension of knowledge resulting in scientific order; such is the order which Mr Ramsay seeks. Mr Ramsay spatializes knowledge:

If thought is like the keyboard of a piano, divided into as many notes, or like the alphabet is ranged in twenty-six letters all in order, then his splendid mind had no sort of difficulty in running over those letters one by one, firmly and accurately, until it had reached, say, the letter Q. He reached Q. . . . But after Q? What comes next? After Q there are a number of letters the last of which is scarcely visible to mortal eyes, but glimmers red in the distance. Z is only reached once by one man in a generation. Still, if he could reach R it would be something.

Here is a logical, scientific procedure toward truth.

Mrs Ramsay, on the other hand, knows by intuition rather than by analysis, and is therefore able to know reality – mobility, qualitative rather than quantitative diversity, time instead of space, movement itself and not merely the path of movement in space.

Matter . . . has no duration and so cannot last through any period of time or change: it simply *is* in the present, it does not endure but is perpetually destroyed and recreated. . . . Just as matter is absolute logical complexity memory is absolute creative synthesis. Together they constitute the hybrid notion of creative duration whose 'parts' interpenetrate which, according to Bergson, comes nearest to giving a satisfactory description of the actual fact directly known which is, for him, the whole reality.[11]

Mr Ramsay – matter – and Lily Briscoe – memory – undergo such an 'interpenetration' in the novel's castastrophe, and by doing so give a satisfactory description of Mrs Ramsay's truth.

'The Window' is a statement of that truth. This first part of the novel seems complete in itself. It begins: ' "Yes, of course, if it's fine tomorrow," said Mrs Ramsay'; and concludes, again with Mrs Ramsay speaking: 'Yes, you were right. It's going to be wet tomorrow. You won't be able to go.' The conflict is projected as a question about the weather. It is a fact, stated by Mr Ramsay at once, that 'it won't be fine'. Charles Tansley – 'the little atheist', as he is called – backs up this fact. But Mrs Ramsay will not accept it as truth, because it hurts James, who wants nothing more than to go out to the lighthouse. Instead she says, 'But it may be fine – I expect it will be fine', and calls her husband's fact nonsense. At the conclusion of this part, when she agrees with her husband that it will rain tomorrow, it is not because she attaches importance to his truth, but because she knows that he wishes her to say 'I love you', and chooses to say it in this way. In neither case is the fact itself of any importance whatsoever to her.

Her disregard of factual truth enrages Mr Ramsay. After all, he *is* right. Mrs Ramsay's truth is one that must trample upon her husband's, however; but his truth – factual truth – is so short-lived that she can distort or deny it without compunction. He himself realizes its fragility; in a generation, he thinks, he will be forgot; even Shakespeare will some day be forgot. It is for this reason that his wife is so essential to him; although he 'exaggerated her ignorance, her simplicity, for he liked to think that she was not clever, not book-learned at all', he nevertheless 'wanted, to be assured of his genius, first of all, and then to be taken within the circle of life, warmed and soothed, to have his senses restored to him, his barrenness made fertile, and all the rooms of the house be made full of life. . . . He must be assured that he too lived in the heart of life.' Therefore he must from time to time leave off his metaphysical speculations and return to his wife, to 'life itself', for sympathy; Mrs Ramsay can communicate to her husband that 'if he put his implicit faith in her, nothing should hurt him; however deep he buried himself or climbed high, not for a second should he find himself without her. So boasting of her capacity to surround and protect, there was scarcely a shell of herself left for her to know herself by;

all was so lavished and spent.' Mrs Ramsay's apparent illogicality is actually the certainty of intuition. For her husband her truth is a false truth, but without it he would perish. 'She knew then – she knew without having learnt. Her simplicity fathomed what clever people falsified. Her singleness of mind made her drop plumb like a stone, alight exact as a bird, gave her, naturally, this swoop and fall of the spirit upon truth which delighted, eased, sustained – falsely perhaps.' 'Falsely perhaps', because her perception of true time has not yet been proved correct. She has been seen only through a window, and the reader has seen her concept of truth only through the window of her own 'room'. She has identified her truth with the lighthouse. 'There is a coherence in things, a stability; something . . . is immune from change, and shines out . . . in the face of the flowing, the fleeting, the spectral, like a ruby'; this can be glimpsed at certain moments, and 'of such moments, she thought, the thing is made that endures'. Just as Mr Ramsay's Z 'glimmers red in the distance', so the 'something' that Mrs Ramsay feels stable shines like a ruby. Her way of meeting it is different from her husband's way – hers being really an end, and his a means. 'Losing personality, one lost the fret, the hurry, the stir . . . things came together in this peace, this rest, this eternity; and pausing there she looked out to meet that stroke of the Lighthouse, the long steady stroke, the last of the three, which was her stroke.'

Seven times in this part of the novel, the phrase 'Someone had blundered' is repeated. Either Mr Ramsay or Mrs Ramsay is wrong, and the remainder of the novel shows that it is Mr Ramsay who 'had blundered'.

The short second part, 'Time Passes', has been praised by almost every critic of the novel as a masterpiece of description. According to Brewster and Burrell, 'It would be hard to find anything in twentieth century English prose to surpass [this part]';[12] others join them in ranking it one of the great passages of English prose. This is all very well, but to remove the part from the whole is to run the risk of ignoring its function. 'Time Passes' must not be thought of as a piece of impressionistic writing; it is actually the testing of Mrs Ramsay's vision by Mr Ramsay's facts, and the apparent triumph of those facts. Simply, it describes the effects of ten years' time upon the little house. The books become moldy; Mrs Ramsay's beloved garden is choked with weeds; toads, swallows, and mice invade the rooms; the wood rots; above all, Mrs Ramsay's truth – symbolized by the shawl she had wrapped around a frightening skull in the children's bedroom – falls victim to 'the facts'. Gradually the folds of the shawl loosen, so that the skull emerges a skull, and not the fairy garden she had called it when it annoyed Cam and James. There is no eternity, no permanence; there are only dust, death, decay. Indeed, Mrs Ramsay herself dies during this ten-year interval; her son Andrew is killed in the war; her daughter Prue dies in childbirth (just as Mrs Ramsay had lived for childbirth). It would seem, then, that Mr Ramsay was correct, for the facts of this spatialized time confirm his pessimism and prove his wife's optimism illusory. When Mrs McNab, who has come now and then to dust the empty house, is suddenly asked to have it ready for occupancy, she labors for days with two other workers to repair the ravages of time. Finally Mr Ramsay, the remaining children, Lily, and Mr Carmichael (who has become a famous poet despite his addiction to drugs) return.

'Le temps passe, et peu à peu tout ce qu'on disait par mensonge devient vrai',[13] wrote Proust. 'The Lighthouse' is, in a sense, testimony to this statement, for here Mrs Ramsay's 'lies' are proved to have been – and still to be – the truth, capable of refuting Mr Ramsay's 'facts'. Time passes, and yet true time does not pass.

Throughout the first part of the novel, Lily Briscoe had been absorbed in her attempt to capture reality in a painting. She did not see the scene as the fashionable Mr Paunceforte had painted it. He had rendered the violent colors about her as pastels, and it was now the custom to see them as he had seen them, to ignore the reality. Despite Paunceforte's distortion, Lily managed 'to clasp some miserable remnant of her vision to her breast, which a thousand forces did their best to pluck from her'.[14] In Lily's picture the real and not the apparent Mrs Ramsay was to be captured; Mrs Ramsay there was represented abstractly as a triangular purple shape (the shadow that, seated in the window, she cast upon the step), and not as a woman in a gray dress. Indeed, Mrs Ramsay thought of herself as 'a wedge-shaped core of darkness, something invisible to others'; and it was this wedge-shaped core, she felt, that would remain permanent and eternal.

Lily had been unable to complete her painting. 'A mother and child might be reduced to a shadow without irreverence. A light here required a shadow there.' But she could not solve the problem of form: 'Mrs Ramsay . . . as she sat in the wicker arm-chair in the drawing-room window . . . wore, to Lily's eyes, an august shape; the shape of a dome. . . . It was a question, [Lily] remembered, how to connect this mass on the right hand with that on the left.'

Now, ten years later, Lily tries again to capture her vision by formalizing it. Her attitude at the beginning of the third part enables the reader to become aware of the symbolic meanings of the circumstance. 'The question was of some relation between those masses', and Lily now feels that she has the solution. The painting causes her to remember Mrs Ramsay, and to recall certain moments of the past. Meanwhile Mr Ramsay comes to her demanding the sympathy his wife used to give him, but Lily can do nothing except remark that his boots are beautiful – just as Mrs Flanders had evaded the central problem in *Jacob's Room* by switching her attention to Jacob's shoes.

Mr Ramsay leaves for the lighthouse, and Lily begins her painting. 'Here she was again, she thought, stepping back to look at it, drawn out of gossip, out of living, out of community with people into the presence of this formidable ancient enemy of hers – this other thing, this truth, this reality, which sud-denly . . . emerged stark at the back of appearances and com-manded her attention.' More and more she thinks of Mrs Ramsay as she continues to paint.

Pour entrer en nous, un être a été obligé de prendre la forme, de se plier au cadre du temps; ne nous apparaissant que par minutes successives, il n'a jamais pu nous livrer de lui qu'un seul aspect à la fois, nous débiter de lui qu'une seule photographie. Grande faiblesse sans doute pour un être de consister en une simple collection de moments; grande force aussi; il relève de la mémoire, et la mémoire d'un moment n'est pas instruite de tout ce qui s'est passé depuis; ce moment qu'elle a enregistré dure encore, vit encore et avec lui l'être qui s'y profilait. Et puis cet émiettement ne fait pas seulement vivre la morte, il la multiplie.[15]

In just the same way, Mrs Ramsay rises from death and lives again. Lily, as she paints, 'exchanged the fluidity of life for the concentration of painting'; she loses consciousness of her personality, her name, her separateness. She remembers Mrs Ramsay

bringing them together; Mrs Ramsay saying, 'Life stand still here'; Mrs Ramsay making of the moment something permanent (as in another sphere Lily herself tried to make of the moment something permanent) – this was of the nature of a revelation. In the midst of chaos there was shape; this eternal passing and flowing (she looked at the clouds going and the leaves shaking) was struck into stability. Life stand still here, Mrs Ramsay said. . . . She owed it all to her.

What Mrs Ramsay had accomplished with the living moment, like a misty or a stark tower holding the light still and illumining with it, Lily is accomplishing with her painting. Lily cries out for Mrs Ramsay to come back, to return; but 'nothing happened', for 'the vision must be perpetually remade'. She wants to get hold of 'the thing itself before it has been made anything' and so to give it expression from its source. She goes on thinking of Mrs Ramsay, bringing the past into the present in a recollection in tranquillity.

Suddenly the window at which she was looking was whitened by some light stuff behind it. At last then somebody had come into the drawing-room; somebody was sitting in the chair. . . .

Mercifully, whoever it was . . . had settled by some stroke of luck so as to throw an odd-shaped triangular shadow over the step. . . . One must keep on looking without for a second relaxing the intensity of emotion, the determination not to be put off, not to be bamboozled. One must hold the scene – so – in a vise and let nothing come in and spoil it.

Lily too is saying, 'Life stand still here.' Then, quietly, it is Mrs Ramsay sitting at the window. Lily finishes her painting. 'Yes, she thought, laying down her brush in extreme fatigue, I have had my vision.' Lily has made her journey to the lighthouse.

Mr Ramsay's own journey to the lighthouse, accompanied by James and Cam, is naturally a literal and factual one. He reads a book during the voyage, and finishes reading it as the boat arrives at the literal lighthouse. He has, so to speak, reached Z by making this trip in memory of his wife – by forcing James finally to go to the lighthouse. During this third part of the novel, the phrase 'We perished, each alone' is repeated just as 'Some one had blundered' was repeated in the first part. Mr Ramsay reaches the lighthouse. 'He sat and looked at the island and he might be thinking, We perished, each alone, or he might be thinking, I have reached it. I have found it; but he said nothing. Then he put on his hat . . . he sprang, lightly like a young man, holding his parcel, on to the rock.' During the journey to the lighthouse, Mr Ramsay has been hearing of the terrible shipwrecks caused by a storm in the winter. He himself, however, carrying a package of presents for the lighthouse man, has finally been able to communicate, to give instead of take, to reach the lighthouse.

The novel itself is comparable to Lily's painting, for its purpose too is to capture and render stable and permanent the essence of Mrs Ramsay. For a long time Lily 'could not achieve that razor edge of balance between two opposite forces; Mr Ramsay and the picture; which was necessary. There was something perhaps wrong with the design? Was it . . . that the line of the wall wanted breaking?' The third part of the novel does precisely what Lily's finished painting does: it connects the masses – matter and memory – and by connecting them is able to illustrate 'life itself' as Virginia Woolf envisioned it. Moving from Lily to Mr Ramsay and back, 'The Lighthouse' not only explains but also dynamically depicts the process by which 'life itself' is discovered.

There is an interesting and perhaps not entirely superficial resemblance between *To the Lighthouse* and E. M. Forster's *Howards End*. As in *To the Lighthouse*, the house Howards End is a unifying force in Forster's novel. It is occupied during Ruth Wilcox's life, then empty and cared for by Miss Avery, then occupied again. Further, Ruth Wilcox dominates *Howards End*, although she dies early in the book. Forster's dualism of love and truth – the passion and the prose – although not identical with the matter-memory of *To the Lighthouse*, is nevertheless the cause of a similar pattern. Forster's *Where Angels Fear to Tread* also carries a hint – not nearly so important as Proust's – of the problem treated here. If Forster offers a suggestion, the way in which Marcel's mother 'becomes' his dead grandmother in *Sodome et Gomorrhe* – mentally re-creating and rediscovering her – is of course a far more significant suggestion of Lily's re-creation of Mrs Ramsay.

The role of the narrator or central intelligence is both more important and less noticeable in *To the Lighthouse* than in *Mrs Dalloway*. As in the earlier novel, the narrator is a means by which the reader attains a unity of response to the diverse personalities within whose consciousnesses he has the illusion of being; he is objectively unconscious of a narrator, but the narrator makes possible both the artistic validity of the novel's statement and his acceptance of it. Far from being a stream-of-consciousness novel, *To the Lighthouse* is the objective account of a central intelligence that approaches and assumes the characters' consciousnesses (just as Clarissa and Mrs Ramsay enjoin themselves vicariously to all life) but does not become completely identified with any one consciousness. This central intelligence is thus free to comment upon the whole in what seems a completely impersonal manner, as this short passage shows:

'It is a triumph,' said Mr Bankes, laying his knife down for a moment. He had eaten attentively. It was rich; it was tender. It was perfectly cooked. How did she manage these things in the depths of the country? he asked her. She was a wonderful woman. All his love, all his reverence, had returned; and she knew it.

'It is a French recipe of my grandmother's,' said Mrs Ramsay, speaking with a ring of great pleasure in her voice. Of course it was French. What passes for cookery in England is an abomination (they agreed). It is putting cabbages in water. It is roasting meat until it is like leather. It is cutting off the delicious skins of vegetables. 'In which,' said Mr Bankes, 'all the virtue of the vegetable is contained.'

Here the central intelligence is reporting a part of the dinner conversation. The remark in parentheses is a popular device by which the author assures the reader that she too agrees with what is being said. The sentences that follow are both a digest of the conversation and an opinion expressed by the central intelligence; the reader, regarding them as an oblique report of the conversation, also reacts toward what the people say with a sympathy seemingly caused by the situation – he has been hoping that Mr Bankes will approve the *bœuf en daube* – but actually caused by the informing personality of the central intelligence. Further, 'She was a wonderful woman' is read as Bankes's thought; 'All his love . . .' is somewhere between his thought and a statement by the narrator, being in the third person; 'and she knew it' is, finally, a direct transitional statement by the central intelligence. But the illusion is so well sustained that Mr Bankes's final remark ('In which . . . all the virtue . . . ') seems to spring only from an abstract of the conversation. Thus the technique serves to instill a common reaction into the diverse reactions of the characters – to affect precisely that unity in diversity of the theme – and so to make certain the reader's response to the book as a whole. It is also compatible with Virginia Woolf's idea of characterization: her belief that there is a common element beneath the diversity, that fundamentally it is 'all one stream'. For this reason Virginia Woolf 'learnt to . . . annihilate the clear line between narrator and character, creating mind and created scene, to take the frame from the picture . . . to make of all – time, place, person, self and other self – a unity. . . .'[16]

Most critics consider *To the Lighthouse* Virginia Woolf's masterpiece, mainly because of the technical ability it displays, the unity of effect, masterful structure. Often it is described in the words with which Lily Briscoe thinks of her painting: 'Beautiful and bright it should be on the surface, feathery and evanescent, one colour melting into another like the colours on a butterfly's wing; but beneath the fabric must be clamped together with bolts of iron. It was to be a thing you could ruffle with your breath; and a thing you could not dislodge with a team of horses.' This novel also fulfils, in the use to which it puts its materials, Lily's postimpressionistic intention that 'one wanted . . . to be on a level with ordinary experience, to feel simply that's a chair, that's a table, and yet at the same time, It's a miracle, it's an ecstasy'. As she was finishing this novel, Virginia Woolf considered it by far her best – more subtle and human than *Jacob's Room* or *Mrs Dalloway*, more interesting, more successful in method. But she was already thinking of a further development of that method, and had a vague idea for a book in which time would be completely abolished, 'my theory being that the actual event practically does not exist – nor time either'.[17] This theory she also developed, and only one year after *To the Lighthouse* she published, in 1928, her next novel, *Orlando, a biography*.

SOURCE: *The Glass Roof* (1954).

NOTES

1. A. B. Goldenveizer, *Talks with Tolstoi*, translated by A. B. Koteliansky and Virginia Woolf (1923) pp. 91–4.

2. See, for example, Joan Bennett, *Virginia Woolf: her art as a novelist* (Cambridge, 1945) p. 79, and the *Times Literary Supplement* review, 30 Oct 1919, p. 607, of *Night and Day*. It is perfectly in

accord with Virginia Woolf's thought that she should ignore or distort the facts: her roses bloom in December, not because she is careless, but because she considers the resulting artistic effect more important than factual accuracy.

3. H. K. Russell, 'Woolf's *To the Lighthouse*', in *Explicator*, VIII (March 1950) 9, 11.

4. *Virginia Woolf*, pp. 103–4.

5. David Daiches, *Virginia Woolf* (New York, 1942) p. 36.

6. 'The Lighthouse, Face to Face', in *Accent*, X (Winter 1950) 108.

7. 'Time in the Novels of Virginia Woolf', in *University of Toronto Quarterly*, Jan 1949, p. 151.

8. E. M. Forster, *Virginia Woolf* (Cambridge, 1942) p. 28.

9. 'Leslie Stephen: Cambridge Critic', in *Scrutiny*, March 1939, p. 405. Q. D. Leavis goes far beyond the realm of literary criticism in her statements about Virginia Woolf's work. She praises *To the Lighthouse*, oddly enough, admiring its formal achievement and complex effects, in *Fiction and the Reading Public*.

10. Mr Ramsay resembles Leslie Stephen, and Mrs Ramsay resembles Virginia Woolf's mother. Julia Stephen had seven children; she was, according to Maitland's *Life* (1906) of Leslie Stephen, much interested in young people – in their friendships or love makings – and was loved by them in return (p. 323); she was a woman of really astounding beauty; a practical nurse; she died nine years before her husband. ('A photograph taken by M. Loppé in the 'Bear' shows Mrs Stephen looking out of the window. . . . That picture became a treasured relic', p. 397.) The very setting of the novel was suggested by the house at St Ives where young Virginia spent her summers. 'It is a shame to leave the place to itself for so long a time as our absence', Stephen wrote, a year before his wife's death (p. 384).

11. Karin Stephen, *The Misuse of Mind: a study of Bergson's attack on intellectualism* (New York, 1922) p. 78.

12. D. Brewster and A. Burrell, 'The Wild Goose: Virginia Woolf's Pursuit of Life', in *Adventure or Experience* (New York, 1930) p. 108.

13. *Albertine disparue* (Paris, 1927) I 74.

14. There is obviously a more than casual similarity between Mr Paunceforte and the Edwardian novelists, and between Lily and the Georgians.

15. *Albertine disparue*, I 100.

16. R. L. Chambers, *The Novels of Virginia Woolf* (Edinburgh, 1947) p. 7.

17. 'Le Journal inédit de Virginia Woolf', in *Roman*, Jan 1951, pp. 11–12. [Editor's note: see *A Writer's Diary* (1953) p. 102.]

Norman Friedman

DOUBLE VISION IN
TO THE LIGHTHOUSE (1955)

So much depends then, thought Lily Briscoe, looking at the
sea which had scarcely a stain on it . . . upon distance: whether
people are near us or far from us. (p. 284)[1]

WHILE there is general agreement that *To the Lighthouse*
centers on questions of order and chaos, permanence and change,
intellection and intuition, male and female, critical unanimity
disappears in the actual tracing out of these themes and the
analysis of the patterns of imagery evoking them. Thus, for
example, it is clear that the simultaneous completion of Lily
Briscoe's painting and the arrival of Mr Ramsay, James, and
Cam at the Lighthouse are somehow functioning together to
finish the book, but no two commentators have agreed as to
what that function *means* as an ending of what has gone
before. One claims that Mr Ramsay is undergoing a transition
from his former intellectual personality to a newly discovered
intuitive view;[2] another that Lily is moving from a concern
with form (art) to a concern with content (life);[3] still another
sees a shift from time to the timeless;[4] while a fourth sees an
allegory of Christ's Ascension, involving a movement from the
god of Wrath to the God of Mercy;[5] yet another sees a transition
from egoism to selflessness;[6] while a sixth thinks of this simultaneous convergence as a clumsy device which resolves nothing.[7]
These examples could be multiplied, but the dominant tendency
is clear: to interpret the thematic conflict – whatever it may be –
as an antithesis of two mutually exclusive terms, one of which
must be rejected in favor of the other. The trip to the Lighthouse, in other words, is too often seen as a one-way ride.

But since the symbolism of the book as well as its structure suggests a rather different set of possibilities, there still seems to be room for an interpretive framework comprehensive enough to embrace them. A single view, an either-or strategy, will hardly prove adequate for dealing with the multiplicity of points of view through which each character is seen in the first section, the descending and ascending movement of the second section, and the shifting simultaneity of event which shapes the third. In order to discern here the intricate web of image, attitude, and idea which Mrs Woolf has woven on her four-dimensional loom, the critic must develop a more complex tactic.

I

'Subject and object and the nature of reality,' Andrew had replied to Lily's question about the content of his father's books (p. 38), and it is exactly this problem which works its way through the novel on three perceptible levels: human relations, metaphysics, and aesthetics. Thus, although Mr Ramsay's problem is technically an epistemological one, the novel itself can also be seen to have been built around the problem of how the known looks to the knower: of one person to another, of nature to man, and of life to the artist. Further, the over-all quality of this relationship may be subsumed under the headings of order, a triumph over life's meaningless flux, and chaos, a giving way to its all but irresistible force or a blank confrontation of its stark emptiness.

The point is, as we shall see, that a dialectic order is achieved by those who manage to focus their apprehension of the nature of reality simultaneously from two different perspectives – that of subject, or involvement in flux, and that of object, or detachment therefrom – and that 'the nature of reality', through which one must pass in making his transition from one perspective to the other, finds its image in *water* as a symbol of surrender. From whatever viewpoint one regards life (thesis), then, whether it be that of the detached philosopher ironically contemplating from a height man's smudge and his smell, or that of the busy mother and housewife frantically involved in the fever and fret of daily routine, one must give it up in favor of the other (antithesis), becoming immersed in the waters of transition, and emerging with a double perspective (synthesis). To lose this perilous balance, to keep out of the wet, is ulti-mately to give way to the chaos of a black and lonely darkness on the one side or to the disorder of a terrifying and senseless force on the other.

An interesting passage in which this theme of the double vision and its accompanying water imagery occurs is found almost half-way through the book:

Brooding, she changed the pool into the sea, and made the minnows into sharks and whales, and cast vast clouds over this tiny world by holding her hand against the sun, . . . and then took her hand away suddenly and let the sun stream down. . . . And then, letting her eyes slide imperceptibly above the pool and rest on that wavering line of sea and sky, . . . she became with all that power sweeping savagely in and inevitably withdrawing, hypnotised, and the two senses of that vastness and this tininess (the pool had diminished again) flowering within it made her feel that she was bound hand and foot and unable to move by the intensity of feelings which reduced her own body, her own life, and the lives of all the people in the world, for ever, to nothing-ness (Nancy: pp. 114–15).

Section one deals chiefly with the first level – the relation of self to other – and it soon becomes evident that no one single trait or characteristic of a person can be seized upon and cherished as a way of 'knowing' him or her. Mrs Ramsay, for example, is a charmingly warm and beautiful woman, yet annoyingly concerned with ordering the lives of others (many of her circle resent her mania for marriage); although she is maternal, intuitive, involved in life's common cares, and capable of an unreasoning fear when she allows herself to dwell upon the tragic fragility of human life, she nevertheless is capable also of a triumphantly mystical detachment wherein life's inscrutable mystery appears ordered and revealed. And the significance of her portrayal, as it emerges from the attitudes of others toward her

as well as from her own broodings, is that the truth about Mrs
Ramsay encompasses both these aspects of her personality.

Or consider Mr Ramsay: he is a self-dramatizing domestic
tyrant, yet he is also admirable as a lone watcher at the dark
frontiers of human ignorance. A detached and lonely philosopher,
he nevertheless craves the creative contact of wife and children;
grim, yet optimistic; austere, yet fearful for his reputation, petty
and selfish, yet capable of losing himself completely in a novel by
Scott; aloof, yet he thrives on the simple company and fare of
humble fishermen.

Lily likewise is a complex figure: a spinster disinterested
in ordinary sexual attachments, she is nevertheless capable of
a fierce outburst of love; an artist perpetually terrified by a
blank canvas, she still manages to approach a solution to the
complex problem of the art-life relationship. Mr Bankes, to
consider another, is an unselfish friend and a dedicated scientist,
yet he is also a cranky food-faddist; a self-sufficient bachelor,
he is nevertheless a lonely widower craving the affection of
children. Or again, Charles Tansley is an irritating and self-
centered pedant, yet he is also a sympathetic human being – a
complexity which Mrs Ramsay herself sums up: 'Yet he looked
so desolate; yet she would feel relieved when he went; yet she
would see that he was better treated tomorrow; yet he was
admirable with her husband; yet his manners certainly wanted
improving; yet she liked his laugh . . . ' (p. 174).

And the climax of the first section occurs at the dinner, a
brilliantly dramatic communion-meal where each solitary ego,
with its petty aggravations and resentments, is gradually
blended with the others into a pattern of completion and
harmony.

Personality, then, can be known only in terms of a multiple
perspective – 'One wanted fifty pairs of eyes to see with. . . .
Fifty pairs of eyes were not enough to get round that one
woman with' (p. 294) – and section one provides just such
a perspective. Including his or her own interior monologues,
each character is presented from at least two points of view:
Mr Ramsay is seen chiefly through the eyes of Mrs Ramsay,

young James, Lily, and Mr Bankes; Mrs Ramsay through those of Lily, Tansley, and Mr Bankes; Mr Bankes himself through those of Lily; Lily herself through those of Mrs Ramsay; and Tansley through the eyes of Mrs Ramsay and Lily. It is by this technique of alternation that each is rendered more or less in the round.

Section two deals mainly with the second level – the relation of man to nature – and it does not, as has been frequently supposed, portray merely the ravages of time and tide afflicting the family and their summer home. In addition to the almost complete destruction of the house, we are also shown its equally dramatic renewal. And its focus is on the comic-epic figure of Mrs McNab, who lurches through the house dusting and wiping, breathing a long dirge of sorrow and trouble, yet who leers, 'looking sideways in the glass, as if, after all, she had her consolations, as if indeed there were twined about her dirge some incorrigible hope' (p. 197). It is she and her helpers who fetch up from oblivion all the Waverley novels and who rescue the house from annihilation.

The fortunes of the family undergo several severe setbacks: Mrs Ramsay dies, Andrew is killed in the war, and Prue dies in childbirth. Yet we are given to understand that Mr Ramsay's work will endure (the fate of his books was somehow tied up with that of the Waverley novels) and, as the next section proceeds to demonstrate, the family continues to develop and mature. The central section of *To the Lighthouse*, therefore, dramatizes not the victory of natural chaos over human order, but rather the reverse: the forces of destruction are defeated by man's power and will to live.

Section three is concerned chiefly with the third level of our theme – the relation of art to life – and continues in the knowledge of loss as well as the achievement of gain. Its structure is based upon the shuttling back and forth between Lily on the island watching those in the boat get farther away, and those in the boat watching the island in turn get farther away. This is accompanied by the corresponding movements of those in the boat getting closer to the Lighthouse, and

of Lily getting closer to the solution of her aesthetic problem.
And the determining factor in each case is love (the 'art' of
life), which might perhaps be defined as order or the achievement of form in human relations through the surrender of
personality: Lily finishes her painting as she feels the upsurge
of that sympathy for Mr Ramsay which she had previously
been stubbornly unable to give, James and Cam surrender
their long-cherished antagonism toward their father as they
reach the Lighthouse, while Mr Ramsay himself attains at
the same time a resolution of his own tensions and anxieties.
The point is not that they have made a one-directional transition from this attitude to that, but rather that, since each is
aware simultaneously both of what is receding and of what
is approaching, each has received in his way a sense of what
I have called the double vision.

II

The presence of this duality can be further demonstrated by
a closer look at the particular imagery of the book – its figures
of speech, its scene, and its plot. The Lighthouse itself as
the most conspicuous image, to begin with, functions in two
ways: as something to be reached, and as the source of a flashing
light. The former aspect is to be considered when we discuss
plot; the latter suggests that the Lighthouse has a symbolic
role of its own to play. In this aspect it appears in two connections: first as it impinges upon the consciousness of Mrs
Ramsay in section one after she has finished reading to James
and is sitting quietly alone for a moment, and second as it
flashes upon the empty house in section two.

The busy mother of eight children, a woman of grace and
ease who delights in social intercourse, and one who visits
the poor as well, she often feels the need 'To be silent; to be
alone'. And as she sits knitting, the relief of abstraction from
'All the being and doing' grows upon her; it is in this mood
that she muses upon the alternating flashes of the light. It is
a mood of detachment, peace, rest, and of triumph over life;

she identifies herself with the third stroke – the long steady stroke – which becomes for her an image of purity and truth, of strength and courage, searching and beautiful: her 'self having shed its attachments was free for the strangest adventures. When life sank down for a moment, the range of experience seemed limitless. . . . Losing personality, one lost the fret, the hurry, the stir; and there rose to her lips always some exclamation of triumph over life when things came together in this peace, this rest, this eternity; and pausing there she looked out to meet that stroke of the Lighthouse, the long steady stroke, the last of the three, which was her stroke. . . .'

This is the 'thesis' of her emotional cycle; the 'antithesis' is evoked as her mood soon modulates into one of grim recognition of the inevitable facts of 'suffering, death, the poor', and she gradually descends from her state of triumphant abstraction from the fret, the hurry, and the stir, by seizing upon the light from a different perspective, 'for when one woke at all, one's relations changed'. Looking now at the steady light, it is 'the pitiless, the remorseless'.

But the cycle is not yet complete until these two moods become synthesized. The second view seems 'so much her, yet so little her'; and then her meditations are crowned, in their third phase, by 'exquisite happiness, intense happiness', and she cries inwardly, 'It is enough! It is enough!' As if, by seeing that long steady flash in two different aspects – first as an image of expansion and release, and then of contraction and confinement – she has received a final intuition of the essential truth of the nature of reality: that one must be both subjectively involved in and objectively detached from life, and that true happiness rests neither in the one sphere nor in the other exclusively, but rather in achieving a harmonious balance – however fragile – between the two. Now she can rest, if but for the moment, content. And to her husband, who is striding up and down the terrace outside the window behind which she sits, 'She was aloof from him now in her beauty, in her sadness' (pp. 94–100).

In the middle section, portraying the death and rebirth of the deserted house, the light makes its second appearance by gliding over the rooms 'gently as if it laid its caress and lingered stealthily and looked and came lovingly again'. That this is only one side of its doubleness is evidenced by the sentence immediately following: 'But in the very lull of this loving caress, as the long stroke leant upon the bed, the rock was rent asunder; another fold of the shawl loosened; there it hung, and swayed' (pp. 199–200). And a few pages on, just preceding the arrival of the forces of renewal in the house, in 'that moment, that hesitation when dawn trembles and night pauses' (p. 208), the Lighthouse beam, as an image of expansion and release (life-love-hope) and contraction and confinement (death-destruction-terror) held in relation, 'entered the rooms for a moment, sent its sudden stare over bed and wall in the darkness of winter, looked with equanimity at the thistle and the swallow, the rat and the straw' (pp. 207–8).

Finally, it is worth noticing in section three that, as Lily begins her painting a second time (while those in the boat are embarking for the Lighthouse), her brush descends in stroke after stroke: 'And so pausing and so flickering, she attained a dancing rhythmical movement, as if the pauses were one part of the rhythm and the strokes another, and all were related.' Thus, in echo of the Lighthouse beam itself, her vision begins to emerge from stroke and pause in alternation, and 'this truth, this reality, which suddenly laid hands upon her, emerged stark at the back of appearances and commanded her attention' (p. 236).

III

Having seen that the Lighthouse beam – stroke and pause in alternation – symbolizes quite clearly that the problem of subject and object and the perception of the nature of reality is a matter of opposites held in dialectic relation, we may now proceed to investigate more closely the specific embodiment of the objective-detachment and subjective-involvement theme in the water imagery which obviously permeates the novel on both the literal and figurative levels as scene and as metaphor. And as this theme and this imagery begin to take root together and grow as one, we shall see a second, more pervasive symbol emerging: the act of immersion as surrender and transition.

The fact is, as we have seen, that whatever his attitude toward life may be, whether objectively detached or subjectively involved, each character must immerse himself in the doubleness of reality by making a transition to the opposite attitude, and that this process in one way or another usually finds its image in water. Taking the three or four chief characters, then, in their apparent order of importance, we can begin with Mrs Ramsay.

Searching for a picture in the illustrated catalogue of the Army and Navy Stores for James to cut out, she suddenly becomes aware that the gruff murmur of talk out on the terrace has ceased and that now, coming to the foreground of her consciousness, the waves are falling monotonously on the beach. Stationed as she is in a moment of domestic involvement, this sound at first 'beat a measured and soothing tattoo to her thoughts and seemed consolingly to repeat over and over again as she sat with the children the words of some old cradle song, murmured by nature, "I am guarding you – I am your support".' The passage continues, however, through the dialectic of transition: 'but at other times suddenly and unexpectedly, especially when her mind raised itself slightly from the task actually in hand, [it] had no such kindly meaning, but like a ghostly roll of drums remorselessly beat the measure of life, made one think of the destruction of the island and its engulfment in the sea. . . .' And the cycle is complete as this sound is once again accompanied by that of her husband's voice chanting poetry: 'She was soothed once more, assured again that all was well, and looking down at the book on her knee found the picture of a pocket knife with six blades which could only be cut out if James was very careful' (pp. 27–9).

As the Lighthouse beam had come to her when she was in a state of detachment, and had spoken to her of triumph and fulfilment, and then of failure and frustration, thereby annihilating her abstracted bliss and bringing her back down to the

sphere of life's fretful involvements, so too the sea – reversing
the process – comes to her when she is in a state of involvement, and speaks of consolation and sympathy, and then of
terror and remorseless power, thereby annihilating her con-
tented involvement and carrying her up to the sphere of blank
and meaningless abstraction. The synthesis which ensues, however, in each case produces a sense of equanimity, peace, and rest.
Thus the double vision involves indeed a two-way process:
depending upon which direction you are going, whether from
subject to object or vice versa, detachment is either joy or fear,
involvement either consolation or despair. And also, depending
upon the direction, the water imagery becomes now a symbol
of the search for human contact and warmth, or of the brute
force of the natural cycle, now a symbol of the search for
intellectual stability and certitude, or of the bottomless ignorance of the race of men and the profound vanity of their puny
knowledge.

Thus, proceeding chronologically through the book, we
discover another aspect of the water imagery in connection
with Mrs Ramsay – that of the fountain as a symbol of feminine
creativity to which the male must resort in order that his fatal
sterility be redeemed. The intellectual husband becomes immersed in the waters of human sympathy and devotion figura-
tively issuing from the intuitive wife. Emotionally exhausted and
depleted, however, by this effort of consolation, she sinks back
down into herself, her fountain pulsing feebly, and hearing 'dully,
ominously, a wave fall', she doubts all that she had said to him
(pp. 58–61).

Reading the tale of The Fisherman and his Wife to James,
she senses some relation of the story to her concurrent meditations, for the tale 'was like the bass gently accompanying a
tune, which now and then ran up unexpectedly into the melody'
(p. 87). In the fairy tale, the sea becomes increasingly more
turbulent each time the poor fisherman arrives to deliver his
wife's insatiable demands upon the enchanted fish. How much,
after all (Mrs Ramsay might be thinking) can one ask of the sea?
For if one presses it too far in one direction, forgetting the

necessity of giving oneself up in turn to the sea in exchange for its gifts, one will lose everything.

Hearing at dinner of the Mannings, old friends she has not seen or thought of for many years, she broods over the relation of past to present, the stasis of the former being imaged as a placid lake and the flux of the latter as water shooting down into the room in cascades. In so far as we are out of the past, we are detached and the water image is a static one; in so far as we are in the present, we are involved and the image is a dynamic one. A few pages later, however, the present also achieves form – in terms of the harmony of all those at the table – so 'that here, inside the room, seemed to be order and dry land; there, outside, a reflection in which things wavered and vanished, waterily' (p. 147). Here it is the human order as dry land which is being opposed to natural flux as water. We shall see below how Lily comes to feel the necessity of deserting the land for the sea.

Finally, as the perfection of this moment becomes in turn a thing of the past, the party disperses and Mr and Mrs Ramsay are in the study reading. Thinking of her husband's anxiety over the fragility of his fame, and of her concern over encouraging him, she feels once more a sense of detachment as she knits and watches him read Scott: 'It didn't matter, any of it, she thought. A great man, a great book, fame – who could tell?' (p. 177). Then, 'dismissing all this, as one passes in diving now a weed, now a straw, now a bubble, she felt again, sinking deeper . . . There is something I want – something I have come to get, and she fell deeper and deeper without knowing quite what it was, with her eyes closed' (p. 178). Brooding over snatches of poetry, she picks up a volume and reads of love lasting and time passing: 'her mind felt swept, felt clean. And then there it was, suddenly entire; she held it in her hands, beautiful and reasonable, clear and complete, the essence sucked out of life and held rounded here – the sonnet' (p. 181: Shakespeare's no. 98). Once again the emotional cycle is complete, and she has reached a point of stability (the aftermath of the meal) by alternating from involvement (her anxious preparations for the meal) to detachment

(the consummation of the meal and the resultant separation
from natural flux), the transition being imaged as an immersion
in water.

IV

Mr Ramsay's uncompromising honesty and unflinching courage
in the face of the perennial mystery of life and the tragic incapacity of the human mind is imaged as a stake driven into the
sea to guide the frail barks which founder out there in the
darkness: 'It was his fate, his peculiarity, whether he wished it
or not, to come out thus on a spit of land which the sea is
slowly eating away, and there to stand, like a desolate sea-bird,
alone' (pp. 11, 68). His masculine detachment from the commonplace – he doesn't notice little things, the shape of a flower, the
texture of a sunset – is here a positive act, a gesture of defense
against the tides of time and ignorance. Yet, as we have seen,
this standpoint becomes ultimately sterile without a periodic
immersion in the feminine waters of life. Or, to take it the other
way round, his withdrawal from the life around him into his
abstracted solitude finds *its* image also in immersion: 'and
then, as if he had her leave for it, with a movement which oddly
reminded his wife of the great sea lion at the Zoo tumbling
backwards after swallowing his fish and walloping off so that
the water in the tank washes from side to side, he dived into the
evening air' (p. 52).

Or again, his children and his domestic attachments (which
somehow signify to Mr Bankes a betrayal of their friendship),
rather than his philosophical solitude, seem to provide the
buttress against the floods: 'That was a good bit of work on
the whole – his eight children. They showed he did not damn the
poor little universe entirely, for on an evening like this, he
thought, looking at the land dwindling away, the little island
seemed pathetically small, half swallowed up by the sea' (p. 106).
He needs both the sense of involvement and of detachment, and
the water imagery functions now in one direction, now in the
other. His demand for the sympathy of women, we may notice,

pours and *spreads* itself in *pools* at their feet, and Lily Briscoe, resenting him, draws her skirts a little closer around her ankles for fear of becoming wet – of becoming involved (p. 228).

And lastly, as if he has reached a more complex state of mind than hitherto, Mr Ramsay thinks to himself, as the boat nears the Lighthouse and while he and Macalister are discussing the local shipwrecks and drownings: 'But why make a fuss about that? Naturally men are drowned in a storm, but it is a perfectly straightforward affair, and the depths of the sea (he sprinkled the crumbs from his sandwich paper over them) are only water after all' (p. 306). Having cast his bread upon the waters and surrendered to the 'destructive element', his anxieties as to his fame and his courage in the face of the inevitable dissolution of human endeavors are resolved in one final symbolic gesture. *Cast your bread upon the waters: for you shall find it after many days. He that observes the wind shall not sow; and he that regards the clouds shall not reap. In the morning sow your seed, and in the evening withhold not your hand: for you know not whether shall prosper, either this or that, or whether they both shall be alike good* (Eccl. 11: 1, 4, 6).

V

For Lily, likewise, the water imagery functions in its double capacity as destroyer and preserver. She and Mr Bankes stroll down to the shore, drawn regularly by some need. 'It was as if the water floated off and set sailing thoughts which had grown stagnant on dry land, and gave to their bodies even some sort of physical relief.' And they both feel a common hilarity, a sort of exhilaration at the sight. But characteristically, the mood turns, 'and instead of merriment [they] felt come over them some sadness – because the thing was completed partly, and partly because distant views seem to outlast by a million years (Lily thought) the gazer and to be communing already with a sky which beholds an earth entirely at rest' (pp. 33–4).

To Lily, the old-maid painter, the great mystery is love: 'Love had a thousand shapes. There might be lovers [i.e. artists]

whose gift it was to choose out the elements of things and place
them together and so, giving them a wholeness not theirs in life,
make of some scene, or meeting of people (all now gone and
separate), one of those globed compacted things over which
thought lingers, and love plays' (p. 286). But the lover in art
cannot help being fascinated by the artists of life who *do* achieve
a wholeness in their lives; so Lily, vicariously seeing the world
through the eyes of human love – the love of Mr and Mrs
Ramsay – feels 'how life, from being made up of little separate
incidents which one lived one by one, became curled and whole
like a wave which bore one up with it, and threw one down with
it, there, with a dash on the beach' (p. 73).

She resented Mrs Ramsay's judgement that an unmarried
woman has missed the best of life, and 'she would urge her
own exemption from the universal law; plead for it; she liked
to be alone; she liked to be herself; she was not made for that'
(p. 77). Yet the love of Paul and Minta is keenly felt as a contrast
to her own barren state: 'How inconspicuous she felt herself by
Paul's side! He, glowing, burning; she, aloof, satirical: he,
bound for adventure; she moored to shore; he, launched, in-
cautious; she, solitary, left out' (p. 153). So, coming back on
that evening ten years later, Lily goes to sleep lulled by the sound
of the sea, for 'Messages of peace breathed from the sea to the
shore'. And she feels, 'why not accept this, be content with this,
acquiesce and resign?' (pp. 213–14).

But the next morning she stubbornly sets up her canvas and
starts to paint. Like Mr Ramsay, the philosopher confronting
the mystery of nature, she too, the artist confronting life, is
imaged as a figure isolated and facing the sea of mystery and
chaos alone: 'Out and out one went, further and further, until at
last one seemed to be on a narrow plank, perfectly alone, over
the sea' (p. 256). But as she gives herself up to her art, as Mrs
Ramsay did to her husband, she loses consciousness of outer
things, 'her name and her personality and her appearance', and
her mind throws up from its depths images, memories, ideas,
'like a fountain spurting over that glaring, hideously difficult
white space, while she modelled it with greens and blues' (p.

238). While her ego is held in abeyance, the creative waters of life, welling up within her, help to shape her picture.

She thinks of Mrs Ramsay, who died in the interval between the two visits, and she remembers Mrs Ramsay's mania for marriage. Suddenly she recalls Paul and Minta, whose marriage has not worked out well after all, and thinks of the glow which love had caused to shine from their faces: 'It rose like a fire sent up in token of some celebration by savages on a distant beach. She heard the roar and the crackle. The whole sea for miles round ran red and gold.' She feels a headlong desire to fling herself down into this sea and be drowned. But the mood shifts, 'And the roar and crackle repelled her with fear and disgust, as if while she saw its splendour and power she saw too how it fed on the treasure of the house, greedily, disgustingly, and she loathed it' (p. 261).

The cycle, however, has yet to be completed. She continues her meditation while painting, and thinks again of Mrs Ramsay. She sees something stir in the window where Mrs Ramsay used to sit, and has a poignant sense of her living presence there beside her. Her tears well up in an anguish of love and grief, and she cries aloud, 'Mrs Ramsay! Mrs Ramsay!' Called out of her reverie by the unexpected sound of her own voice, she looks around embarrassed. 'She had not obviously taken leave of her senses. No one had seen her step off her strip of board into the waters of annihilation. She remained a skimpy old maid, holding a paint-brush' (pp. 268–9). But she has taken the plunge.

Some further light is cast upon the key phrase – 'the waters of annihilation' – in this passage by its recurrence in another work by Mrs Woolf which will perhaps help to clinch our definition of the symbolic function of the water imagery in *To the Lighthouse*. That work is a little book of less than thirty pages, which appeared just three years after *To the Lighthouse*, entitled *On Being Ill*,[8] wherein she speaks of how 'tremendous' is 'the spiritual change' which illness effects: 'how astonishing, when the lights of health go down, the undiscovered countries that are then disclosed . . . how we go down into the pit of death and feel the waters of annihilation close above our heads and

wake thinking to find ourselves in the presence of the angels
and the harpers. . . .' Clearly here the act of immersion is a symbol of rebirth, or, as we have styled it, of *transition* from one
state to another – in the novel under examination, of transition
from the single view, whether it be that of objective detachment
or subjective involvement, to the double vision which appre-
hends the nature of reality simultaneously from both points of
view.

VI

It now remains to tie our strands together by analyzing the
significance of the alternating points of view around which
the final section of the novel is built. As we have seen, its
structure is determined by the double vision of Lily on the
island watching the boat approach the Lighthouse while she
finishes her painting, and of those in the boat watching the island
recede from view while they near the completion of their trip.
'So much depends then, thought Lily Briscoe, looking at the sea
which had scarcely a stain on it . . . upon distance: whether
people are near us or far from us; for her feeling for Mr Ramsay
changed as he sailed further and further across the bay' (p. 284).

Similarly James, in the boat, thinks, as they get closer to
their destination, of his childhood and of the time he had hated
his father for saying they would not be able to go to the Lighthouse next morning:

The Lighthouse was then a silvery, misty-looking tower with
a yellow eye, that opened suddenly, and softly in the evening.
Now –
James looked at the Lighthouse. He could see the white-
washed rocks; the tower, stark and straight; he could see that it
was barred with black and white; he could see windows in it; he
could even see washing spread on the rocks to dry. So that was
the Lighthouse, was it?
No, the other was also the Lighthouse. For nothing was
simply one thing. The other Lighthouse was true too. (pp.
276–7)

Dramatically, there is a double tension to be resolved here, each aspect somehow centered around the gaunt figure of Mr Ramsay. First there is in Lily a curious feeling of frustration due to her long-standing inability to give Mr Ramsay the feminine sympathy he craves – probably because this would entail performing a more sexual role than she will allow in her desire to keep her artist-spinsterhood intact – and this is somehow tied up with the trip to the Lighthouse and the completion of her painting. As the third section proceeds, 'She felt curiously divided, as if one part of her were drawn out there – it was a still day, hazy; the Lighthouse looked this morning at an immense distance; the other fixed itself doggedly, solidly, here on the lawn' (pp. 233–4). She is seeking that 'razor-edge of balance between two opposite forces; Mr Ramsay and the picture; which was necessary' (p. 287).

So too James, in league with Cam, is stubbornly trying to keep a firm hold on his long-standing resentment against his father, to resist tyranny to the death. But 'Cam looked down into the foam, into the sea with all its treasure in it, and its speed hypnotized her, and the tie between her and James sagged a little. It slackened a little' (p. 246).

Back on the island, Lily continues her painting, raising in her mind the question of artistic detachment from the common sympathies of life and the consequent lack of emotional stability which has been haunting her all along: 'No guide, no shelter, but all was miracle, and leaping from the pinnacle of a tower in the air? Could it be, even for elderly people, that this was life? – startling, unexpected, unknown?' (p. 286). As James's childhood resentment against his father prevents him from yielding to his father's emotional demands, thereby standing in the way of the son's identification with the father and consequently blocking his normal growth towards maturity, so too Lily's aloofness from life's routine involvements prevents her from yielding to Mr Ramsay's demand for feminine sympathy, thereby standing in the way of her acceptance of her sexual role and consequently blocking her achievement of artistic maturity.

Meanwhile James, who has been steering the boat, nursing his resentment, is praised for his navigational skill by his father just as they reach their goal. 'There! Cam thought, addressing herself silently to James. You've got it at last. For she knew that this was what James had been wanting, and she knew that now he had got it he was so pleased that he would not look at her or at his father or any one.' Mr Ramsay sits expectantly, waiting to disembark: 'What do you want? they both wanted to ask. They both wanted to say, Ask us anything and we will give it you' (pp. 306–8).

Similarly Lily, as a result of the parallel course run by her emotional cycle, the progress of her painting, and her awareness of Mr Ramsay in the boat reaching the Lighthouse, feels her tension resolving at the same time:

'He must have reached it,' said Lily Briscoe aloud, feeling suddenly completely tired out. For the Lighthouse had become almost invisible, had melted away into a blue haze, and the effort of looking at it and the effort of thinking of him landing there, which both seemed to be one and the same effort, had stretched her body and mind to the utmost. Ah, but she was relieved. Whatever she had wanted to give him, when he left her that morning, she had given him at last.
'He has landed,' she said aloud. 'It is finished.'

Mr Carmichael stood beside her, the ageing poet 'looking like an old pagan god, shaggy, with weeds in his hair and the trident (it was only a French novel) in his hand', and repeated: 'They will have landed.' She feels that this is a moment of communion – one to match, we might add, the similar moment which occurred during the meal in section one – and she thinks: 'He stood there as if he were spreading his hands over all the weakness and suffering of mankind; she thought he was surveying, tolerantly and compassionately, their final destiny. Now he has crowned the occasion, she thought. . . .' And, under the spell of this benediction, 'Quickly, as if she were recalled by something over there, she turned to her canvas. There it was – her picture' (pp. 308–9).

James has come into manhood by identifying himself with his father's attitude of grim and solitary acceptance of the uncompromising reality: 'So it was like that, James thought, the Lighthouse one had seen across the bay all these years; it was a stark tower on a bare rock. It satisfied him. It confirmed some obscure feeling of his about his own character. . . . He looked at his father reading fiercely with his legs curled tight. They shared that knowledge. "We are driving before a gale – we must sink." he began saying to himself, half aloud, exactly as his father said it' (pp. 301–2).

Finally, Lily has come to see the need of holding art and life in relation by means of the double vision: 'One wanted, she thought, dipping her brush deliberately, to be on a level with ordinary experience, to feel simply that's a chair, that's a table, and yet at the same time, It's a miracle, it's an ecstasy' (pp. 299–300). And this complex perspective, we recall, was gained by both James and Lily, as well as Mr Ramsay, by means of a yielding – whether literal or figurative – to the watery element of transition.[9]

SOURCE: *English Literary History*, XXII, no. 1 (1955).

NOTES

1. The page references throughout are to the Harbrace Modern Classics edition.

2. S. H. Derbyshire, 'An Analysis of Mrs Woolf's *To the Lighthouse*', in *College English*, III (1942) 353–60.

3. Cf Dorothy M. Hoare, *Some Studies in the Modern Novel* (1938) pp. 53–61, and John Hawley Roberts, ' "Vision and Design" in Virginia Woolf', in *PMLA* LXI (1946) 835–47.

4. Dayton Kohler, 'Time in the Modern Novel', in *College English*, X (1948) 15–24.

5. F. L. Overcarsh, 'The Lighthouse, Face to Face', in *Accent*, X (1950) 107–23.

6. David Daiches, *Virginia Woolf* (1942) pp. 84–8 (see pp. 90–104 of this volume).

7. D. S. Savage, *The Withered Branch* (1950) pp. 87–96; and Deborah Newton, *Virginia Woolf* (Melbourne, 1946) pp. 37–40.

For further comments on this novel see also Winifred Holtby, *Virginia Woolf* (1932) pp. 137–60; Edwin Muir, 'Virginia Woolf', in *Bookman*, LXXIV (1931) 362–7; Joseph Warren Beach, 'Virginia Woolf', in *English Journal*, XXVI (1937) 603–12; R. L. Chambers, *The Novels of Virginia Woolf* (London and Edinburgh, 1947) pp. 29–35; Bernard Blackstone, *Virginia Woolf: a commentary* (New York, 1949) pp. 100–30; James Southall Wilson, 'Time and Virginia Woolf', in *Virginia Quarterly Review*, XVIII (1942) 267–76; Joan Bennett, *Virginia Woolf: her art as a novelist* (New York, 1945) pp. 118–19; William Troy, 'Virginia Woolf and the Novel of Sensibility', in *Symposium*, III (1932) 53–63, 153–66 (see pp. 85–9 of this volume); L.B.S., 'Virginia Woolf's *To the Lighthouse*', in *Explicator*, VIII (Nov 1949) Q. 2; Charles G. Hoffman, 'Woolf's *To the Lighthouse*', in *Explicator*, X (Nov 1951) 13; H. K. Russell, 'Woolf's *To the Lighthouse*', in *Explicator*, VIII (March 1950) 38; Conrad Aiken, 'The Novel as a Work of Art', in *Dial*, LXXXIII (1927), 41–4 (see pp. 76–80 of this volume); N. Elizabeth Monroe, 'The Inception of Mrs Woolf's Art', in *College English*, II (1940) 217–30; William York Tindall, 'Many-leveled Fiction: Virginia Woolf to Ross Lockridge', in *College English*, X (1948) 65–71; and John Hawley Roberts, 'Toward Virginia Woolf', in *Virginia Quarterly Review*, X (1934) 587–602.

8. Printed and published by Leonard and Virginia Woolf at the Hogarth Press, 1930, p. 9. Grateful thanks are due to my colleague, Mr Edward W. Manchester, for the loan of this valuable book, one of a limited edition of 250 copies signed by the author who also set the type.

9. After this essay was completed, I read Erich Auerbach's treatment of this novel in *Mimesis: the representation of reality in western literature*, Willard R. Trask. Trans. (Princeton, 1953) ch. 20, and wish now to make reference to it here. (See pp. 105–32).

Joseph L. Blotner

MYTHIC PATTERNS IN
TO THE LIGHTHOUSE (1956)

I

THE impulses and convictions which gave birth to *Three Guineas*
and *A Room of One's Own* carried over into Virginia Woolf's
fiction. Their most powerful expression is found in *To the Lighthouse*. But something, probably her strict and demanding
artistic conscience, prevented their appearance in the form of the
intellectual and argumentative feminism found in the first two
books. In this novel Virginia Woolf's concept of woman's role
in life is crystallized in the character of Mrs Ramsay, whose
attributes are those of major female figures in pagan myth. The
most useful myth for interpreting the novel is that of the Primordial Goddess, who 'is threefold in relation to Zeus: mother
(Rhea), wife (Demeter), and daughter (Persephone)'. One of the
major sources of the myth is the Homeric 'Hymn to Demeter',
in which the poet compares Rhea with her daughter Demeter,
and makes it clear that Demeter and her daughter Persephone
'are to be thought of as a *double figure*, one half of which is the
ideal complement of the other'.[1] This double figure is that of the
Kore, the primordial maiden, who is also a mother. Also useful
in interpreting the novel is the Oedipus myth.

In using myth as an approach to a work of literature, the
critic can make one of two assertions: the artist knowingly used
myth as a basis for his creation; or, all unaware, he used it as it
welled up out of the subconscious layers of his psyche where it
resided as forgotten material, as an archetypal pattern or a
fragment of the collective or racial unconscious. But one of these
assertions leads to a dilemma when it is applied to *To the Lighthouse*, and the other is fundamentally unsound for either fruitful

criticism or sound scholarship. First, Virginia Woolf's diary shows that she read Greek, and 'On Not Knowing Greek' shows that she venerated it. And, even had she not read Jung, Freud, and Frazer prior to 1927,[2] she would have known about them through other members of the Bloomsbury Group. However, there is no direct evidence that she consciously used myth in the writing of this novel. Therefore, to assert that she did would be only speculation. Second, because of the relatively large number of these patterns as presented by Frazer, Jung, and Freud, and because of the enormous number of variations into which they can be differentiated by particular cultures, one is able to find some sort of referent in them for major elements of many novels. Then, any parallel between the mythic pattern and the work of art, by virtue of invoking the supposedly forgotten, or the archetypal patterns in the artist's unconscious, is argued as sufficient basis for claiming that a causative relationship exists. Virginia Woolf in her diary reiterated the role of her 'subconscious' in the germination of a novel and noted 'how tremendously important unconsciousness is when one writes'.[3] However, this proposition is susceptible of neither proof nor disproof. These myths may well have risen from Virginia Woolf's subconscious to form the framework of her novel, but this can be shown by neither critic nor psychologist. There is, however, a third position. When meaningful, coherent, and illuminating parallels are discerned, the work may be interpreted in terms of the myth. Often what appears fragmentary or only partly disclosed in the work may be revealed as complete and explicit through the myth.

This method is used from the outside, so to speak. It is not an interior approach asserting that myth was present at the conception and execution of the work; it rather asserts that myth may be brought to the work at its reading. It is like laying a colored transparency over a sheet covered with a maze of hues to reveal the orderly pattern which otherwise resides within them unperceived. Thus, in *To the Lighthouse* the myths of Oedipus and the Kore, superimposed momentarily upon the novel, provide a framework within whose boundaries and by virtue of whose spatial ordering the symbolic people, passages, and phrases of the book can be seen to assume a relationship to each other which illuminates their reciprocal functions and meanings. But since one key may open several doors in a house while leaving several more still locked, the mythic approach will not be urged as a Rosetta Stone for fathoming all the meanings of *To the Lighthouse*. However, this interpretation has several advantages. It shows that this is not, as has often been asserted, a novel which is poetic but plotless.[4] The poetry is certainly there but so is the plot, if one reads the novel with all its striking parallels against these myths which are so strong in plot. This is not to suggest that Mrs Woolf is consciously or unconsciously indebted to *The Golden Bough*, Bulfinch's mythology, or the sources of these works for her plot, but rather that the mythic approach helps to show that this novel has in fact a clear and coherent narrative beneath its enchanting poetry and evocative prose. In this interpretation Mrs Ramsay is not merely Goodness (Blackstone, p. 112), or light, spirit, and spell (Roberts, p. 596). She is more than this and more than the mainspring of the novel: she is the meaning of the novel. This interpretation also relates this work, Virginia Woolf's finest as an artist, to her fundamental convictions as a woman.

Although it has been suggested that *To the Lighthouse* can be explained in terms of Christian myth,[5] there is much evidence, both external and internal, which argues against this interpretation. Virginia Woolf's agnosticism appears on many pages of her diary. And Christian symbolism is quite as inappropriate for Mrs Ramsay. When the phrase, 'We are in the hands of the Lord', enters her mind, she rejects it: 'instantly she was annoyed with herself for saying that. Who had said it? Not she; she had been trapped into saying something she did not mean.'[6] This has been 'an insincerity slipping in among the truths . . .' (98). The beam from the Lighthouse sweeps over her, 'purifying out of existence that lie, any lie' (97). If there is a place in the novel for a male deity, he is not Christ, but Zeus. This deity would appropriately be he, linked with the hidden malevolence Mrs Ramsay sometimes senses in life, for Zeus was the god who

connived with Hades in the abduction of Persephone, and was
himself the bridegroom by violence of Demeter.

That Mrs Woolf's characters are symbolic is quite clear. Mrs
Ramsay and her husband stand watching their children when
suddenly a meaning descends upon them, 'making them representative . . . made them in the dusk standing, looking, the
symbols of marriage, husband and wife' (110–11). But Mrs
Ramsay is a symbol of much more than this. She is a symbol of
the female principle in life. Clothed in beauty, an intuitive and
fructifying force, she opposes the logical but arid and sterile
male principle. Her influence works toward the mating of men
and women, toward their becoming fruitful like herself. Her
function is the same on the intellectual level, for she gives her
protection and inspiration to both art and science. To Lily
Briscoe the painter she gives stimulus and understanding; to
Carmichael the poet she gives haven from squalor and a shrewish
wife; to Ramsay the philosopher she supplies love, comfort,
and reassurance; to Tansley the graduate student she offers
protection for a personality rubbed raw by insecurity; to Bankes
the botanist she renders affection and respite from a widowed
life and priestlike devotion to science. 'Indeed, she had the whole
of the other sex under her protection; for reasons she could not
explain . . . finally, for an attitude towards herself which no
woman could fail to feel or to find agreeable, something trustful,
childlike, reverential . . . ' (13).

II

Comparing her feelings upon completing *The Waves* with those
she had when she finished *To the Lighthouse*, Virginia Woolf
wrote that 'What interests me in the last stage was the freedom
and boldness with which my imagination picked up, used and
tossed aside all the images, symbols *which I had prepared* [italics
mine]. I am sure that this is the right way of using them – not in
set pieces, as I had tried at first coherently, but simply as images,
never making them work out; only suggest. Thus I hope to
have kept the sound of the sea and the birds, dawn and garden

subconsciously present, doing their work underground' (*Writer's Diary*, p. 165). This penetrating introspection gives the keynote for interpretation of Virginia Woolf's use of image and symbol. One must not expect a point-for-point correspondence between symbol and referent, and, by implication, no exact parallel between character and plot on the one hand and mythic personage and mythic pattern on the other. However, there are surprisingly strong correspondences between the two.

Rhea was the oldest of the gods, the child of Gaea, Mother Earth, and Ouranos, Father Heaven. When her brother Cronos overthrew Ouranos, Rhea became Cronos' wife and queen of the universe. Since Gaea was not actually a divinity, however, nor ever separated from the earth and personified, her daughter Rhea is the primal pagan goddess antedating the male gods. Although Cronos was said to have brought in the Golden Age in Italy when he fled there from the victorious Zeus, he cuts a poor figure beside Rhea. Having attained power by mutilating and dethroning his father, he attempted to keep it by swallowing his children. This he did with each of the first five Rhea bore him, attempting to thwart the prophecy that one of his children would overthrow him. By contrast, Rhea is the completely good and loving mother. Wrapping a stone in swaddling clothes and substituting it for Zeus, she has the child spirited to Crete. It is he who later delivers his brothers and sisters by forcing Cronos to disgorge them.

Whereas Rhea has six children, three boys and three girls, Mrs Ramsay has eight, four boys and four girls. Like Cronos, Mr Ramsay was sometimes 'like a lion seeking whom he could devour . . .' (233). He has power and authority: 'Let him be fifty feet away, let him not even speak to you, let him not even see you, he permeated, he prevailed, he imposed himself. He changed everything' (233). In each family the youngest child, a male, is the one who opposes the father. Zeus, alone in his exile on Crete, might have reflected like James, 'I shall be left to fight the tyrant alone' (250). As Rhea protected Zeus from physical harm, so Mrs Ramsay tries to guard James from psychological wounds. When Mr Ramsay declares that the weather will not permit the trip to the Lighthouse which James so passionately desires, Mrs Ramsay tries to induce her husband to modify his pronouncement. She reflects that children never forget; 'she was certain that he was thinking, we are not going to the Lighthouse tomorrow; and she thought, he will remember that all his life' (95).

Mrs Ramsay has many of the physical attributes of a goddess. To Lily's eyes she seems to wear 'an august shape . . .' (80). She has a 'royalty of form . . .' (47). Lily perceives that Mr Bankes 'worshipped' Mrs Ramsay (75). When Mr Bankes hears her voice, he visualizes her as 'very clearly Greek' (47), and feels that 'the Graces assembled seemed to have joined hands in meadows of asphodel to compose that face' (47). Augustus Carmichael bows as if to do her 'homage' (167). When Charles Tansley glimpses her standing motionless, a picture of Queen Victoria behind her, he realizes that she is 'the most beautiful person he had ever seen' (25). He visualizes her 'stepping through fields of flowers and taking to her breast buds that had broken and lambs that had fallen; with the stars in her eyes and the wind in her hair . . .'(25). And her glance comes from 'eyes of unparalleled depth' (77). Even as he speaks of prosaic things, 'one would be thinking of Greek temples, and how beauty had been with them there in that stuffy room' (291). Even her bearing is regal: 'like some queen who, finding her people gathered in the hall, looks down upon them, and descends among them, and acknowledges their tributes silently, and accepts their devotion and their prostration before her . . . she went down, and crossed the hall and bowed her head very slightly, as if she accepted what they could not say: their tribute to her beauty' (124).

Mrs Ramsay's psychic qualities are also those of a goddess. She is possessed of an intuitive knowledge and wisdom, and exercises a dominion over those around her, seeming almost to cast a spell upon them. Lily Briscoe, particularly sensitive to this aspect of her character, struggles with ambivalent feelings. She sees Mrs Ramsay as 'unquestionably the loveliest of people . . . the best perhaps' (76), yet she chafes at her imperiousness. Lily laughs at her, 'presiding with immutable calm over destinies which she completely failed to understand' (78). But at the same time she divines, in the heart of this woman 'like treasures in the tombs of kings, tablets bearing sacred inscriptions, which if one could spell them out, would teach one everything . . .' (79). When Mrs Ramsay exercises her powers, her domination, Lily is moved to reflect that 'there was something frightening about her. She was irresistible' (125). Her perceptions are clearly psychic: 'She knew then – she knew without having learnt. Her simplicity fathomed what clever people falsified. Her singleness of mind made her drop, plumb like a stone, alight exact as a bird, gave her, naturally, this swoop and fall of the spirit upon truth . . . ' (46). Her grey eyes seem to penetrate the thoughts and feelings of others. Her domination pulls them all together, makes them interact as she wants them to do. But, 'directly she went a sort of disintegration set in . . .'(168).

III

If Mrs Ramsay resembles Rhea, she appears almost an incarnation of Demeter. This divine being, the Goddess of the Corn, was the daughter of Cronos and Rhea and the sister of Zeus. But unlike him and the other Olympians, she was, with Dionysus, mankind's best friend. Hers was the divine power which made the earth fruitful. It was she 'who was worshipped, not like the other gods by the bloody sacrifices men liked, but in every humble act that made the farm fruitful. Through her the field of grain was hallowed, "Demeter's holy grain".'[7] Even when the originally simple rites in her honor evolved into the Eleusinian Mysteries, their effect was still beneficent. The quality of these observances survived even the decline of Greece and the rise of Rome, for Cicero wrote that 'among the many excellent and indeed divine institutions which . . . Athens has brought forth and contributed to human life, none, in my opinion, is better than those mysteries. For by their means we have been brought out of our barbarous and savage mode of life and refined into a state of civilization, and as the rites are called "initiations", so in very truth we have learned from them the beginnings of life, and have gained the power not only to live happily, but also to die with a better hope.'[8]

Symbols of fruitfulness cluster around Mrs Ramsay. She plants flowers and sees that they are tended. The others, thinking of her, associate flowers with her instinctively. She adorns herself with a green shawl. Running throughout the book, through her own stream of consciousness, is an almost obsessive concern that the greenhouse shall be repaired and preserved. Many of the figures of speech used to describe her relate to nature. Concentrating, 'she grew still like a tree . . .' (177). In solitary meditation she reflects 'how if one was alone, one leant to inanimate things; trees, streams, flowers; felt they expressed one; felt they became one; felt they knew one, in a sense were one . . .' (97). At times she even thinks in terms of myth. Contemplation of a cornucopia-like dish of fruit 'made her think of a trophy fetched from the bottom of the sea, of Neptune's banquet, of the bunch that hangs with vine leaves over the shoulder of Bacchus . . .' (146).

She is an ardent matchmaker, giving Paul Rayley the impetus and encouragement to propose to Minta Doyle, determining to marry Lily Briscoe to William Bankes. She insists that 'Minta must, they all must marry . . . an unmarried woman had missed the best of life. The house seemed full of children and Mrs Ramsay listening . . .' (77). And her attitude toward marriage seems more pagan than Christian. The elaborate dinner over which she presides, coming immediately after Paul's successful proposal to Minta, gives her mixed feelings, a sense 'of celebrating a festival, as if two emotions were called up in her, one profound – for what could be more serious than the love of man for woman, what more commanding, more impressive, bearing in its bosom the seeds of death; at the same time these lovers, these people entering into illusion glittering eyed, must be danced round with mockery, decorated with garlands' (151). And this mockery is not at all inconsistent with the character of Demeter. Kerényi writes that in the figure of the Kore 'There is, for instance, the strange equation of marriage and death, the bridal chamber and the grave. Marriage in this connexion has the character of murder; the brutal ravisher is the god of death himself. On the other hand, marriage retains its proper and primary meaning as the union of man and woman. But not only does it call forth the lamentations of the celebrants, it also calls forth obscene speech and laughing at obscene actions' (pp. 179–80).

An important characteristic of Mrs Ramsay in her Demeter aspect is her complete femininity. As Demeter was worshipped more by men than women, as the sacrifices to her were humble and restrained rather than fierce and bloody like those of men, so Mrs Ramsay in all her aspects is feminine and opposed to that which is undesirable in masculinity. When she gives to Mr Ramsay the sympathy and reassurance he begs, the action is symbolic: 'into this delicious fecundity, this fountain and spray of life, the fatal sterility of the male plunged itself, like a beak of brass, barren and bare' (58). By this act, Mr Ramsay is 'taken within the circle of life . . . his barrenness made fertile . . .' (59). This characteristic is not exclusively Mr Ramsay's: 'she felt, as a fact without hostility, the sterility of men . . . ' (126). With her quick intuition, her special knowledge, she is at the opposite pole from them. Although she does not possess their analytical reasoning powers, she is far more perceptive than they. 'How much they missed, after all, these very clever men! How dried up they did become, to be sure' (150). There is little doubt that these sentiments are inherent in Virginia Woolf's feminism. In Mrs Ramsay's thoughts one finds an echo of those of her creator, who wrote, 'the egotism of men surprises and shocks me even now', who found that 'the male atmosphere is disconcerting to me . . . I think what an abrupt precipice cleaves asunder the male intelligence, and how they pride themselves upon a point of view which much resembles stupidity' (*Writer's Diary*, pp. 135, 12). Jung concludes his essay on the psychological aspects of the Kore with the comment that 'Demeter-Kore exists on the plane of mother-daughter experience which is alien to man and shuts him out. In fact, the psychology of the Demeter cult has all the features of a matriarchal order of society where the man is an indispensable but on the whole disturbing factor' (p. 245).

Even the story of the Fisherman and His Wife, which Mrs

Ramsay reads to James, reflects this attitude. To perceive it, however, one must do what Virginia Woolf did in *Orlando*: change the sex of the principal character. In *To the Lighthouse* the individual who makes the insatiable demands is not the wife but the husband. Mr Ramsay, the philosopher, has driven himself to the Q of mental effort and understanding. He is plunged into melancholy despair at his inability to reach Z. He is described as standing desolate in darkness on a narrow spit of land, the black seas nearly engulfing him. It is his wife who is content with that which they have already received, who accepts their portion and cherishes their gift of love.

The figures of Demeter and Mrs Ramsay are linked in another important way. They are characterized not only by fruitfulness, but by sorrow as well. This element also serves to point up the transition from the Demeter to the Persephone component of this multiple myth. Demeter's sorrow is caused, of course, by her loss of Persephone. Mrs Ramsay's sorrow is neither so continuous nor so specifically focused as that of Demeter. But when she falls prey to it, her sorrow is genuine and pervasive, and highly suggestive of that of the goddess: 'Never did anybody look so sad. Bitter and black, half way down, in the darkness, in the shaft which ran from sunlight to the depths, perhaps a tear formed; a tear fell; the waters swayed this way and that, received it, and were at rest. Never did anybody look so sad' (46). And this is not a simple *weltschmerz*, but a genuine reaction to a frightening vision of a real antagonist, for 'she felt this thing that she called life terrible, hostile and quick to pounce on you if you gave it a chance' (92). Another of Mrs Ramsay's interior monologues might be that of the goddess implored to make the earth fruitful again: 'Why, one asked oneself, does one take all these pains for the human race to go on? Is it so very desirable?' (134).

IV

In the familiar story, Demeter's only child, Persephone, was abducted by Hades and spirited down to the underworld to reign with him over the souls of all the dead. In her anguish for her daughter, the Goddess of the Corn 'withheld her gifts from the earth, which turned into a frozen desert. The green and flowering land was icebound and lifeless because Persephone had disappeared' (Hamilton, p. 57). Finally compelled to intervene, Zeus sent Hermes to Hades with the order that Persephone must be released. Hades complied, but first forced her to eat a pomegranate seed, whose magical properties would insure her return to him for a third of each year. Zeus also sent Rhea to Demeter to tell her that Persephone would be released and to ask Demeter to make the earth fruitful again. Demeter, of course, complied. Edith Hamilton writes:

In the stories of both goddesses, Demeter and Persephone, the idea of sorrow was foremost. Demeter, goddess of the harvest wealth, was still more the divine sorrowing mother who saw her daughter die each year. Persephone was the radiant maiden of the spring and the summertime. . . . But all the while Persephone knew how brief that beauty was; fruits, flowers, leaves, all the fair growth of the earth, must end with the coming of the cold and pass like herself into the power of death. After the lord of the dark world below carried her away she was never again the gay young creature who had played in the flowery meadow without a thought of care or trouble. She did indeed rise from the dead every spring, but she brought with her the memory of where she had come from; with all her bright beauty there was something strange and awesome about her. She was often said to be 'the maiden whose name may not be spoken'. (pp. 53–4)

Many allusions in *To the Lighthouse* suggest the Persephone–Mrs Ramsay correspondence. Barely nine pages into the novel one reads that she had 'in her veins the blood of that very noble, if slightly mythical, Italian house, whose daughters, scattered about English drawing rooms in the nineteenth century, had lisped so charmingly, had stormed so wildly, and all her wit and bearing and her temper came from them . . .' (17).

Early in the novel Mrs Ramsay has premonitions, foreshadowings of her departure from the green and flowering loveliness of the Isle of Skye, of her descent into the world of shades. As she sits in the gathering dusk, she looks out upon her garden: 'the whitening of the flowers and something grey in the leaves conspired together, to rouse in her a feeling of anxiety' (93–4). Her mood deepens until 'all the being and the doing, expansive, glittering, vocal, evaporated; and one shrunk, with a sense of solemnity, to being oneself, a wedge-shaped core of darkness, something invisible to others' (95). Yet at times these depths are briefly pierced by shafts of light. The sound of the waves on the beach 'seemed of some old cradle song, murmured by nature, "I am guarding you – I am your support" ' (27). It is as if Persephone, sensing the imminence of her rape and abduction, divined also that her salvation would come from her who had sung a cradle song, her mother, Demeter, the goddess so close to nature.

Mrs Ramsay's death is communicated to the reader with shocking suddenness and brevity, as though it were not the event itself which was important, but rather its consequences. In Lily Briscoe's reflections in 'The Lighthouse' section of the novel, however, the reader is given Lily's special vision of Mrs Ramsay's departure. And, of course, it is Lily who is most sensitive to Mrs Ramsay, to her essence and her function. As Lily paints, the images sweep in on her mind: 'It was strange how clearly she saw her, stepping with her usual quickness across fields among whose folds, purplish and soft, among whose flowers, hyacinths or lilies, she vanished. It was some trick of the painter's eye. For days after she had heard of her death she had seen her thus, putting her wreath to her forehead[9] and going unquestioningly with her companion, a shade across the fields . . . all had been part of the fields of death' (269–70). When Persephone had wandered away from her companions, thus isolating herself for Hades' attack, she had been attracted by banks of narcissus, hyacinths, and lilies (Frazer, p. 36). As she was abducted, she dropped the lilies she had gathered.[10] Thirty pages later in the novel, Lily's vision of Mrs Ramsay's departure is resumed: 'She let her flowers fall from her basket, scattered and tumbled them on to the grass and, reluctantly and hesitatingly, but without question or complaint . . . went too. Down fields, across valleys, white, flower-strewn . . . the hills were austere. It was rocky; it was steep. The waves sounded hoarse on the stones beneath. They went, the three of them together . . . ' (299). The identity of the third figure is problematical. The daughter to whom Mrs Ramsay is closest, the lovely Prue, follows her mother in death.[11] It may be that Lily's unconscious mind has joined Prue to her mother in this symbolic vision. Since the unity of the two divine persons is central to the concept of the Kore, this is a workable hypothesis for this interpretation.[12] But in terms of the myth, Mrs Ramsay's failure to question or complain does not seem apt. In view of the other detailed correspondences – the falling flowers, the rocky steepness so clearly suggestive of the chasm out of which Hades rose to seize his prey – this is perhaps one point upon which one might invoke Virginia Woolf's avowed intention of making her symbols work 'not in set pieces . . . but simply as images, never making them work out; only suggest' (*Writer's Diary*, p. 165).

The very first pages of 'Time Passes', the middle section of the novel, may be seen as symbolic of the transformation of the earth when Demeter withheld her gifts: 'a downpouring of immense darkness began. Nothing, it seemed, could survive the flood, the profusion of darkness . . . ' (189). There is not only darkness, but also dissolution as 'fumbling airs' creep into the house; 'wearily, ghostlily . . . they . . . blanched the apples . . . fumbled the petals of roses . . . ' (191). 'Divine goodness' displays the treasures which might be given to men if they deserved them, but 'it does not please him; he covers his treasures in a drench of hail, and so breaks them . . . the nights are now full of wind and destruction . . . ' (193).

Then, as this section of the novel progresses, vegetation springs up in the solitude as time passes. But there is a horror beneath this growth, now blind, purposeless, and even destructive: 'the flowers standing there, looking before them, looking up, yet beholding nothing, eyeless, and so terrible' (203). The house becomes a moldering shell, in the process of dissolution. Finally, 'If [a] feather had fallen, if it had tipped the scale downwards, the whole house would have plunged to the depths to lie upon the sands of oblivion' (209). This once pleasant place, now reft of the force which had made it beautiful, 'would have turned and pitched downwards to the depths of darkness' (208). The time of catastrophes, private and public, has come; Andrew is killed by a piece of shrapnel; Prue dies in childbirth; and the first World War sweeps across the face of Europe.[13]

v

The reappearance of Persephone has its symbolic equivalent in the novel in the return of the force which Mrs Ramsay represented. Mrs McNab receives orders to have the house restored. The predominant activity in the last section of the book is the expedition to the Lighthouse, upon which Mr Ramsay is determined almost as if it were a rite of propitiation toward Mrs Ramsay's spirit. And clearly, her spirit has a profound effect upon Lily. In this, Virginia Woolf may have been influenced by *A Passage to India*, the novel of her intimate friend E. M. Forster. This book, which she felt represented Forster in 'his prime',[14] appeared three years before *To the Lighthouse*. The central female figure in Forster's novel is Mrs Moore, an old Englishwoman. Through her influence, felt returning after her death, some of the wounds inflicted during the conflict between the British and the Indians in Chandrapore are healed. Earlier in *To the Lighthouse*, Mrs Ramsay has performed an act symbolic of Demeter's role in the rescue of Persephone. Going to the nursery, she has covered the boar's skull which has kept her daughter Cam awake until eleven o'clock at night – covered the skull with her own green shawl. The symbol of death is banished and obliterated by the symbol of fertility. In Lily's first night in the house after her return, she reflects that 'peace had come' (213). If the guests were to go down to the darkened beach, 'They would see then night flowing down in purple; his head crowned; his sceptre jewelled; and how in his eyes a child might look' (213). This dark and kingly deity, whose symbol had earlier frightened a child from sleep, has now been disarmed. The feminine principle, the Kore, has triumphed over the dark underworld with her release from it.

As the day passes, Lily invokes Mrs Ramsay, fruitlessly at first. But then she feels her imminence. ' "Mrs Ramsay! Mrs Ramsay!" she repeated. She owed it all to her' (241). At times Lily's longing is so intense that 'she called out silently, to that essence which sat by the boat, that abstract one made of her, that woman in grey, as if to abuse her for having gone, and then having gone, come back again. It had seemed so safe, thinking of her. Ghost, air, nothingness, a thing you could play with easily and safely at any time of day or night, she had been that, and then suddenly she put her hand out and wrung the heart thus' (266).

But finally, of course, as the boat reaches the Lighthouse and the rapport is achieved between James, Cam, and Mr Ramsay, Lily completes her picture, becomes, in this individual work, fruitful as an artist. Just as Mrs Ramsay's spirit has been the force which brings about the consummation of the trip to the Lighthouse, so her spirit brings about Lily's epiphany. In that famous passage, 'With a sudden intensity, as if she saw it clear for a second, she drew a line there, in the centre. It was done; it was finished. Yes, she thought, laying down her brush in extreme fatigue, I have had my vision' (310). The return of Persephone is thus twofold. Mrs Ramsay, in the Persephone aspect of the Kore, has returned as an almost palpable presence to the Isle of Skye from which she had been snatched by death. Persephone has also returned through Lily's final achievement of the artistic vision and triumph denied her ten years earlier.[15] As clear as the existence of the relationship between Mrs Ramsay and Lily is the function of this relationship: 'Demeter and Kore, mother and daughter, extend the feminine consciousness both upwards and downwards. They add an "older and younger", "stronger and weaker" dimension to it and widen out the narrowly limited conscious mind bound in space and time, giving it intimations of a greater and more comprehensive personality which has a share in the eternal course of things' (Jung, p. 225). Both the mother-figure and the daughter-figure are united in that they are artists – the one in paints and the other in human relationships – and in that they are bound to each other by psychic bonds which remain firm even beyond death. Demeter has effected the liberation of Persephone.

VI

Sigmund Freud's interpretation of the Oedipus myth is almost as famous as the myth itself. This pattern, Freud says, dramatized in the legend of the Greek youth who unwittingly kills his father, marries and begets children with his mother, and then blinds himself in atonement, is fundamental in human experience. It is so basic that 'the beginnings of religion, ethics, society, and art meet in the Oedipus complex'. We are moved by Sophocles' play, Freud says, by the consciousness that Oedipus' fate 'might have been our own. . . . It may be that we were all destined to divert our first sexual impulses toward our mothers, and our first impulses of hatred and violence toward our fathers; our dreams convince us that we were.'[16]

That the relationship between James, Mrs Ramsay, and Mr Ramsay reflects this pattern is so clear as to be almost unmistakable. The intense adoration which James cherishes for his mother has its opposite in an equally strong hatred for his father, 'casting ridicule upon his wife, who was ten thousand times better in every way than he was (James thought) . . . ' (10). Virginia Woolf says of Mr Ramsay that 'his son hated him' (57). This emotion is thoroughgoing: 'Had there been an axe handy, or a poker, any weapon that would have gashed a hole in his father's breast and killed him, there and then, James would have seized it' (10). Mrs Ramsay is solicitous and fearful for James as Jocasta might have been for the young Oedipus: 'what demon possessed him, her youngest, her cherished?' (43).

James's jealousy and feelings of rivalry with his father are intensified by his perhaps unconscious knowledge of the sexual aspect of the relationship between his parents. He is made acutely aware of it in the episode early in the novel in which Mr Ramsay comes to his wife for the sympathy and reassurance he demands. The imagery used to describe this action is patently sexual. James, standing between his mother's knees, feels her seem 'to raise herself with an effort, and at once to pour erect into the air a rain of energy . . . and into this fountain and spray of life, the fatal sterility of the male plunged itself, like a beak of brass, barren and bare' (58). Then James feels shut out when, the demand complied with, 'Mrs Ramsay seemed to fold herself together, one petal closed in another, and the whole fabric fell in exhaustion upon itself, so that she had only strength enough to move her finger, in exquisite abandonment to exhaustion . . . while there throbbed through her, like a pulse in a spring which has expanded to its full width and now gently ceases to beat, the rapture of successful creation' (60–1).

Into the third section of the novel, across the space of ten years, James carries these same emotions undiminished in intensity. Of his mother he thinks, 'She alone spoke the truth; to her alone could he speak it' (278). Contemplating his father, James realizes that 'He had always kept this old symbol of taking a knife and striking his father to the heart' (273). The pattern is so strong that now James and his father compete in another triangle in which Cam has been substituted for Mrs Ramsay. The two children have made a compact to resist their father's tyranny, but James feels that he will lose to him again just as he had before. As Mr Ramsay begins to win Cam over, James acknowledges his defeat. ' "Yes," thought James pitilessly . . . "now she will give way. I shall be left to fight the tyrant alone" ' (250). An instant later, the antecedent of the present experience is dredged up out of the recesses of his memory: 'There was a flash of blue, he remembered, and then somebody sitting with him laughed, surrendered, and he was very angry. It must have been his mother, he thought, sitting on a low chair, with his father standing over her' (251).

Freud writes of the ambivalence the child feels toward his father, the conflict between tenderness and hostility. He concludes that unless the child is successful in repressing the sexual love for the mother and hostility for the father, while concomitantly allowing the natural affection for the father to grow, neurosis will be the result. Significantly, at the end of the finally accomplished journey to the Lighthouse, James experiences his

rapport with Mr Ramsay. Cam addresses herself silently to
James: 'You've got it at last. For she knew that this was what
James had been wanting . . . He was so pleased that he was not
going to let anybody share a grain of his pleasure. His father had
praised him' (306).

VII

The Oedipus myth is consonant with the Persephone myth in its
application to *To the Lighthouse* and both are reflections of
fundamental patterns of human experience. The two old antagon-
ists testify to this judgment of their importance, Freud to the
former and Jung to the latter. Appropriately, the symbol for one
section of the novel, 'The Window', is female, and that for another section, 'The Lighthouse', is male. Exalting the feminine
principle in life over the masculine, Virginia Woolf built her
novel around a character embodying the life-giving role of the
female. In opposition, she shows the male, both in the father and
son aspect, as death-bearing – arid, sterile, hateful, and 'fatal'
(58). The female principle in life is exalted in all its aspects of
love which are opposed to the harsh and critical aspects of the
male principle, of fertility with its pattern of triumph over death
in rebirth. What, then, becomes of the single obvious central
symbol, the Lighthouse? Its use is simply this: in its stability, its
essential constancy despite cyclical change which is not really
change at all, this symbol refers to Mrs Ramsay herself. This
meaning is revealed to the reader explicitly: Mrs Ramsay 'looked
up over her knitting and met the third stroke and it seemed to
her like her own eyes meeting her own eyes, searching as she
alone could search into her mind and heart . . . She praised herself
in praising the light, without vanity, for she was stern, she was
searching, she was beautiful like that light' (97). And just as
there are three persons combined in the Primordial Goddess, so
there are three strokes to the Lighthouse beam, and 'the long
steady stroke, the last of the three . . . was her stroke . . . ' (96).
    As Mrs Ramsay gives love, stability, and fruitfulness to her
family and those in her orbit, so the female force should always

function. It serves to ameliorate or mitigate the effects of male violence, hate, and destructiveness. And should the physical embodiment of this force pay her debt to the world of shades, this is not an ever-enduring loss, for it returns through those whom it has made fruitful and thus drawn into the rebirth pattern. Or it may be sought, found, and embraced as, in their separate ways, James, Cam, and Mr Ramsay experience it at the end of their ritual and symbolic voyage to the Lighthouse.

SOURCE: *PMLA* LXXI (1956).

NOTES

1. C. G. Jung and C. Kerényi, *Essays on a Science of Mythology*, trans. R. F. C. Hull (New York, 1949) pp. 25, 152.

2. *A Writer's Diary: being extracts from the diary of Virginia Woolf*, ed. Leonard Woolf (New York, 1953) pp. 205–6. Leonard Woolf, in a recent letter, informs me that he doubts that Virginia Woolf ever read any of Freud's works, but that he (Woolf) had discussed them with her, having read them as he published them in England under the imprint of the Hogarth Press.

3. Ibid.

4. For a statement of this position see Bernard Blackstone, *Virginia Woolf* (London and New York, 1949) p. 99; Edwin B. Burgum, 'Virginia Woolf and the Empty Room', in *Antioch Review*, III (Dec 1943) 596–611; and John H. Roberts, 'Toward Virginia Woolf', in *Virginia Quarterly Review*, x (Oct 1934), 587–602.

5. F. L. Overcarsh, 'To the Lighthouse, Face to Face', in *Accent*, x (Winter 1950) 107–23.

6. Virginia Woolf, *To the Lighthouse* (New York: Harcourt, Brace Modern Classics, 1927) p. 97. The pages from which further quotations are drawn are indicated in the text.

7. Edith Hamilton, *Mythology* (Boston, Mass., 1942) p. 54.

8. *De Re Publica, De Legibus*, trans. Clinton W. Keyes (1928) pp. 414–15. (*Laws* II xiv 36.)

9. 'In ancient art Demeter and Persephone are characterized as goddesses of the corn by the crowns of corn which they wear on their heads and by the stalks of corn which they hold in their hands' (J. G. Frazer, *The Golden Bough*, 3rd ed., 1912, VII 43).

10. *The Reader's Encyclopedia*, ed. William R. Benét (New York, 1948) p. 886.

11. Prue's death had come as a result of childbirth. This in itself suggests the inextricable connection of birth and death in the Kore myth.

12. Kerényi and Jung describe versions of the Persephone myth in which Demeter, as well as her daughter, was a victim of rape (pp. 170, 197, 251). Thus, in another variation, Mrs Ramsay and her daughter would signify Demeter and her daughter.

13. In 'The Eleusinian Festival' Schiller describes Demeter's wanderings:

> No refreshing corn or fruit
> Her distressing need await,
> Human bones the fanes pollute,
> And the altars violate.
> Wheresoe'er her footsteps turned
> Nought but sorrow could she scan,
> And her lofty spirit burned,
> Grieving for the fall of man.

Poetical Works of Friedrich Schiller, ed. Nathan H. Doyle, trans. Percy E. Pinkerton (1902) p. 198. Perhaps a better translation is that recited by Ivan to Alexey in Dostoevsky's *The Brothers Karamazov*, trans. Constance Garnett (New York: Mod. Lib., 1950) p. 125.

14. Virginia Woolf, 'The Novels of E. M. Forster', in *Atlantic Monthly*, CXL (Nov 1927) 642–8.

15. There is another factor which confirms Lily's role as a Persephone figure in this interpretation. Mrs Ramsay's characterization of her as prim and old-maidish is nothing more than emphasis and re-emphasis of a characteristic of Persephone, 'whose salient feature was an *elemental virginity*' (Jung and Kerényi, p. 207).

16. *The Basic Writings of Sigmund Freud*, ed. and trans. A. A. Brill (New York, 1938) p. 308.

Sharon Kaehele and Howard German

TO THE LIGHTHOUSE: SYMBOL AND VISION (1962)

VIRGINIA WOOLF'S *To the Lighthouse* is a study of personality, of the relationship between the sexes, of time, death, nature
and art. In this novel, however, these concerns are unified in a
way no cataloguing can suggest, for Mrs Woolf possessed to an
unusual degree that gift which she feels is essential to the novelist,
'the power of combination – the single vision'. The diversity of
interpretation among critics of *To the Lighthouse* suggests that,
in this case, a discernible 'single vision' may be lacking.[1] Yet we
feel that a careful reading of the three parts of the novel with
attention to details of character, action and imagery will reveal
how successfully Mrs Woolf has combined these diverse themes
into a unified whole. This unity can best be shown by an analysis
of the Lighthouse symbol in part I and of Lily Briscoe's vision in
part III. Mrs Woolf's ability to concentrate so much of her meaning in a symbol and an episode is dependent upon a careful use of
patterns of details. Throughout *To the Lighthouse* one feels her
exhibiting the trait she recommends to writers in *A Room of One's
Own*: she is capable at the appropriate time of 'beckoning and
summoning' so that there rise up in memory, 'half-forgotten,
perhaps quite trivial things in other chapters dropped by the
way'.[2] When assembled, these 'trivial things' awaken within the
reader of *To the Lighthouse* a sense of the whole, of the complex
but cohesive vision of reality created by the book.

I

Part I of *To the Lighthouse* deals with ideas about personality,
the relationship between the sexes, and modes of escape from
time. Primarily, these ideas are expressed through the Ramsays,

whom Mrs Woolf has endowed with qualities she believed typical
of the basic masculine and feminine characters. Their traits are
complementary: Mrs Ramsay's creative, intuitive femininity
balances her husband's courageous, intellectual masculinity. At
its best the man–woman relationship is strengthened by the
union of these characteristics. Several passages demonstrate the
interdependence of the Ramsays; those we have chosen also
provide descriptive details – 'trivial things' – which contribute
to an understanding of the symbols and other themes. Through
these details, for example, we see that Mr Ramsay is frequently
compared to the blade of a knife and Mrs Ramsay to a tree and
that the traits of *both* the Ramsays are to be identified with the
major symbol, the Lighthouse.

With her sensitivity to the needs of others, Mrs Ramsay serves
Mr Ramsay primarily through her capacity for sympathy and her
ability to give him a sense of being 'at the heart of life'. These
qualities are demonstrated in the description of their encounter
at the window.

Mrs Ramsay, who had been sitting loosely, folding her son in
her arms, braced herself, and, half-turning, seemed to raise
herself with an effort, and at once to pour erect into the air a
rain of energy, a column of spray, looking at the same time
animated and alive as if all her energies were being fused into
force, *burning and illuminating* . . . and into this delicious fecundity, this fountain and spray of life, the fatal sterility of the male
plunged itself, like a *beak of brass*, barren and bare. He wanted
sympathy. He was a failure, he said. Mrs Ramsay *flashed her
needles*. . . . *Flashing her needles*, confident, upright, she created
drawing room and kitchen, set them all aglow; bade him take his
ease there, go in and out, enjoy himself. . . . James felt all her
strength flaring up to be drunk and quenched by the *beak of brass*,
the arid *scimitar of the male*. . . . She assured him [Mr Ramsay]
beyond a shadow of a doubt, by her laugh, her poise, her com-
petence (as a nurse *carrying a light* across a dark room assures a
fractious child), that it was real; the house was full . . . and James
. . . felt her rise in a *rosy-flowered fruit* tree laid with leaves and
dancing boughs into which the *beak of brass*, the arid *scimitar* of

his father, the egoistical man, plunged and smote, demanding sympathy. (pp. 58–60)[3]

The imagery of this passage tends to equate Mrs Ramsay with both trees and the Lighthouse; other passages can easily be found to complete these identifications. At the dinner, for example, Mrs Ramsay picks up and repeats to herself the lines about trees in Charles Elton's poem, 'Come Out and Climb the Garden Path'; going upstairs later she unconsciously uses the elm trees outside the window to orient herself because 'her world was changing; they were still'; and, finally, when she returns to the room where her husband sits reading, she glows 'still like a tree which has been tossing and quivering but now settles leaf by leaf into quiet'. However, Mrs Ramsay consciously tends to identify herself most closely with the Lighthouse, or rather with its beam:

She looked up over her knitting and met the third stroke and it seemed to her like her own eyes meeting her own eyes, searching as she alone could search into her mind and her heart, purifying out of existence that lie, any lie. She praised herself in praising the light, without vanity, for *she was stern, she was searching, she was beautiful like that light*. It was odd, she thought, how if one was alone, one leant to inanimate things; *trees*, streams, flowers; felt they expressed one; felt they became one; felt they knew one, in a sense were one. . . . (p. 97)

This passage also shows Mrs Ramsay's concern with the truth of her inner life. On the other hand, she acquires a sense of security against chaos and time from Mr Ramsay's intellect, which is intent upon external reality. His conversation with Tansley outside the window comforts her by concealing the sound of the waves – those symbols of flux which 'remorselessly beat the measure of life'.[4] Again, at the dinner described in this first part, Mr Ramsay's conversation enables Mrs Ramsay to feel that she has for a moment escaped time; 'she let it uphold and sustain her, this admirable fabric of the masculine intelligence, which ran up and down, crossed this way and that, like iron

girders spanning the swaying fabric, upholding the world'. Mr
Ramsay's particular contribution to his wife's world is summed
up in the following passage describing him walking on the lawn
alone.

It was his fate, his peculiarity, whether he wished it or not, to
come out thus on a spit of land which the sea is slowly eating
away, and there to stand, like a desolate sea-bird, alone. It was his
power, his gift, suddenly to shed all superfluities, to shrink and
diminish so that he looked barer and felt sparer, even physically,
yet lost none of his intensity of mind, and so to stand on his little
ledge facing the dark of human ignorance, how we know nothing
and the sea eats away the ground we stand on – that was his fate,
his gift. But having thrown away . . . all gestures and fripperies,
all trophies of nuts and roses, and shrunk so that not only fame
but even his own name was forgotten by him, he kept even in
that desolation a vigilance which spared no phantom and luxuriated in no vision, and it was in this guise that he inspired . . ·
in his wife . . . reverence, and pity, and gratitude too, as *a stake
driven into the bed of a channel* upon which the gulls perch and
the waves beat inspires in merry boatloads a feeling of gratitude
for the duty it is taking upon itself of *marking the channel out
there in the floods alone.* (pp. 68–9)

The italicized words of this passage suggest the image of the
Lighthouse, and one or two additional details make clear that
it can be associated with Mr Ramsay also. For instance, during
one of his meditations Mr Ramsay is unable to solve a problem
that disturbs him; yet he resolves that 'he would not die lying
down; he would find some crag of rock, and there, his eyes fixed
on the storm, trying to the end to pierce the darkness, he would
die standing'. Also, Mr Ramsay's stature ('lean as a knife,
narrow as the blade of one', 'very straight and tall') and his
professional habit as a philosopher of seeking colorless essences
suggest the Lighthouse, which is described as being 'stark and
straight, glaring white and black' in the daytime.

The Lighthouse, then, in part symbolizes both Mr and Mrs
Ramsay. This interpretation is confirmed by a passage in part III

in which James contrasts his early impressions of the Lighthouse, which he recalls in thinking of his mother, with the Lighthouse he sees and likens to his father as they near it in the boat.

> The Lighthouse was then [in his childhood] a silvery, misty-looking tower with a yellow eye, that opened suddenly, and softly in the evening. Now –
> James looked at the Lighthouse. He could see the white-washed rocks; the tower, stark and straight. . . . So that was the Lighthouse, was it?
> No, the other was also the Lighthouse. For nothing was simply one thing. The other Lighthouse was true too. (pp. 276–7)

James's ability to reconcile his two views of the Lighthouse reminds us, however, that it symbolizes not only the individual traits of the Ramsays, but the harmonious union of their complementary qualities – courage with sympathy, intellect with intuition, endurance with fertility.

Such harmony, however, does not always exist. Both the younger Ramsays and their parents make clear the possibilities for discord in the inherent differences between the masculine and feminine natures. Clashes occur more frequently among the children because their need for the strength of the opposite sex is seldom great enough to overcome the antagonism aroused by their conflicting perspectives. The quarrel between James and Cam in the nursery exhibits those traits which occasionally mar the relationship of the adult Ramsays. James takes the same satisfaction in looking at the skull that his father takes in confronting delusion with fact. Cam, on the other hand, in refusing to look at the horned shadows cast by the skull, shrinks from a reminder of death and, perhaps, from her own female inheritance which will subject her to future attacks by beaked assailants. Showing her skill in eliminating discord, Mrs Ramsay satisfies both their natures by wrapping the skull in her green shawl – fact is still there but concealed by the fertility of life. Similarly, as the quarrel over the trip to the Lighthouse illustrates, strife does occur between Mrs Ramsay and her husband. But Mrs Ramsay's skill and their mutual need succeed in subduing such clashes of temperament, and their marriage is not harmed. Mr Ramsay's catchword, 'someone has blundered', suggests his sense of the human predicament rather than a judgement of his marriage. And the Grimm fairy tale of 'The Fisherman and His Wife', which Mrs Ramsay reads to James, does not accurately reflect her relationship with her husband; it hints at Mrs Ramsay's tendency to manage, a fault which occasionally contributes a discordant note to the marital song 'like the bass gently accompanying a tune which now and then ran up unexpectedly into the melody'.[5] Although both the Ramsays are sometimes egoistic, their significant characteristics are those admirable traits which we have suggested merge in the Lighthouse symbol.

A discussion of the androgynous nature of the Lighthouse symbol does not reveal its full meaning, for it is also associated with ideas about time, flux, death and egoism. Just as an actual Lighthouse functions to mark a fixed spot in moving waters, so the Lighthouse in this novel symbolizes fixed points or ways of creating fixed points in the flux of human life. In the previously quoted paragraph comparing Mr Ramsay to a stake 'marking the channel out there in the floods alone', Mrs Woolf suggests the plight of all individuals before the harassing flux of nature and relentless time. Mr Ramsay's confrontation of chaos represents the efforts of man's intelligence to control flux and to create at least a temporary order. Although occasionally 'petty, selfish, vain, egoistical', Mr Ramsay casts aside all traces of egoism during his vigil on the spit of land; 'even his own name was forgotten by him'. The object of Mr Ramsay's regard is not only flux but death itself, for he is constantly aware of man's mortality and refuses to accept comforting visions which ignore this terminus of flux 'where our frail barks founder in darkness'. This suggestion of the Lighthouse as death is reinforced by the frequent equating of Mr Ramsay to a knife blade and by the description of the loss of personality and the physical shrinking he undergoes when he is 'marking the channel'. Death as a mode of escape from egoism seems terrifying; but, as some of the following passages describing Mrs Ramsay reveal, the release from personality promised by death is occasionally felt to be desirable; death can be seen as a consummation as well as an extinction.

Considerably more of the Lighthouse imagery dealing with flux is found in passages describing Mrs Ramsay. For the most part, Mrs Ramsay finds life 'terrible, hostile, and quick to pounce upon you'. The sound of the waves reminds her that even her own day is 'as ephemeral as a rainbow' and makes her think of 'the destruction of the island and its engulfment in the sea'. In her battle with life Mrs Ramsay admits, however, that there have been great 'reconcilement scenes' when she seems to have triumphed over flux and time to enjoy a fleeting contact with eternity. The passage already quoted in which she identifies herself with the Lighthouse makes clear that such victories occur when she has relinquished her own egoistic concerns. This loss of personality seems to occur most often in three circumstances: when she is engaged in introspection, when she is with her husband, or when she is with a group of congenial people. For example, indulging in introspection before dinner, Mrs Ramsay thinks:

Not as oneself did one find rest ever, in her experience . . . but as a wedge of darkness. Losing personality, one lost the fret, the hurry, the stir; and there rose to her lips always some exclamation of triumph over life when things came together in this peace, this rest, this eternity; and pausing there she looked out to meet that stroke of the Lighthouse, the long steady stroke . . . which was her stroke. . . . (p. 96)

Watching the Lighthouse beam, she recalls the way in which it bends across their bed, stroking the floor, and she feels as if 'it were stroking with its silver fingers some sealed vessel in her brain whose bursting would flood her with delight'. She thinks then that she has 'known happiness, exquisite happiness, intense happiness'.

The imagery of this description is faintly sensual and connects this moment of impersonality with her love for her husband. The best illustration of the way in which their love contributes to a triumph over time is found in the last scene in part I when Mrs Ramsay finds herself inexplicably drawn to the room where her husband sits reading. Feeling a need for his voice, she is comforted by his asperity in rebuking her for trying to finish the stocking that night. Reassured, she in turn answers his need by artfully but indirectly assuring him of her love. Sensing the completeness of their rapport, Mrs Ramsay turns toward the Lighthouse which is shining outside the window and thinks to herself that 'nothing on earth can equal this happiness'.

A similar sense of release is felt by Mrs Ramsay during the final moments of the dinner party which begins so badly. At the outset Mrs Ramsay feels tired and dissatisfied with her life; she realizes that 'nothing seemed to have merged. They [the guests] all sat separate and the effort of merging and flowing and creating rested upon her.' Lifted from her own personal concerns by an interest in other people, she manages to make the dinner a success by uniting her guests and her family into a harmonious group. Her reward comes when, in a moment of peace, she thinks:

There is a coherence in things, a stability; something, she meant, is immune from change, and shines out (she glanced at the window with its ripple of reflected lights) in the face of the flowing, the fleeting, the spectral, like a ruby. . . . Of such moments, she thought, the thing is made that endures.

These added details, then, round out the meaning of the Lighthouse and enable us to define more exactly some of the central themes of part I. Symbolizing both Ramsays, the Lighthouse shows Mrs Woolf's belief in the existence of certain basic masculine and feminine traits which are valuable to the opposite sex and contribute to a harmonious union. At the same time, these androgynous traits enable individuals to deal with chaos and time. The method of dealing with chaos may be that of Mr Ramsay, who uses his intelligence to face the irrationality of external nature, or that of Mrs Ramsay, who uses her intuition to control the chaos of personality and society. The escape from time occurs as the result of a subordination of or release from egoism in various ways: in unselfish concentration upon one's work (reaching 'Z' for Mr Ramsay), in an identification with an inanimate object, in a mystical contemplation, or in a harmonious merging with another individual or group. Finally, among the escapes from time and self is death, which, while frightening, occasionally suggests a desirable release to the eternal flux or, as Mrs Ramsay's reveries imply, to a more stable eternity which defeats both time and change.

II

Part II is designed to reveal the force of time and flux upon man and his works and to emphasize the indifference of nature to man's fate. At the same time this section of the novel demonstrates the value, but limited power, of the best Ramsay traits, largely through showing what happens in a world devoid of these characteristics. In 'Time Passes' Mrs Ramsay's fear of the remorseless waves and her veneration of the masculine intellect for trying to control chaos are seen to be justified when flux in various forms (floods of darkness, curious winds, drenching rain) begins its assault. Within a few years Mrs Ramsay, Prue and Andrew are dead. Uninhabited for ten years, the Ramsay home in the Hebrides enjoys a brief period of loveliness and stillness, but this reign is broken by the noisy visits of Mrs McNab and soon by the unlovely deterioration of the house. The Lighthouse beam watches with equanimity the invasion of thistle, rat and swallow and protects the house no more effectively than does Mrs McNab's recollection of Mrs Ramsay in her grey cloak stooping over the flowers. The house verges on ruin before the forces of time because 'nothing now withstood them, nothing said no to them'. What eventually saves the house is neither reason nor intuition, but chance, perhaps abetted by feminine concern; a timely letter from the Ramsay girls again puts Mrs McNab in motion.

The indifference of the Lighthouse to the ravages of time upon the Ramsay household is shared by all nature. As the torn leaves and tumultuous seas show, nature itself is vulnerable to the assaults of time and flux, but nature is endowed with an insensible fertility which enables it to resist time and also to overpower the works of man. When confronted with the elements in their more beautiful phases, man ignores nature's encroachments; he longs to believe that parts of nature have been purposely assembled to reflect his inner vision and to prove that 'good triumphs, happiness prevails, order rules'. But Mrs Woolf makes clear that nature looks on man's misery, meanness and torture 'with equal complacency' and that his optimistic inferences reflect only his own hopes and beliefs. If harmony exists between man and nature, it is fleeting and achieved only when man tries to impose order on the chaos of the elements. Only after Mrs McNab and her aides have stayed 'the corruption and the rot' and rescued the house and its grounds from the 'pool of time' is there heard an 'intermittent half-harmony' between man and nature. And only with the restoration of the house does Mrs McNab have a vision of Mr Ramsay standing on the lawn.

The stress in part II is upon nature, but enough attention is given to people to emphasize the merit of the Ramsay values. Man himself is responsible for some of the destruction during this period, for his irrationality and egoism claim Andrew in war. Like the egoism that powered the hammer blows that Tansley would have let fall at the dinner party, 'the gunpowder' that is in man explodes into the furor of war. Like winds and waves, nations

disported themselves like the amorphous bulks of leviathans whose brows are pierced by no light of reason, and mounted one on top of another, and lunged and plunged in the darkness or the daylight (for night and day, month and year ran shapelessly together) in idiot games, until it seemed as if the universe were battling and tumbling, in brute confusion and wanton lust aimlessly by itself. (pp. 202–3)

Mrs McNab, the main character in part II, seems to be the embodiment of womankind at one remove from the insensible fertility of nature. She reveals the virtues of pertinacity and occasional humor, but her indifference to the world and her witlessness (her facial expression is an evasive leer which slides off even her own reflection in the mirror) make her the antithesis of the Ramsays. Like the old street-singer in *Mrs Dalloway* who 'rocks and creaks and moans in the eternal breeze', Mrs McNab lurches through life like a drifting ship. Content to float eternally on a sea of gossip and drink, she suggests the power of flux over human beings who lack Mr Ramsay's regard for fact and Mrs Ramsay's desire for moments of inner truth.

III

In 'The Lighthouse' Mrs Woolf's interest in human relationships and her emphasis upon the transience of life are combined with a concern for the problems of art and the artist. The action of this part is presented in two strands; one of these deals with the journey of Mr Ramsay, Cam and James to the Lighthouse, provides ideas about character and time, and contributes to an understanding of Lily's final vision. Presented in alternate chapters, the other sequence of events describes Lily's thoughts while she paints on the terrace. This action culminates in her vision, which draws together the major ideas in the novel.

The first strand of action begins when Mr Ramsay, showing that masculine ability to 'rule India', marshals his reluctant brigade – Cam and James – into the boat to make the journey cancelled ten years earlier. For Mr Ramsay the journey is a rite in memory of the dead, but some of the details indicate that it is also a voyage into the future, perhaps to death itself, one of the states symbolized by the Lighthouse. Mr Ramsay's frequent repetition of the catchword from Cowper ('we perished, each alone'), his final farewell to Lily and the boat's departure 'shrouded in profound silence' support this interpretation of the voyage. More important, however, than the conjectural aspects of the voyage as a journey into the future are the ideas presented about character, emotion and memory. In their appearance in part III, Cam and James reaffirm the existence of their basic feminine and masculine traits suggested in part I. For example, Cam, like her mother, is bewildered by facts – the points of the compass are as alien to her as was the square root of 1253 to Mrs Ramsay. En route to the Lighthouse Cam recalls her childhood feeling of safety in the library where her father and his friends read, and because of Mr Ramsay's presence in the boat, Cam feels free to imagine herself involved in all sorts of daring adventures. Like his father, James believes that 'life is difficult', and he senses that he and his father share a 'loneliness which was for both of them the truth about things'. The austere Lighthouse confirms 'some obscure feeling of his about his own character', and nearing it, James says half aloud and exactly like his father, 'we are driving before a gale – we must sink'.

The voyage to the Lighthouse illustrates the difficulty of judging others and the way in which each new set of sensations has the power to alter a judgement. Both Cam and James begin the day hating their father for his past tyranny and for forcing them to make the trip, but during the journey their opinions of him change, and they become reconciled to him – just as Lily does in her meditations on the shore. At sea, Mr Ramsay seems so much in his element that Cam comes to admire him for his bravery, 'his oddity and his passion', and finds the feeling of security he emits overpowering. James's hatred for his father has been gradually eroding with his increased awareness of their similarities; it is obliterated when his father, after making 'some mathematical calculation', praises his steering. The younger Ramsays' attitude towards their father is influenced by the pace of the boat: their hatred mounts at times when the wind is still, but when the boat begins to move through the water they both have 'a sense of escape and exaltation, what with the speed and the change'. The rush of water and the welter of sensation, like the passage of time, weaken the tie between Cam and James, and the force of their original hatred abates. Paradoxically, while this journey shows clearly the power of time and flux to weaken emotion, it also shows the power of emotion to transfix a moment of time in the memory. Mrs Ramsay's belief that 'children don't forget' is shown to be true for moments connected with some emotional experience. Daydreaming in the boat, Cam silently repeats the description of the imaginary land created by her mother in the nursery. James's memories make clear the power of hate to fasten an episode in the mind, for he succeeds in tracing his hatred of his father back to the early scene in the window.

The two strands of action in part III are arranged to parallel and contrast with each other in various ways. For example, they provide verbal echoes. On shore Lily thinks that there is 'no guide, no shelter, but all was miracle and leaping from the pinnacle of a tower into air'. A few pages later, Mr Ramsay's appearance in the bow of the boat prompts James to think of him saying 'there is no God' and simultaneously makes Cam think that he looks 'as if he were leaping into space'. The two lines of action provide ironic commentaries on each other: Cam's thoughts about the people on shore having no feelings bracket the descriptions of Lily's anguished longing for Mrs Ramsay. When Lily wonders about life: 'what did it mean, could things thrust their hands up and grasp one; could the blade cut, the fist grasp'; an answer is supplied on the same page by a description of Macalister's boy grasping a fish and cutting a square out of its side to bait his hook with. Both plot lines explore reality – one probing space, the other time. While Cam muses about the *receding* island, Lily thinks of Mrs Ramsay *receding* in time. The use of words such as 'recede' and 'distance' both in Cam's thoughts about space and in Lily's thoughts about time invites the reader to apply the individual reflections to both dimensions. Cam's ideas deny any essential reality to the distant in space (and, because of the ambiguity of language, to the distant in time as well). She reflects that the shore quickly takes on a 'composed look of something receding in which one has no longer any part' and that 'all those paths and the lawn, thick with the lives they had lived there, were gone; were rubbed out; were past; were unreal and now this was real, the boat and the sail. . . .' As they near the Lighthouse, Cam concludes that 'the sea [is] more important now than the shore'. The existence of Lily back on the shore refutes the validity of Cam's ideas about space, and Lily's own thoughts contain important ideas about the reality of time.

As Lily paints on the terrace and reminisces about her visits to the Ramsays, she has a series of revelations which involve Mrs Ramsay. Through these revelations the reader is reminded that the Ramsays serve as 'lighthouses' for other people as well as for each other. Lily finds herself, for example, able to recall very vividly a pleasant afternoon on the beach with Charles Tansley and Mrs Ramsay. Because of Mrs Ramsay's influence Lily's customary antagonism for Tansley had dissolved, and ten years later the memory of that afternoon exists complete in Lily's mind. Lily realizes that Mrs Ramsay has created order and permanence out of chaos just as Lily tries to create stability in art. In her earlier visit Lily exulted in the atmosphere the Ramsays created, 'that unreal but penetrating and exciting universe which is the world seen through the eyes of love'; now she comprehends as well the power of love to etch experience upon the mind. Lily thinks, 'Love had a thousand shapes. There might be lovers whose gift it was to choose out of the elements of things and place them together and so, giving them a wholeness not theirs in life, make of some scene, or meeting of people (all now gone and separate), one of those globed compacted things over which thought lingers, and love plays.'[6]

After arriving at this insight, Lily continues to paint and meditate until she has her final vision: she suddenly sees Mrs Ramsay seated in the window knitting. To discuss this vision requires consideration of three questions: why does Lily have a vision; what is its significance; and what is the meaning of the line Lily draws in the center of her painting? The first question can be answered by showing that Lily has become more like Mrs Ramsay (i.e. more feminine) in appreciating the value of intuition and in feeling sympathy for others. In part 1 Lily attempts to *understand* Mrs Ramsay: she sits at her knee, but those 'tablets bearing sacred inscriptions' which she imagines enshrined in Mrs Ramsay's heart remain hidden from Lily so that the desired intimacy is never forthcoming. Lily's realization of her fondness for intellect is shown by her thoughts about Mrs Ramsay's acts of charity.

She [Mrs Ramsay] never talked of it [an act of charity] – she went, punctually, directly. It was her instinct to go, an instinct like the swallows for the south . . . turning her infallibly to the human race, making her nest in its heart. And this, like all instincts, was a little distressing to people who did not share it; to Mr Carmichael perhaps, to herself certainly. Some notion was in both of them about the ineffectiveness of action, the supremacy of thought. (pp. 291–2)

In part III, however, Lily comes closer to adopting Mrs Ramsay's willingness 'to rest in silence, uncommunicative, to rest in the extreme obscurity of human relations'. Her change in attitude is shown by her acceptance of her intuitive relationship with Mr Carmichael and by the way she *senses* a change in him because of Andrew's death.

More noticeable in Lily is the change in her attitude toward men. With her little Chinese eyes, white puckered-up face and skimpy figure, Lily has never commanded a retinue of admirers as has Mrs Ramsay, whose beauty makes Mr Bankes think of the Greek Graces, barbarity tamed and chaos subdued. Because of her lack of sexual feeling and her inability to give sympathy and praise even when genuinely merited, Lily's relations with men are largely 'neutral': Mr Bankes admires her neat appearance and good sense. Lily resists Mrs Ramsay's constant attempts to make her marry because she enjoys being unmarried and has found a satisfactory purpose in art, even though she realizes that her paintings will probably lie unviewed in an attic somewhere. Therefore Lily has no feelings about the mutual social needs of the sexes; when faced with an unmanageable human situation, Lily turns to her painting, 'the one dependable thing in a world of strife'. At the dinner Lily feels no sympathy for the suffering ego of Tansley but speculates sceptically about the social interdependence of the sexes. She notices, however, that Mrs Ramsay 'pities men as if they lacked something – women never, as if they had something'. Almost at this moment Mrs Ramsay is briefly pitying Lily for the contrast she makes with Minta Doyle. The juxtaposition of these reflections points to Lily's dominant masculinity early in the book.

Ten years later Lily begins to change; 'the war had drawn the sting of her femininity. Poor devils, one thought, of both sexes.' At the beginning of part III, Lily still feels that every time Mr Ramsay approaches her in his hunger for sympathy, ruin and chaos come with him; she thinks of him as a man who takes and to whom she will be forced to give. But they are drawn together by their mutual admiration of his boots, and when he ties her shoe, she feels great sympathy for him. This feeling is intensified when she sees him apparently shed his ambition, his worries and his personality as he concentrates on leading the children to the Lighthouse. Several times during the morning Lily's burden of undischarged sympathy draws her to the cliff to seek Mr Ramsay's boat. During this time she comprehends more fully the nature of his longing when she herself cries out for Mrs Ramsay and discovers how 'anguish could reduce one to such a pitch of imbecility'. The clearest evidence of a change in Lily is seen in her reaction to her vision of Mrs Ramsay: 'And as if she had something she must share, yet could hardly leave her easel, so full her mind was of what she was thinking, of what she was seeing, Lily went past Mr Carmichael holding her brush to the edge of the lawn. Where was that boat now? And Mr Ramsay? She wanted him.' Lily's feeling about Mr Ramsay here is quite different from her earlier veneration of a man who writes books on 'subject and object and the nature of reality'; this passage suggests an urgency more like that which inexplicably draws Mrs Ramsay to her husband at the end of part I. Lily's reaction shows a considerable change in the woman who in part I wonders rather idly 'how would it be' if neither sex aided the other, and at the beginning of part III regards Mr Ramsay's approach as the onslaught of havoc. No doubt, then, Lily's increased femininity accounts for her seeing Mrs Ramsay, for this vision represents a glimpse of eternity which hitherto in the novel has been realized only by Mrs Ramsay's feminine intuition.

What is the significance of Lily's vision? To say that Lily's seeing Mrs Ramsay is merely a projection of the mind's eye, a natural consequence of Lily's thinking of and longing for Mrs Ramsay, would be to misrepresent the vision. Admittedly Mrs Ramsay had hoped to fix herself in the memories of those who succeeded her. As she ascends to the nursery after the dinner party, Mrs Ramsay thinks of its after-effect for her guests.

They would, she thought . . . however long they lived, come back to this night; this moon; this wind; this house; and to her too. It flattered her . . . to think how, wound about in their hearts, however long they lived she would be woven; and this [her mother's sofa], and this [her father's rocking chair], and this [a map of the Hebrides], she thought, going upstairs, laughing. . . . (p. 170)

Lily's earlier reveries in 'The Lighthouse' indicate how success-ful Mrs Ramsay has been. Mrs Ramsay has achieved a type of immortality and from the standpoint of philosophical realism has, in Lily's mind, an existence as palpable as that of any chair or table. But Lily's ultimate vision is something else. It is the result of her adopting an attitude which combines the perspectives of both Mr and Mrs Ramsay and makes reality simultaneously factual and miraculous, and it has the immediacy of a fresh sen-sory impression. Lily's vision is a momentary glimpse of an absolute eternity – 'a divine goodness had parted the curtain'. That the object of this vision should be Mrs Ramsay is appro-priate, for she herself was a creator of moments of eternity. The vision completes the parallel between the action in the boat and that on shore. The former sequence revealed the fallaciousness of Cam's belief that spatial reality was limited to the area compre-hended by her consciousness. Lily's vision makes clear that for Mrs Woolf reality also includes a temporal element ordinarily beyond the finite consciousness of the individual.

The significance of the line Lily draws on her canvas can best be shown by considering Mrs Woolf's ideas about the artist and by analyzing the role of Lily's art in the novel. Mrs Woolf's concept of the human mind and the creative act is found in a passage from *A Room of One's Own.*

In each of us two powers preside, one male, one female; and in the man's brain, the man predominates over the woman, and in the woman's brain, the woman predominates over the man. The normal and comfortable state of being is that when the two live in harmony together, spiritually co-operating. If one is a man, still the woman part of the brain must have an effect; and a woman also must have intercourse with the man in her. Coleridge perhaps meant this when he said that a great mind is androgynous. It is when this fusion takes place that the mind is fully fertilized and uses all its faculties.[7]

These statements suggest that the individual mind contains a fusion of sexual traits just as the Lighthouse represents the composite traits of Mr and Mrs Ramsay. The passage makes clear why as an artist, an aspiring creative mind, Lily is described with details suggestive of both the Ramsays. For example, just as Mr Ramsay respects facts, so Lily reveres colors and thinks it dishonest to 'tamper' with them. The description of Lily painting echoes that of Mr Ramsay during his vigil: 'giving up the fluidity of life for the concentration of painting', Lily seems at these times 'like an unborn soul, a soul reft of body, hesitating on some windy pinnacle and exposed without protection to all the blasts of doubt'. When beginning to paint, Lily thinks of the reality she is after as a 'formidable ancient enemy' in the same way that Mrs Ramsay thinks of life as a 'terrible, hostile' foe. As Mr and Mrs Ramsay occasionally discard their personalities, so Lily, when painting, loses 'consciousness of outer things, and her name and her personality and her appearance'. Mrs Woolf's belief in the androgynous fusion which produces the creative moment is suggested by the imagery used in describing Lily painting: 'the mass loomed before her; it protruded'; then, 'as if some juice necessary for the lubrication of her faculties were spontaneously squirted'; 'it [the brush] was now heavier and went slower, as if it had fallen in with some rhythm'; and 'her hand quivered with life'.

Throughout the book Lily's thoughts about painting have implications for the novel as a whole. Talking with Mr Bankes about her painting of Mrs Ramsay at the window, Lily analyzes the problem of composition in these terms: 'It was a question, she remembered, how to connect this mass on the right hand with that on the left. She might do it by bringing the line of the branch across so; or break the vacancy in the foreground by an object (James perhaps) so. But the danger was that by doing that the unity of the whole might be broken.' For the reader this discussion of unity applies not only to the painting but to the Ramsays (or the sexes) as well; they are the 'masses' to be connected by a 'branch' or James. The later scene of the Ramsays watching Prue play catch provides a tableau composed very much like the painting, and inspires Lily to envisage the grouping as an image of marriage; 'so that is marriage, Lily thought, a man and a woman looking at a girl throwing a ball'.

But the details of Lily's painting which have the greatest interest for the reader are her two solutions to this problem of composition. At the dinner in part I Lily determines that the solution is to put the tree in the middle of the picture. Since so much of the imagery in 'The Window' identifies Mrs Ramsay with trees, this solution seems to emphasize the role of the female; it reflects Lily's attitude before the 'sting of her femininity had been drawn'. This decision may be a satisfactory answer for the painting, but several of the details indicate ironically its inadequacy as a *modus vivendi*. Its shortcomings are implied by the imagery used in one of Lily's meditations on painting. Lily wants a picture 'feathery, evanescent, one color melting into another like the color of a butterfly's wing; but beneath the fabric must be clamped together with bolts of iron'; these 'bolts of iron' are reminiscent of the 'iron girders' of masculine intellect which Mrs Ramsay feels uphold the world. Furthermore, immediately after Lily has decided upon her solution, Charles Tansley is described as 'laying down his spoon precisely in the middle of the plate' and sitting 'precisely in the middle of the view'. This description stresses both the existence of the opposite sex, which Lily's solution ignores, and the type of egoistic considerations under-lying her decision.

Lily's final solution – the *line* down the middle – restores the balance. So many of the details identify Mr Ramsay with a blade or tower that this second solution seems to imply that Lily has come to accept the importance of the opposite sex or has come to realize both the feminine and masculine parts of her own personal-ity. These parts have fused in the creative moment and enabled her as an individual to have her vision of Mrs Ramsay and as an artist to complete her painting. The line down the middle of the painting is her tribute to Mr Ramsay so that 'whatever she had wanted to give him . . . she had given him at last'. Of course, the book implies that neither solution, the tree nor the blade, is ade-quate in itself. Both solutions, which incidentally follow the implications of the titles of parts I and III ('The Window' and 'The Lighthouse'), must be fused or set in a harmonious relation-ship to each other – just as Chinese paintings on long rolls of silk depend for their effect upon the harmonious relationship of each successive element with the preceding one.

In *To the Lighthouse,* then, Virginia Woolf has challenged the forces of time, space and change with ideas of human relationships and artistic perception. While chaotic time may pass and human beings be denied full comprehension of existence, Mrs Woolf suggests that intermittently the right focus composes life into the final vision – the glimpse of reality which is Lily's 'miserable rem-nant' made whole.

Source: *Bucknell Review*, x (May 1962).

NOTES

1. A brief analysis of some earlier interpretations of the Lighthouse as a symbol can be found in James Hafley, *The Glass Roof* (Berkeley and Los Angeles, 1954) pp. 79–80 (see this volume, pp. 135–6). See also William York Tindall, *The Literary Symbol* (Bloomington, 1955) pp. 156–63.

2. *A Room of One's Own* (New York, 1929) p. 162.

3. *To the Lighthouse* (New York, 1927). All subsequent references to the novel are to this Harcourt, Brace edition; any italics in quoted passages are ours.

4. The same kind of complexity seen in the Lighthouse symbol is found in the references to the waves. At one point Mrs Ramsay finds the sound of the waves comforting; at another they are reminders of time and death (pp. 27–8). A similar example of this ambiguity is found in part III when Lily contrasts the neat pattern of the waves seen from a distance with their foamy complexity for the swimmer (p. 235). In the novel water seems to have about it either an unpleasant suggestion of the chaos of nature and the relentlessness of time, or a pleasant connotation of immersion, of escape from a fixed egoistic world of personality into an impersonal external world or a harmonious social situation.

5. For a discussion of the novel which stresses Freudian details and regards Mrs Ramsay's personality as the destructive element in the Ramsay household, see Glenn Pedersen, 'Vision in *To the Lighthouse*', in *PMLA* LXXIII (Dec 1958) 585–600.

6. The imagery of this passage is clearly chosen to stress the way in which both love and art create lasting forms ('globed compacted things'). Mrs Woolf also shows several times in the novel that art creates a 'community of feeling' which draws people together. Lily and Mr Bankes, for example, are drawn together ('surrounded in a circle forever') when they contemplate her painting; and part of Mrs Ramsay's ease at the dinner comes from the pleasure she shares with Mr Carmichael as they contemplate the artful arrangement of fruit in a bowl on the table. Mrs Woolf's emphasis upon love and art follows the conclusions of G. E. Moore, one of the guiding spirits of the Bloomsbury Group, who argued that personal relationships and aesthetic apprehension are the two ultimate goods in human existence. An excellent discussion of Moore's influence upon the Bloomsbury Group can be found in J. K. Johnstone, *The Bloomsbury Group* (New York, 1954) pp. 20–45.

7. *A Room of One's Own*, pp. 170–1.

Morris Beja

MATCHES STRUCK IN THE DARK: VIRGINIA WOOLF'S MOMENTS OF VISION (1964)

The great revelation had never come. The great revelation perhaps never did come. Instead there were little daily miracles, illuminations, matches struck unexpectedly in the dark. . . .

To the Lighthouse

READING the published version of Virginia Woolf's diary, one is especially impressed by the many moments of vision she recorded throughout the volume. Sometimes these experiences seem to have had an unusually, even an abnormally powerful effect – at times they even seem to have had an almost mystical quality, as if there were some great revelation hovering nearby, ready to be grasped. Apparently, however, the great revelation never actually came, and in any case most of Mrs Woolf's moments of vision were, instead, little daily miracles, illuminations. But for all their trivial and everyday character, they are essential to a full understanding of her work. Like James Joyce, who believed 'that it was for the man of letters to record these epiphanies with extreme care, seeing that they themselves are the most delicate and evanescent of moments',[1] Mrs Woolf used her records of evanescent moments as the bases for works of art.

At one point in her diary she reflects on the possibility of writing 'a book of characters; the whole string being pulled out from some simple sentence, like Clara Pater's "Don't you find that Barker's pins have no points to them?"' [2] This particular 'simple sentence' was actually transformed into the subtitle and first words of one of Mrs Woolf's most interesting stories, 'Moments of Being: "Slater's Pins Have No Points"'. Julia Craye, an elderly, very genteel music teacher, opens the story by observing, when a pin drops to the floor, 'Slater's pins have no points – don't you always find that?'[3] Her pupil, Fanny Wilmot, is startled by the incongruity of this remark, so domestic as it is, coming from Miss Craye. During the few brief moments she spends searching for the pin, Fanny muses upon this comment, and the story consists of her reflections, which take the form of an imaginative re-creation of Miss Craye's past life. Fanny even dreams up a courtship, and how the young couple had gone out in a small boat, both of them aware that he was determined to propose. Nervous and reluctant, Miss Craye had rebuked him for careless rowing, and her words had produced 'a moment of horror, of disillusionment, of revelation, for both of them' (p. 105). He had gone away angry and without proposing, and she had remained free. Fanny's reverie is suddenly interrupted when she finds the pin: and now her feelings become really complicated, for when she looks up she sees not a lonely old woman, but one who is experiencing 'a moment of ecstasy'. This ecstasy in turn produces for Fanny another revelation: 'All seemed transparent, for a moment, to the gaze of Fanny Wilmot, as if looking through Miss Craye, she saw the very fountain of her being spurting its pure silver drops.' The story ends as Miss Craye, laughing this time, repeats her remark that 'Slater's pins have no points' (pp. 107–8).

Elsewhere in her diary, Mrs Woolf exclaims, 'How many little stories come into my head! For instance: Ethel Sands not looking at her letters. What this implies. One might write a book of short significant separate scenes. She did not open her letters' (p. 114). The 'book of short significant separate scenes' may remind one of a novel Mrs Woolf had already written, *Jacob's Room*, but the incident she remembers here apparently suggested the short story, 'The Lady in the Looking-Glass: A Reflection'. Like 'Moments of Being', this story consists of an imaginative association of ideas, in this case those of the narrator herself, whose thoughts, which dwell on the probable character and background of a woman named Isabella, are provoked by the objects reflected in a mirror in Isabella's home. We get a highly sentimental and romanticized picture of Isabella's profundity, and of the interesting and friendly letters she must receive – until her own reflection finally appears: 'At once the looking-glass began to pour over her a light that seemed to fix her; that seemed like some acid to bite off the unessential and superficial and to leave only the truth. It was an enthralling spectacle. . . . And there was nothing. Isabella was perfectly empty. She had no thoughts. She had no friends. She cared for nobody. As for her letters, they were all bills. Look, as she stood there, old and angular, veined and lined, with her high nose and her wrinkled neck, she did not even trouble to open them' (*Haunted House*, pp. 91–2).

I have compared these passages from Virginia Woolf's diary and fiction in order to give an indication of how, in her art, she made use of those actual experiences from her own life that she called moments of vision; she also gave similar experiences to many of the characters in her novels and stories who, as far as we can tell, had no biographical basis. In fact, despite her many experiments with widely differing fictional forms, the technical device of the moment of vision appears in all her work, from first to last. But although she mentioned and discussed such moments more frequently than Joyce and even Proust, in contrast to them she never evolved anything remotely like a theory to explain her experiences: to her, 'such moments of vision are of an unaccountable nature . . . try to explain them and they disappear; write them down and they die beneath the pen'.[4] But despite their evanescence, or because of it, to a large extent they determined the character and especially the structure of her novels, as one can see from even a cursory reading of such books as *Jacob's Room*, *Mrs Dalloway*, and *To the Lighthouse*. The attitude toward experience which underlies these and her other works is made explicit in *The Waves* – which she once thought of calling 'Moments of Being' – by the novelist Bernard, who distrusts 'neat designs of life that are drawn upon half-sheets of note-paper. . . . I begin to seek some design more in accordance with those moments of humiliation and triumph that come now and then undeniably.'[5]

In her first two novels, *The Voyage Out* and *Night and Day*, although moments of vision appear, they are not yet essential elements of either theme or structure. She was at this time experimenting with the epiphany technique in shorter forms, and in 1921 she put together in a volume called *Monday or Tuesday* a number of sketches that were not so much stories as prose poems, and which therefore enabled her to develop two of her main talents: her lyrical gift and her ability to 'make up situations' or 'instantly make up a scene' – which she contrasted with what she felt was her inability to construct plots (*Diary*, p. 116). Intense moments of illumination continue to appear in her later stories too, where they frequently involve the revelation to a character of his own loneliness, or to the reader of the essential isolation in which we all live. Besides the stories I have mentioned, such illuminations are important in 'An Unwritten Novel', 'Together and Apart', and 'A Summing Up'. But her main interest was not diverted to the short story, and in *Jacob's Room* she produced her first novel to make genuinely major use of epiphanies, which may even be said to be the basis for its structure. *Jacob's Room* consists of many brief sections, each describing a single scene or conversation, a fragment, a slice of Jacob's life, a corner of his room, usually as seen by someone other than Jacob himself; then Mrs Woolf immediately goes on to another fragment, another moment of vision, and in this way Jacob, through a vast series of such moments, is continually revealed to the other characters and to the reader. Obviously, it would have taken a miracle to prevent such an experiment from being choppy and almost incoherent; no miracle occurred. The sketches in *Monday or Tuesday* were not integrated at all, for each had been meant to stand by itself; again in *Jacob's Room,* unfortunately, the scenes are not sufficiently integrated as part of the whole work or related to each other, though now there is a unified subject and a unified (though not yet unifying) technique. *Jacob's Room* therefore stands in an intermediate position between her earlier sketches and the later, successful novels. Of these I shall examine two, *Mrs Dalloway* and *To the Lighthouse,* more closely than the rest.

The number of moments of vision in *Mrs Dalloway*, Virginia

Woolf's first truly major achievement, is amazing; almost every section (there are no chapters) has at least one, usually more. Everyone, like Peter Walsh, is 'a prey to revelations', and like him all the characters are fully conscious of this susceptibility and reflect upon it with an uncanny 'power of taking hold of experience, of turning it round, slowly, in the light'.[6] Septimus Warren Smith notes his 'revelations on the backs of envelopes' (p. 28), and his 'sudden thunderclaps of fear' (p. 96) that he has lost the power to feel are what have driven him mad. Less an actual 'prey' to them than Septimus, Elizabeth Dalloway calmly muses upon those moments when the most surprising and trivial objects have the power 'to stimulate what lay slumbrous, clumsy, and shy on the mind's sandy floor, to break surface, as a child suddenly stretches its arms; it was just that, perhaps, a sigh, a stretch of the arms, an impulse, a revelation, which has its effects for ever, and then down again it went to the sandy floor'. Elizabeth's thoughts are interrupted by her desire to know, 'what was the time? – where was a clock?' (p. 151). In the same way Septimus' revelation that beauty and truth are the same and are 'made out of ordinary things' is interrupted by Rezia's remark, for they have an appointment, that 'it is time'. In quiet desperation, Septimus persists:

The millions lamented; for ages they had sorrowed. He would turn round, he would tell them in a few moments, only a few moments more, of this relief, of this joy, of this astonishing revelation –
'The time, Septimus,' Rezia repeated. 'What is the time?' (pp. 77–8)

Septimus is forced to keep the revelation to himself, though eventually his vision seems to be shared with Mrs Dalloway, and to that extent his essential isolation overcome.

Clarissa Dalloway, of course, is the person most sensitive to what she calls her 'secret deposit of exquisite moments'. In the principal account of moments of vision in this novel, her hidden revelatory experience is cryptically yet unmistakably described as sexual; feeling 'like a nun who has left the world', she thinks of how she has never been able to dispel from her personality 'a virginity preserved through childbirth which clung to her like a sheet' and because of which she has sometimes failed her husband:

... yet she could not resist sometimes yielding to the charm of a woman, not a girl, of a woman confessing, as to her they often did, some scrape, some folly. And whether it was pity, or their beauty, or that she was older, or some accident – like a faint scent, or a violin next door (so strange is the power of sounds at certain moments), she did undoubtedly then feel what men felt. Only for a moment; but it was enough. It was a sudden revelation, a tinge like a blush which one tried to check and then, as it spread, one yielded to its expansion, and rushed to the farthest verge and there quivered and felt the world come closer, swollen with some astonishing significance, some pressure of rapture, which split its thin skin and gushed and poured with an extraordinary alleviation over the cracks and sores. Then, for that moment, she had seen an illumination; a match burning in a crocus; an inner meaning almost expressed. But the close withdrew; the hard softened. It was over – the moment. (pp. 33, 36)

In one sense, Clarissa's revelations of 'what men felt' correspond to an experience Virginia Woolf had herself undergone, and which she recorded in *A Room of One's Own*. She had seen a man and a woman get into a taxi and depart together, and the sight, 'ordinary enough' in itself, had an extraordinary effect on her imagination – so extraordinary, in fact, that she later used a very similar scene as the climax of *The Years*. As a result of this vision, Mrs Woolf sketched a view of the soul as a fusion between male and female elements in which one or the other sex predominates. When there is a complete balance, we have the utmost power, and this may be what Coleridge meant by saying that the great mind is 'androgynous'.[7] In *Mrs Dalloway*, however, there is a quality to Clarissa's experience that is not simply androgynous, but displays an actual if latent homosexuality. This fact becomes more evident when Clarissa goes on to recall the feeling she used to have many years ago for Sally Seton: 'Had not that, after all, been love?' (p. 37). At first Clarissa is unable to recapture her old emotion, but as she removes her hairpins she recalls how once, while doing her hair, she had felt a moment of ecstasy upon realizing that she and Sally were under the same roof. She then remembers another moment, 'the most exquisite moment of her whole life', when 'Sally stopped; picked a flower; kissed her on the lips. The whole world might have turned upside down! . . . the radiance burnt through, the revelation, the religious feeling!' This incident was innocently cut short by Peter, who was in love with Clarissa; but, fiercely indignant at his interruption, she imagined she could feel 'his hostility; his jealousy; his determination to break into their companionship. All this she saw as one sees a landscape in a flash of lightning. . . .' (pp. 40–1). In the end, however, it was not her love for Sally that separated Clarissa and Peter, but rather her new and greater love for Richard Dalloway (who, Clarissa tells Rachel in *The Voyage Out*, 'gave me all I wanted. He's man and woman as well').[8] For the rest of the novel the subject of Clarissa's latent homosexuality is dropped, and the main interest of this very significant passage finally lies in the Proustian way in which the past experience is revived.

Virginia Woolf realized how, in the 'perfect rag-bag of odds and ends' of which our memory is the seamstress, 'the most ordinary movement in the world . . . may agitate a thousand odd, disconnected fragments'.[9] Thus Clarissa, by performing such a commonplace act as doing her hair, experiences sensations similar to the ones she had felt many years before, and these sensations lead to a complete recapture of the past – significantly, a past which itself had contained a moment of revelation. It is not only the manner of recapture that is Proustian; so is the use to which the recapture is put, for it starts a flashback which provides us with some very important facts about Clarissa's life.

Flashbacks occur more frequently in *Mrs Dalloway* than in any of Virginia Woolf's other novels – as might be expected, since one of its major themes is the complexity of the relationship between the present and the past. Indeed, recollections of the past are so frequent that the action of the novel may be regarded as taking place on two different time levels: the present day in London and the summer at Bourton thirty years before. At the beginning of the novel Clarissa realizes that what she loves is 'life; London; this moment of June' (p. 6). However, she does not live entirely in the present moment, much as she may love it. Throughout the book we are shown her many memories, and in fact only a few pages later she thinks with pleasure of those moments when friends, from whom one may have been parted for years, 'came back in the middle of St James's Park on a fine morning' (p. 9). She does shortly say to herself that anyone could remember, and that 'what she loved was this, here, now, in front of her' (p. 11); but not everyone can remember as vividly as Clarissa Dalloway can. Nevertheless, her feelings about the value of the present moment are sincere; she has an unusual ability to live in both the memory of the past and the here and now. This characteristic is shared by Peter, who after a number of passages during which he recaptures scenes from the past – 'it was extraordinary how vividly it all came back to him' – can still say that life 'here, this instant, now ... was enough' (pp. 84, 88). Clarissa and Peter would both prefer to stress the present, but they are in middle age and worried about growing old, so their minds almost involuntarily turn to their youth. 'If you are young', Mrs Woolf writes elsewhere, 'the future lies upon the present, like a piece of glass, making it tremble and quiver. If you are old, the past lies upon the present, like a thick glass, making it waver, distorting it.'[10] In *Mrs Dalloway*, this remark is verified by the fact that most, though not all, of Clarissa's and Peter's moments of vision now recall the past, while the ones they had experienced when young – such as his 'sudden revelation' that she would someday marry the stranger, Dalloway (p. 68) – had anticipated the future, just as Elizabeth's do now. The exceptions are those of young Septimus, whose disturbed mind cannot forget the war.

Clarissa's fears of old age and her 'horror of death' cause her to develop a transcendental theory which allows her to believe that, once having had contact with people or things, we may survive after death in the memories of this or that person, or even haunt certain places – a notion that anticipates *To the Lighthouse*, and Mrs Ramsay's continuing presence after her death. Peter's sceptical refinements on this theory produce fanciful thoughts on immortality that seem based on what might be called moments of delayed revelation, or 'retrospective' epiphanies:

Looking back over that long friendship of almost thirty years her theory worked to this extent. Brief, broken, often painful as their actual meetings had been, what with his absences and interruptions . . . the effect of them on his life was immeasurable. There was a mystery about it. You were given a sharp, acute, uncomfortable grain – the actual meeting; horribly painful as often as not; yet in absence, in the most unlikely places, it would flower out, open, shed its scent, let you touch, taste, look about you, get the whole feel of it and understanding, after years of lying lost. Thus she had come to him; on board ship; in the Himalayas; suggested by the oddest things (so Sally Seton, generous, enthusiastic goose! thought of *him* when she saw blue hydrangeas). (pp. 168–9)

Such grasping at straws for some sort of survival results from Clarissa's and Peter's intense love of life, a love that is even shared by the suicide, Septimus, who immediately before he kills himself decides to 'wait till the very last moment. He did not want to die. Life was good' (p. 164).

And perhaps we are meant to feel that Septimus does achieve a strange, vicarious immortality through a union with other people. After his death, the ambulance rushing to the scene is heard by Peter, who experiences a moment 'in which things came together; this ambulance; and life and death' (p. 167). That evening, at one of her frequent parties – parties which she gives because 'what she liked was simply life' (p. 134) – Clarissa leaves her guests for a few minutes and goes into a little side room; looking out of the window she is surprised to see the old woman she had seen climbing upstairs earlier in the day, now going to bed and staring 'straight at her' (p. 204). The scene resembles a previous one: at the window just before Septimus had jumped, 'coming

down the staircase opposite an old man stopped and stared at
him' (p. 164). Clarissa cannot know of this similarity, of course,
but as she reflects that death is 'an attempt to communicate',
that there is 'an embrace in death' (p. 202), she sees the old woman
and remembers that someone has mentioned that a young man
has committed suicide:

There! the old lady had put out her light! the whole house was
dark now with this going on, she repeated, and the words came
to her, Fear no more the heat of the sun. She must go back to
them. But what an extraordinary night! She felt somehow very
like him – the young man who had killed himself. She felt glad
that he had done it; thrown it away while they went on living.
The clock was striking. The leaden circles dissolved in the air.
But she must go back. She must assemble. She must find Sally
and Peter. And she came in from the little room. (pp. 204–5)

Although Septimus is dead, the revelation to Clarissa of her
identity with him paradoxically emphasizes life and stills her
fears of death. As so often in Mrs Woolf's novels, the climax of
the book is an integrating epiphany that brings together many of
the important themes and characters; and here it serves the
specific purpose of revealing the triumph of life and the value of
love, of what Sally despairingly calls 'human relationships' (p.
211). As Clarissa deserts the vacant little room and comes into
the party among her friends, her symbolic force does not go
unnoticed:

'. . . What does the brain matter,' said Lady Rosseter, getting up,
'compared with the heart?'
    'I will come,' said Peter, but he sat on for a moment. What is
this terror? what is this ecstasy? he thought to himself. What is
it that fills me with extraordinary excitement?
    It is Clarissa, he said.
    For there she was. (p. 213)

The idea that the brain matters hardly at all compared with the
heart, illustrated here by the figure of Mrs Dalloway, appears

again in Virginia Woolf's next novel, *To the Lighthouse*, where it is illustrated by the figure of Mrs Ramsay. Mrs Ramsay is an instinctive woman who knows things 'without having learnt. Her simplicity fathomed what clever people falsified' (p. 49). Her husband, however, is one of the 'clever people', a distinguished philosopher with an acute intellect that was 'incapable of untruth; never tampered with a fact . . .' (p. 13). Consequently, in a novel in which, once more, everyone is 'a prey to revelations', Mr Ramsay is the major exception. His books are on 'subject and object and the nature of reality', but the irony of the novel is that he has attained less true understanding of his own field than his wife, for he has not yet realized that the brain does not matter compared with the heart.

Although I have no desire to turn *To the Lighthouse* into a treatise on epistemology, it seems to me that here, as in all her work, the strong implications of Mrs Woolf's presentation of the problem of 'subject and object and the nature of reality' are that one can only solve the problem if one grasps two fundamental truths: that when the true nature of reality is perceived, an intuitive union takes place between the subject and the object, that is, the person knowing and the thing being known; and that, because the nature of reality is largely a matter of subjective interpretation, objects are very complex, and nothing can be said to be simply one thing. Despite his intellect, or because of it, Mr Ramsay does not realize these two principles as fully as a number of the other characters in the novel, who are therefore temperamentally more capable than he of experiencing moments of being.

The notion of an intuitive union between subject and object certainly sounds reminiscent of Bergson, but if Mrs Woolf derived it from anyone it was probably from the philosophy of G. E. Moore or from his students, among whom were a number of figures in the Bloomsbury Group. She was especially influenced by Moore's concept of 'states of mind', as were Roger Fry and Clive Bell. And Charles Mauron, in an essay published by Leonard and Virginia Woolf at the Hogarth Press, adapted Fry's aesthetics to literary needs by directly linking the notion of

significant form, to use Bell's term, with Moore's 'states of mind'
– the synthesis that would naturally occur to the members of
Bloomsbury:

The simplest entities that literary art admits are states of mind, or
perhaps one ought to say moments of the spirit. They are what
we are at a given moment: the landscape that we contemplate, the
sentiment which agitates us, the wonderful rhythm of a respira-
tion, the movement of a palm tree. The external reality blends
with the interior, or rather there is only one reality. Those
divisions, useful enough for the life of action, into external
objects, sensation, and sentiment, are abolished.[11]

Such moments are frequently experienced by Mrs Ramsay, who
is, spiritually, the wisest character in *To the Lighthouse*: 'Often
she found herself sitting and looking, sitting and looking, with
her work in her hands until she became the thing she looked at –
that light for example.' 'That light' – the beam from the Lighthouse – exerts an unusual fascination upon her, and she feels
strangely united to it. 'It was odd, she thought, how if one was
alone, one leant to things, inanimate things; trees, streams, flowers;
felt they expressed one; felt they became one; felt they knew one, in
a sense were one; felt an irrational tenderness thus (she looked at
that long steady light) as for oneself' (pp. 100–1).

The second major concept one must grasp in order to understand the nature of reality – that objects are complex and are
actually many things – is also important in *Orlando*, where there
are so many metamorphoses it is hard to keep track of them; Orlando herself realizes that 'nothing is any longer one thing' (p.
305). As Mrs Woolf explains, 'when one has been in a state of
mind (as nurses call it)' – Orlando is pregnant – 'the thing one is
looking at becomes, not itself, but another thing, which is bigger
and much more important and yet remains the same thing. If
one looks at the Serpentine in this state of mind, the waves soon
become just as big as the waves on the Atlantic; the toy boats
become indistinguishable from ocean liners.' In fact, one realizes
that 'that's what it is – a toy boat on the Serpentine, it's ecstasy

– ecstasy' (pp. 286–8). In *To the Lighthouse*, this principle, like the first one, can be demonstrated in a passage centering on Mrs Ramsay; to her, the calm rhythm of the waves breaking upon the beach is usually a soothing comforting sound, a 'cradle song, murmured by nature' – yet at times this same sound produces a horrible fear of destruction and makes her 'look up with an impulse of terror' (p. 30).

However, the most important realization in the novel of this aspect of the apprehension of reality is not Mrs Ramsay's, but the one achieved by her son, who comes to it only after many years. James Ramsay, when we first meet him, is only just out of infancy and is looking forward with childish eagerness to the excitement of the next day's journey to the Lighthouse; but the weather is threatening, and the conflict between what Mr and Mrs Ramsay each represent is shown mainly through their different attitudes toward the chances of their being able to make the trip. Always rational and factual, Mr Ramsay thinks it best that the boy should be discouraged from believing that the weather will be good enough for the boat to go out: James hates him for this logic. Mrs Ramsay, trying to guard the boy from too much pain, can neither give up her own hopes nor completely dash her son's. In the end, Mr Ramsay of course turns out to be correct, yet we are clearly meant to feel that in some more basic way than that of fact it is he who is wrong and his wife right. Even he seems to sense this, so he apologetically approaches the seated Mrs Ramsay and, trying at the same time to humor James by tickling and prodding his bare legs, offers to check the Coastguards for the weather prediction, so they can be sure. But, realizing her husband's discomfort and loving him even more than their son, she yields and admits that of course he is right.

That evening, Mrs Ramsay looks sadly at James as he goes off to bed: 'she was certain that he was thinking, we are not going to the Lighthouse to-morrow; and she thought, he will remember that all his life' (p. 99). And he does, though for a long time it is forgotten and is only remembered ten years later when his father – whom he still resents – has to press him into making the long-postponed trip to the Lighthouse. In the boat James recalls

– very vaguely at first – what had happened on that day years before: 'He began to search among the infinite series of impressions which time had laid down, leaf upon leaf, fold upon fold softly, incessantly upon his brain; among scents, sounds; voices, harsh, hollow, sweet; and lights passing, and brooms tapping; and the wash and hush of the sea, how a man had marched up and down and stopped dead, upright, over them' (pp. 260–1). At last, as they approach the Lighthouse, James recaptures the past and then also realizes that nothing is simple, that the world and reality are much more complex than he has hitherto realized:

Something, he remembered, stayed and darkened over him; would not move . . .
'It will rain,' he remembered his father saying. 'You won't be able to go to the Lighthouse.'
The Lighthouse was then a silvery, misty-looking tower with a yellow eye that opened suddenly and softly in the evening. Now –
James looked at the Lighthouse. He could see the white-washed rocks; the tower, stark and straight; he could see that it was barred with black and white; he could see windows in it; he could even see washing spread on the rocks to dry. So that was the Lighthouse, was it?
No, the other was also the Lighthouse. For nothing was simply one thing. The other was the Lighthouse too. (pp. 285–6)

James is now ready for the revelation that his father must not be interpreted too simply either, that he is not 'simply one thing', a stern, unfeeling tyrant. But that revelation will take another epiphany.
In addition to Mrs Ramsay and James, Lily Briscoe also comes to understand the complex relationship between subject and object and the nature of reality: 'One wanted, she thought . . . to be on a level with ordinary experience, to feel simply that's a chair, that's a table, and yet at the same time, It's a miracle, it's an ecstasy' (pp. 309–10). Of the four major characters, consequently, that leaves only Mr Ramsay in the dark. Yet he is not a stupid man; nor is he completely unemotional – he certainly loves his

wife very much. Why, then, has he failed to learn? And why has
he had no sudden spiritual revelations? The answers to these
questions can, I think, be expressed in terms of James Joyce's
very useful theory of aesthetics. In Mr Ramsay's own terms, he
has managed to reach Q, but not R; in Joyce's, he has reached
the apprehension of *integritas* and *consonantia*, but he has yet to
perceive *claritas*. He has reached the level of 'ordinary experience', as Lily calls it: he feels 'simply that's a chair, that's a table'.
Having realized that an object 'is one integral thing, that it is *a*
thing', he has achieved the phase of perception called *integritas*;
he has also gone on to the next step, *consonantia*, which Joyce
appropriately associates with the 'analysis' of apprehension:
'The mind recognises that the object is in the strict sense of the
word, a *thing*, a definitely constituted entity' (*Stephen Hero*, p.
212). So far so good; but Mr Ramsay's over-rational mind
prevents him from going beyond analysis. At one point in the
novel his wife perceives his limitation: 'His understanding often
astonished her. But did he notice the flowers? No. Did he notice
the view? No. . . . He never looked at things' (pp. 111–12).
What she means is that he does not look at things the way she
does, the way Lily speaks of when she says that one wishes 'to
feel simply that's a chair, that's a table, and yet at the same time,
It's a miracle, it's an ecstasy'. That is, he cannot enter into the
object and experience its radiance, its *quidditas*, its whatness.
Claritas, the phase of apprehension that Joyce associates with
intuition and epiphany, is out of Mr Ramsay's reach. The reason
for this incapacity seems clear: he is too dependent upon his
intellect. It is only at the end of the novel, when he insists upon
performing his quite 'irrational' act of atonement, by going
to the Lighthouse at last, that he apparently experiences the
nature of reality.

The epiphany in which he does so is not his alone; it is shared
by James, Cam, Lily, and even Mr Carmichael. In this way all the
characters attain what Lily had wished for ten years before, when
she leaned on Mrs Ramsay's knee and thought that 'it was not
knowledge but unity that she desired, not inscriptions on tablets,
nothing that could be written in any language known to men, but

intimacy itself, which is knowledge . . .' (p. 83). We need 'only connect', another member of Bloomsbury has told us, and we shall be saved. And in *To the Lighthouse*, as in *Mrs Dalloway* but on a broader scale, Virginia Woolf's characters achieve a measure of union – and salvation – in a climactic moment of being: James and Cam connect with their father, while he unites with them but also with his dead wife, in whose memory he has come to the Lighthouse, and with Lily, who on shore not only connects with him but also with Mr Carmichael and above all with Mrs Ramsay. As the little boat reaches the island, Mr Ramsay unexpectedly praises James's steering, and instantly the boy and his sister drop all their antagonism:

They both wanted to say, Ask us anything and we will give it you. But he did not ask them anything. He sat and looked at the island and he might be thinking, We perished, each alone, or he might be thinking, I have reached it. I have found it, but he said nothing.
Then he put on his hat.
. . . He rose and stood in the bow of the boat, very straight and tall, for all the world, James thought, as if he were saying, 'There is no God', and Cam thought, as if he were leaping into space, and they both rose to follow him as he sprang, lightly like a young man, holding his parcel, on to the rock.

'He must have reached it,' said Lily Briscoe aloud, feeling suddenly completely tired out. . . . Ah, but she was relieved. Whatever she had wanted to give him, when he left her that morning, she had given him at last.
'He has landed,' she said aloud. 'It is finished.' Then, surging up, puffing slightly, old Mr Carmichael stood beside her, looking like an old pagan God, shaggy, with weeds in his hair and the trident (it was only a French novel) in his hand. He stood by her on the edge of the lawn, swaying a little in his bulk, and said, shading his eyes with his hand: 'They will have landed,' and she felt that she had been right. (pp. 318–19)

But, though this is the climactic epiphany, it is not the final one – the last is reserved for Lily alone. Mrs Woolf had been troubled

about how to end the novel, and she indicated her problem in the
Diary: 'I had meant to end with R. climbing on to the rock.
If so, what becomes of Lily and her picture? Should there be a
final page about her and Carmichael looking at the picture and
summing up R.'s character? In that case I lose the intensity of the
moment' (p. 99). She solved her problem through the unifying
epiphany which lets Lily and Carmichael share in 'the intensity of
the moment'; but she also increased that intensity by giving Lily
her own separate vision as well.

   Although she is by no means the main character, Lily Briscoe
has more moments of vision than any other figure in *To the Lighthouse*, even Mrs Ramsay, who serves as her source of inspiration
by 'making of the moment something permanent (as in another
sphere Lily herself tried to make of the moment something
permanent) – this was of the nature of a revelation' (p. 249).
Of course, the sphere in which Lily makes her attempt is the
same as Virginia Woolf's own: art. Lily is acutely aware of the
frustration of trying to translate moments of intensity into
worthwhile art, to capture in her painting 'the thing itself before
it has been made anything' (p. 297). She is a painter, but her
comments on the impossibility of recording the most evanescent
of moments are sometimes expressed in terms that seem more
appropriate to the man of letters. Thus, sensing on the morning
of the trip to the Lighthouse that all words seem to become
symbols that day, she feels that 'if only she could put them together . . . write them out in some sentence, then she would have
got at the truth of things'; but one cannot write the words out:
'The urgency of the moment always missed its mark. Words
fluttered sideways and struck the object inches too low' (pp. 228,
274). Lily's art actually uses not words but visual forms and
colors; that the difficulties remain, however, is shown by the fact
that it takes four separate moments of inspiration over a period
of many years for her to finish her picture. The first had occurred
before the action of the novel starts and is remembered as 'that
vision which she had seen clearly once and must now grope for
among hedges and houses and mothers and children – her picture' (p. 86). While visiting the Ramsays during the first part of

the book she is working on a view of their house, and at dinner in the evening she has her second inspiration: 'In a flash she saw her picture, and thought, Yes, I shall put the tree further in the middle; then I shall avoid that awkward space' (p. 132). The full significance of this moment is not revealed until much later, when we also learn that 'it had flashed upon her that she would move the tree to the middle, and need never marry anybody . . .' (p. 271). But before she can carry out her intention everyone leaves the Ramsays' summer home, Mrs Ramsay dies, Lily loses track of her picture, and ten years pass. Then Mr Ramsay unexpectedly re-opens the house and invites the guests of that summer to visit there again. Confronted with the same scene she had been paint- ing, Lily has her third moment of inspiration when she recalls her previous one. 'Suddenly she remembered. When she had sat there last ten years ago there had been a little sprig or leaf pattern on the table-cloth, which she had looked at in a moment of revelation. . . . She would paint that picture now' (p. 228). After some initial difficulty she works steadily all that morning, and by the moment Mr Ramsay lands at the Lighthouse her new painting is all but complete. She has paused while she seems to share with Mr Carmichael the same thoughts about Mr Ramsay and what he has done, when 'quickly, as if she were recalled by something over there', she turns to her canvas and takes up her brush. She then looks at the steps of the house, where she had earlier felt she could see an image of Mrs Ramsay, but: 'they were empty; she looked at her canvas; it was blurred. With a sudden intensity, as if she saw it clear for a second, she drew a line there, in the centre. It was done; it was finished. Yes, she thought, laying down her brush in extreme fatigue, I have had my vision' (pp. 319–20). With these words, which end the novel, it appears that Lily's hopes of capturing her fleeting inspiration and making of the moment something permanent are at last realized.

I have paid special attention to *Mrs Dalloway* and *To the Lighthouse* primarily because I believe they are Virginia Woolf's greatest novels, but they are also representative of her use of moments of vision in almost all her work after *Jacob's Room*. . . . Although in many ways each of her later novels experiments

with a new departure in fiction, each follows basically the same
pattern that she first used in *Mrs Dalloway*: we encounter many
epiphanies of varying importance throughout the novel and
then at the end we have a climactic moment of vision which
unifies and summarizes a number of the major themes and brings
together the separate threads of the story.

For example, the last words of *Orlando*, a novel largely concerned with the passage of time, tell of the heroine's ecstatic
realization, for the second time that day, that it is the present
moment, 'Thursday, the eleventh of October, Nineteen Hundred
and Twenty-eight' – which also happens to have been the date
on which the first edition of the book was published; as Mrs
Woolf remarks, it is no wonder that Orlando had turned pale
upon making the same discovery earlier in the day, 'for what
more terrifying revelation can there be than that it is the present
moment?' (pp. 329, 298). More serious in tone, *The Waves* has an
especially large number of moments of vision throughout the
novel, many of them almost semi-mystic in character. (Mrs
Woolf has often been called a 'mystic', and she herself occasionally uses the word 'mystical' to describe her feelings or her works
(see the *Diary*, pp. 105, 137). However, her characters seem to
have what might be called 'secular' mystical experiences, in which
a person feels the sensations but not the convictions of the mystic,
the moments themselves being far more important than what
they reveal. As Katharine says in *Night and Day*, it is 'the process
of discovering' that matters, 'not the discovery itself at all'.[12]
In *The Waves*, Bernard, while he is having his hair cut, suddenly
feels himself being annihilated and becoming part of the 'unfeeling universe', but then notices an expression in his hair-
dresser's face: 'It is thus that I am recalled. (For I am no mystic;
something always plucks at me – curiosity, envy, admiration,
interest in hairdressers and the like bring me to the surface)'
(p. 199). What most prevents both him and Mrs Woolf from
experiencing the great revelation is, paradoxically, what most
makes them susceptible to little daily miracles and illuminations:
their intense sensibility to the trivia of experience.) In his final
vision, Bernard senses in the world about him an 'eternal re-

newal', as of waves rising and falling, and then comes to a new awareness that 'death is the enemy', that it is against death that he must fling himself, 'unvanquished and unyielding' (p. 211). In contrast, *The Years* ends with a vision of tranquillity. During a party, Eleanor Pargiter looks out of a window and sees a young man and a girl get out of a taxi, and Eleanor is inexplicably moved when she sees them enter a home together; as she, like Mrs Dalloway, returns to the party, the sky above wears 'an air of extraordinary beauty, simplicity and peace'.[13]

Mrs Woolf's last novel is an exception to this pattern, for *Between the Acts* does not finish with a major, unifying revelation, although toward the end one does climax the outdoor production staged by Miss La Trobe; after having gone through the entire pageant of English history, the actors stop time at 'the present moment' and hold mirrors up to the people in the audience, who are thereby revealed to each other and to themselves; as the audience soon realizes, 'that was her little game! To show us up, as we are, here and now.'[14] Extended quotations from this pageant form the centre of interest in the novel, and just as the portrayal of Lily Briscoe had demonstrated Mrs Woolf's views about the origins of art, so the portrayal of Miss La Trobe indicates her views about its aims and functions. While the pageant is still in progress, Miss La Trobe tries to estimate how much effect it has so far produced: 'Hadn't she, for twenty-five minutes, made them see? A vision imparted was relief from agony . . . for one moment . . . one moment' (p. 117). Like most true artists perhaps, she finally decides that she has failed; but she is at least partially wrong, as we can see from the discomfort of the spectators when confronted with their image in the mirrors, and from the powerful and personal effect the pageant has upon Mrs Swithin. Whatever degree of success Miss La Trobe may have, however, her aim is clear: she wants, if only for a moment, to impart a vision to her audience. That this is also Mrs Woolf's aim is shown by the impressionism of her own literary and critical ideas. To her, the function of a novel has been performed if, when one has read it, 'one sees more intensely afterwards; the world seems bared of its covering and given an intenser life' (*A Room of One's Own*, p. 166). In every great novel there are certain passages which startle you 'into a flash of understanding'; together these passages make up the 'book itself', which is actually the 'emotion which you feel' (*Moment*, pp. 129–30). This affective view of artistic experience can also be found in Joseph Conrad, who states that his aim is to reveal to his readers 'all the truth of life' in 'a moment of vision'. So it is no wonder that Mrs Woolf greatly admired his work, or that she wrote in 1917 that Conrad's moments of vision are in fact 'the best things in his books'.[15]

For Virginia Woolf, too, believes that her task is to make us hear, to make us feel – that it is, before all, to make us *see*.

Source: *Critical Quarterly*, VI (Summer 1964).

NOTES

1. *Stephen Hero*, ed. Theodore Spencer, rev. John J. Slocum and Herbert Cahoon (New York, 1955) p. 211.

2. *A Writer's Diary*, ed. Leonard Woolf (1953) p. 99.

3. *A Haunted House and Other Short Stories* (1953) p. 101.

4. 'Moments of Vision', in *Times Literary Supplement*, no. 853 (23 May 1918) p. 243.

5. Unpublished MS of *The Waves* in the Berg Collection, New York Public Library, title-page; *The Waves* (1955) p. 169.

6. (1958) pp. 69, 88.

7. *A Room of One's Own* (1954) pp. 145–8.

8. (1957) p. 65.

9. *Orlando: a biography* (New York, 1928) p. 78.

10. 'The Moment: Summer's Night', in *The Moment and Other Essays* (1952) p. 9.

11. *The Nature of Beauty in Art and Literature*, trans. Roger Fry (1927) p. 74.

12. (1950) p. 138.

13. (New York, 1937) p. 435.

14. (1960) p. 217.

15. Joseph Conrad, Preface to *The Nigger of the Narcissus* (New York, 1933) p. xvi; Virginia Woolf, 'Lord Jim', in *Times Literary Supplement*, no. 810 (26 July 1917) p. 355.

Jean Guiguet

TO THE LIGHTHOUSE (1962)

ONE afternoon in Tavistock Square, even before *Mrs Dalloway* had reached the public, Virginia Woolf thought out her fifth novel, *To the Lighthouse.*[1] It came to her, as most frequently happened, quite unexpectedly, with sudden urgency, between essays and sketches[2] whose brevity proved both restful and stimulating after the long labour of *Mrs Dalloway*. On 14 May 1925, we find it mentioned for the first time in *A Writer's Diary*, with its principal characteristics:

This is going to be fairly short; to have father's character done complete in it; and mother's; and St Ives; and childhood; and all the usual things I try to put in – life, death, etc. But the centre is father's character, sitting in a boat, reciting We perished, each alone, while he crushes a dying mackerel.

Yet this was only a germ which must be allowed to develop, for she adds:

However, I must refrain. I must write a few little stories first and let the *Lighthouse* simmer, adding to it between tea and dinner till it is complete for writing out.[3]

Sketchy as this project is, it includes two points that are worth noting. On the one hand, the importance given to her characters as characters, if not in the traditional sense, at least in the sense implied in *Mrs Dalloway*; which leads one, from the start, to expect similarity of treatment with the book's predecessor.

On the other hand, the theme of loneliness in death: its importance is emphasized by its association with the central figure; resuming one of the obsessions that haunt *Mrs Dalloway*,[4] it promises an analogy of substance which combined with the analogy of form, will make this novel the natural sequel to the one she has just completed.

A month later, on 14 June, the broad lines of the novel are already laid down, somewhat too precisely perhaps for the author's liking,[5] since she dreads being confined within too narrow a framework which would not allow her latitude for the enrichments and excrescences which constitute the life of writing.[6] Between the superficial, bread-and-butter commitments of criticism consequent on the success of *The Common Reader*, the book takes shape in the depth of her mind,[7] surfacing indiscreetly at times to distract her from her writing.[8] The themes of death, solitude and memory intermingled, the sound of the sea in the background,[9] seem to steep these preliminary meditations in a very special colour, which impregnates the form in anticipation to such a point that Virginia Woolf realises the inadequacy of the word 'novel' and seeks another to describe her work: 'A new —— by Virginia Woolf. But what? Elegy?'[10] This sense of overflowing the limits of the genre is here explicitly expressed for the first time; it grew constantly more marked until the end of her career. By July, a fortnight before leaving for Rodmell, where she hoped to begin her book and complete it during her two months' stay, the project has ripened,[11] the division into three parts is settled: 'father and mother and child in the garden; the death; the sail to the Lighthouse'.[12] Among possible enrichments, those she already envisages are, first, a number of compressed character sketches, then the world of childhood.[13] Meanwhile, however, two problems preoccupy her. The first is the fear of lapsing into the sentimentality which the subject, compact of intimate memories, invites irresistibly. This apprehension is no doubt a highly personal one, the artist's reaction to the natural inclination of her sensibility – and also the origin of its antidote, her humour. But at the same time it is an echo of *Mrs Dalloway*, the discrimination between sensibility and sentimentality being one of the problems raised by the personality of Clarissa.[14]

For the moment she thinks of resorting to a classic remedy,

catharsis; and she considers getting rid of this dangerous propensity by giving vent to it freely in a story.[15] The second problem is a positive one: it concerns 'this impersonal thing, which I'm dared to do by my friends, the flight of time and the consequent break of unity in my design'.[16] This idea involves not only the second chapter – 'seven years passed' at the time, 'Time passes' in the final version – but the whole structure of the novel: it was the basic problem corresponding to that which she had solved for *Mrs Dalloway* by her discovery of the 'tunnelling process'. The interest she takes in it reveals her determination to experiment and improve: 'A new problem like that breaks fresh ground in one's mind; prevents the regular ruts.'[17]

However, once at Rodmell, an attack of depression not only renders her incapable of any steady work during the two months that were to have been devoted to *To the Lighthouse*, but confuses her ideas, undermines her powers of decision and raises doubts on the essential features of the book.[18] In point of fact, being deprived of her zest and energy, she realizes the danger of facile repetition: either a companion piece to *Mrs Dalloway*, a novel dominated by a single character, or else a 'far wider slower book' in which she would 'run the risk of falling into the flatness of *N. & D.* [*Night and Day*]'.[19]

A partial improvement in her health and a brilliant start towards the end of August were short-lived.[20] Not until February 1926[21] do we find her writing with ease and fluency, immersed, save for a brief period in the afternoons, in her novel, the whole of which is now present in her mind.[22] By 29 April she has finished the first part and started on the second,[23] her pace and enthusiasm no whit diminished by the abstract and unusual character of this section, which is completed on 25 May.[24] She expects to finish by the end of July. Difficulties arising over the last pages, time wasted on an essay about De Quincey,[25] and perhaps also too fine and too busy a summer,[26] postpone the completion date to 13 September.

Having completed this task with considerably less effort than *Jacob's Room* and *Mrs Dalloway*,[27] she expresses her usual feelings of 'relief and disappointment'.[28] However, the revision and retyping – three times over for certain passages – which took from 25 October 1926 to 14 January 1927,[29] left her fairly satisfied. She writes that 'it is easily the best of my books: fuller than J's R. [*Jacob's Room*] and less spasmodic, occupied with more interesting things than *Mrs D*. . . . It is freer and subtler, I think.'[30] A second reading, shortly before publication,[31] confirms this judgement, which is scarcely shaken by some friends' criticism[32] or the coolness of a review,[33] amply made up for by the book's success with the public and the enthusiasm of her own circle.[34]

The lighthouse that shines out at night, in the offing from the island where the Ramsays are spending their holidays with a group of friends, is the vanishing point, both material and symbolic, towards which all the lines of *To the Lighthouse* converge. James Ramsay, six years old, cutting out an old catalogue as he sits at the feet of his mother, who is knitting by the window, is going to the lighthouse tomorrow, thus realising his profoundest dream. He shall go if it's fine, Mrs Ramsay says. But it won't be fine, Mr Ramsay declares. The day draws to a close, a day like many other days, made up of nothing; the children play, Lily Briscoe paints, Carmichael dozes and dreams, Tansley argues with his master, Mr Ramsay, Mrs Ramsay knits and James cuts out his catalogue. The dinner gong summons them all to table to enjoy *bœuf en daube*; the children go to bed, the young people go off to the beach, Mr and Mrs Ramsay read. It will rain tomorrow. The evening is as empty and yet as full – and almost as long – as Clarissa Dalloway's day. Whereas the latter took its rhythm from the hours struck by Big Ben, here only the changing light in the garden marks the flow of time, and the unchanging noise of the waves holds the evening motionless. The characters, though their physical closeness creates a multiplicity of contacts, meanwhile withdraw each into his haunted solitude.

Then everybody comes indoors, the lights go out; and that night, that few hours' withdrawal, blends with the darkness and withdrawal of ten years' absence that flow over the empty house in twenty-five pages in which marriages, births and deaths are inscribed in parentheses. This is the second part which, after the personal reign of Duration, asserts the impersonal triumph of Time.

And as morning dawns after these two nights merged into one, corresponding to the evening that had flowed into them, James starts off for the lighthouse with his sister Cam and his father, while Lily Briscoe sets up her easel where it must have stood ten years earlier and completes her painting, realising her vision at the same moment as James realises his dream. In the intensity of this second moment, Duration has revived and triumphed over Time, triumphed even over death since Mrs Ramsay – who has died, in parentheses, under the reign of Time – haunts these pages with a presence that echoes the material permanence of the lighthouse.

When describing the birth and growth of this novel I pointed out those features in its conception which seemed to relate it to *Mrs Dalloway*. Even from the résumé given above, it is patent that this relationship has altered between the initial project and the final achievement. That Mrs Ramsay has usurped the place originally assigned to her husband is a point to which I shall return. What interests us here is rather the way in which the central character dominates the book. Behind the account of Mrs Ramsay's day we find no analysis of her feelings, no generalized interpretation of her attitudes; she is not the centre toward which all elements converge, as was the case with Mrs Dalloway, in order to define her and strengthen her autonomous personality in face of the conflicts that divide her and the contradictory impressions that she arouses around her. On the contrary, by a kind of centrifugal process, Mrs Ramsay radiates through the book, impregnating all the other characters.[35] And it is the relations that emanate from her personality, rather than the personality that emanates from these relations, that becomes the focus of interest in the book. This is an essential alteration of the initial project: in fact, Virginia Woolf has chosen the 'wider slower book', thus escaping from the ghost of Mrs Dalloway and from the danger of repetition. By this choice she has committed herself to the path that she envisaged at the same time, the attempt 'to split up emotions more completely'.[36] Freed from the requirements of cohesion involved in the working out of a single character, she finds herself closer to the 'purely psychological' conception of D. H. Lawrence.[37] The newness of this material, and the subtlety and richness in it, have saved it from the other danger she apprehended: the flatness of *Night and Day*.

On the other hand the obsession with solitude, originally associated with death, as in *Mrs Dalloway*, loses its tragic character. Mr Ramsay's 'We perished, each alone' retains under its declamatory exaggeration a grievous truth and the pain of defeat. But although the words become symbols, as the author is at pains to point out[38] – perhaps unnecessarily – they do not efface the memory of a different, triumphant solitude, that of Mrs Ramsay, the solitude and silence into which the human being withdraws in order to become 'a wedge-shaped core of darkness', piercing to the heart of things in peace and eternity.[39] This meditation of Mrs Ramsay's, when she is alone for a moment, the only time in the whole evening, seems to be the happiest peak to which Virginia Woolf's thought ever attained. It corresponds on the plane of sensibility and life to Lily Briscoe's vision,[40] which completes it on the plane of rational and aesthetic thought. This enables one to say that *To the Lighthouse*, deriving from *Mrs Dalloway*, not only continues it but replies to the questions it asked. Septimus died in solitude, and one guessed that Clarissa's sense of communion might be a victory over that solitude and that death – but one could only guess it. Clarissa answered the riddle that she asked by her mere presence, which was unexplained except by the words 'she was'. Mrs Ramsay is the explicit expression of such a presence. And at the same time the survival of that presence beyond death, the dramatic character of which is relegated to the domain of literature that obtrudes in Mr Ramsay's declamations, abolishes solitude and brings about the communion that Clarissa had only suggested. Without denying those two ineluctable truths, solitude and death, *To the Lighthouse* makes of them the two fundamental experiences through which the human being, aspiring towards a single truth, a single light, reaches these and fulfils himself.

This progress from one book to the next is the result neither of literary artifice nor of abstract speculation. We have seen that Virginia Woolf had really begun her novel in January 1926, and it is on 27 February of that year that she writes in her diary the important analysis of her 'moments of vision'. The essential thing that lies behind the appearances and the superficial individualities of Lily Briscoe and Mrs Ramsay is derived not from Julia Stephen or the painter Vanessa,[41] but from Virginia Woolf herself. Does this mean that this 'elegiac' book which inevitably drew its substance from memories – even at the risk of becoming 'sentimental' – slips into that 'self-centred dream' to which, at this period, the author was accused of succumbing?[42] The boundary between one's present self and one's past is so imprecise that they inevitably merge into one another. Moreover, these two complementary realities are not mutually exclusive; the first envelops and conceals the second. Virginia Woolf had to pass through the present moment in order to recover time past, without betraying either aspect of reality in her painting of it. Her sister's opinion is reliable evidence: 'Nessa enthusiastic – a sublime, almost upsetting spectacle. She says it is an amazing portrait of mother; a supreme portrait painter; has lived in it; found the rising of the dead almost painful.'[43]

Thus, in addition to whatever else it has become, the novel actually is that evocation of the past that it sought to be. The close involvement of the author's whole being with that past is further confirmed by the liberating function ascribed by Virginia Woolf to her book, when on the ninety-sixth anniversary of her father's birth she writes: 'I used to think of him and mother daily: but writing the *Lighthouse* laid them in my mind.'[44]

The Ambroses, the Hilberys,[45] Mrs Dalloway were too sketchy, too much mingled with foreign elements to free her from the burden of all that she inherited from father and mother; only the completion of their portraits could exhaust both the feeling that clung to them and the literary temptation that gave a parasitical life to their memories.

It remains to be asked why the respective positions of Mr and Mrs Ramsay have been inverted. *A Writer's Diary* says nothing about this alteration, which seems significant enough to justify some comment, even if the reasons adduced remain mere hypotheses.

Mr Ramsay, it must be admitted, is not a sympathetic character; his originality, his anxiety and loneliness, his need for admiration and sympathy do not suffice to redeem his intransigent positivism, his selfishness and brusquerie. No doubt it is of the unflattering side of her portrait that Virginia Woolf is thinking when she writes: 'People will say I am irreverent. . . .'[46] The picture of Leslie Stephen in her *Times* article of 1932[47] is certainly recognizable as Mr Ramsay, but in a gentler and more lovable form. If we compare these two portraits with the one that emerges from Annan's book[48] we realize that both are true. Their difference is that which separates an intimate relationship from a more impersonal acquaintance. Mr Ramsay is the father figure which had to be exorcised; it was his despotism in all its forms, over mind and heart, that had to be overthrown. And no doubt the domination he exercized over his entourage gave rise to the initial idea that he should dominate the book. But the element of antagonism between the author and her protagonist eclipsed their affinities, and would have condemned the book to a certain externality, acceptable perhaps for the short, swift book originally planned, but incompatible with the longer, slower book eventually chosen.

Of Virginia Woolf's relations with her mother we know little. Yet from the violence of the shock which the 13-year-old girl felt at her loss[49] we may conclude that between mother and daughter there were certain deep affinities which became fixed and idealized at the same time through this premature death. *To the Lighthouse*, being an elegy, could only have as its central figure a being wholly and unreservedly loved. Moreover, if Leslie Stephen could represent that rational quest of truth and that feeling of solitude which the author sought to express, only Julia Stephen could represent that unfailing intuition, that sensibility, that gift of sympathy which, for Virginia Woolf, are the supreme human qualities, those which give a person that intensely radiant power that illuminates our darkness like a lighthouse beam. Finally, in this novel which is above all an analysis of the relations that connect and mingle human beings beneath the words and gestures whose value as communication is so inadequate, a medium was needed who could scarcely be imagined save as a woman endowed with 'some secret sense, fine as air'.[50] No doubt Virginia Woolf would be the first to protest against the artificial element in the traditional opposition between men's and women's natures. Yet she usually respects their broad lines, and in *To the Lighthouse* she stresses the opposition and exploits it.[51] And one can even see in this exploitation a certain bias which reflects tendencies that were strongly marked in her: on the one hand, her feminism, in the broad sense of the word, which might be defined as a defiant belief in woman's superiority in the quest for truth and the almost occult knowledge of life: on the other hand, a kind of nostalgic yearning for a relation between women, opposed to love between man and woman. I have tried to define, with all the prudence necessitated by the lack of precise documents, Virginia Woolf's conception of love;[52] Ruth Gruber[53] has pointed out the interest she showed in Lesbianism, as witness the relations between Sally Seton and Clarissa Dalloway, Elizabeth and Miss Kilman, and the ambiguity of Orlando. While writing *Mrs Dalloway*, she drops a hint in her diary: 'Yesterday I had tea in Mary's room and saw the red lighted tugs go past and heard the swish of the river: Mary in black with lotus leaves round her neck. If one could be friendly with women, what a pleasure – the relationship so secret and private compared with relations with men. Why not write about it? Truthfully?'[54]

Without seeking to extract from this passage more than it contains, one cannot help being aware of the emotional burden it betrays and the uneasiness that emanates from it. No doubt it is merely something instantaneous, as fleeting as Sally's kiss on Clarissa's lips or Lily Briscoe's impulse of affection for Mrs Ramsay. No doubt, these lines only express aspiration and longing, but at the same time they admit concealment and tabu. In the summer of 1926, when *To the Lighthouse* was nearing completion, Virginia Woolf saw a great deal of Victoria Sackville-West,[55] as she did again the following summer, when the idea of *Orlando* occurred to her.[56] In January 1927 she went to Knole.[57]

And it was in September 1928, after the publication of *Orlando*, that the two friends went to France together, by themselves.[58] The biographical enigma posed by these facts, these allusions, these literary transpositions can only be answered . . . by Mrs Ramsay's reflection: 'Love had a thousand shapes.'[59] And this assertion, while it answers our enquiry, however inadequately, also replies to the doubt that flashed through Rachel twenty years earlier, when she thought about her feeling for Helen Ambrose, about Richard Dalloway's kiss, or about any other man she might meet later on: 'she could not possibly want only one human being'.[60] *Orlando* and *The Waves*, later, assert the same conviction, which moreover is complementary to those inter- mittences of the heart to which Virginia Woolf's psychology allotted so important a place.

The analysis of the married relation which Blackstone, for instance, tends to consider the chief focus of interest in *To the Lighthouse*,[61] is in fact only one particular case of the instability and complexity of our feelings. The paragraph in her Diary on 'The married relation',[62] written in the summer of 1926, sug- gests that by then, after fourteen years of marriage, Virginia Woolf had decided to take her bearings. However, if certain elements of personal experience have unquestionably been trans- posed into the novel, this has a significance that goes far beyond what it can tell us about the Ramsays or the Rayleys, and it is at least as plausible to take the Diary paragraph as a hybrid com- ment, scribbled in the margin of the book and of life, rather than as the sign of a dominant preoccupation underlying the book.

Since I propose to study the problem of Time and the ques- tion of structure elsewhere, I shall merely allude to the im- portance of these two points, which I have tried to bring out in my summary of *To the Lighthouse*. I shall only mention that the change of tone, of style, of movement in the second part caused the author some anxiety.[63] Perhaps Roger Fry's dis- approval[64] was partly responsible; unless it was her awareness of the audacity represented by this technical process and the inevitable hostility it would arouse among critics and readers. It is not surprising to find Arnold Bennett condemning this second

part.[65] There is no doubt that the virtuosity of these pages
emphasizes their strangeness. Yet they are neither irrelevant
ornament nor a purely technical device. Their aim is precisely
to set in the very centre of the book, in a significant fashion, the
essential, ambiguous protagonist: Time-Duration. Whereas
under the aspect of Duration it plays its role in the two other
sections, discreetly merged into the consciousness of the *dramatis
personae*, in this second part, under the aspect of Time, it achieves
its inhuman task as cosmic agent.

No doubt Virginia Woolf implicitly admits a heterogeneity,
the dangers of which she did not minimize: 'The lyric portions of
To the Lighthouse are collected in the 10-year lapse and don't
interfere with the text so much as usual.' But declaring in the
next sentence that the book fetched its circle pretty completely
this time,[66] she asserts thereby that its heterogeneity, far from
interrupting the line of the work, is an integral part of it. Without
contesting that the dual nature of the tone is evidence of a
duality in the author's personality, what has been called (by R.
Las Vergnas) her androgynousness, I should like to suggest that
To the Lighthouse, by its structure, its movement, as also by its
essential subject, attempts to resolve that duality, and that *The
Waves* only develops and carries to the limits of their potential
the resources of style and composition which are exploited here.

Such as it is, retaining enough traditional elements and characters and a semblance of a plot to satisfy the common reader, yet
brimming with inward life and with a lyricism which give it a
density characteristic of Virginia Woolf, *To the Lighthouse*, by
the synthesis which it achieves and the balance it maintains between contradictory tendencies, won the favour of the reading
public[67] and at the same time, if it did not gain unanimous
approval from the critics, was at least granted indulgence by
some who unhesitatingly condemn her other novels.[68]

SOURCE: *Virginia Woolf and Her Works* (1962; translated, by
Jean Stewart, 1965).

NOTES

1. Cf *A Writer's Diary* (London, 1953; New York, 1953) p. 106 (105): 'so I made up the *Lighthouse* one afternoon in the Square here'. In the notes the figures in parentheses refer to pages in American editions of the works. *A Writer's Diary* will be abbreviated as *AWD*.

2. Cf *AWD* p. 74 (73): Monday, 20 April (1925): 'I have now at least 6 stories welling up in me. . . .'

3. *AWD* pp. 76–7 (75).

4. Cf *Mrs Dalloway* (1950) p. 103 (140): 'Besides, now that he was quite alone, condemned, deserted, as those who are about to die are alone, there was a luxury in it, an isolation full of sublimity . . .', and p. 202 (280–1): 'Death was defiance. Death was an attempt to communicate, people feeling the impossibility of reaching the centre which, mystically, evaded them; closeness drew apart; rapture faded, one was alone. There was an embrace in death.'

5. Cf *AWD* p. 78 (77): '[I] have thought out, perhaps too clearly, *To the Lighthouse*.'

6. Cf *AWD* p. 80 (79): 'I think, though, that when I begin it I shall enrich it in all sorts of ways, thicken it; give it branches – roots which I do not perceive now.'

7. Cf *AWD* p. 80 (78): 'slipping tranquilly off into the deep water of my own thoughts navigating the underworld. . . .'

8. Cf *AWD* p. 80 (78): 'But while I try to write, I am making up *To the Lighthouse*.'

9. Cf *AWD* p. 80 (78): 'the sea is to be heard all through it'.

10. Cf *AWD* p. 80 (78).

11. Cf *AWD* p. 80 (79): 'having a superstitious wish to begin *To the Lighthouse* the first day at Monk's House. I now think I shall finish it in the two months there.'

12. *AWD* p. 80 (79).

13. Cf *AWD* p. 80 (79): 'It might contain all characters boiled down; and childhood. . . .'

14. Cf *Mrs D* p. 41 (53–4): 'She owed him words: "sentimental", "civilised"; they started up every day of her life as if he guarded her. A book was sentimental. . . . "Sentimental", perhaps she was to be thinking of the past.' And p. 210 (292): was 'Clarissa pure-hearted; that was it. Peter would think her sentimental. So she was.'

15. Cf *AWD* p. 80 (79): 'The word "sentimental" sticks in my gizzard (I'll write it out of me in a story . . .). But this theme may be sentimental. . . .' The anxiety was to persist until the book was in print, cf *AWD* pp. 100 (98), 101 (100), 107 (106).

16. *AWD* p. 80 (79).

17. *AWD* pp. 80–1 (79).

18. Cf *AWD* p. 81 (79–80): 'I am intolerably sleepy and annulled and so write here. I do want indeed to consider my next book, but I am inclined to wait for a clearer head. The thing is I vacillate between a single and intense character of father; and a far wider slower book. . . .'

19. Cf *AWD* p. 81 (80).

20. Cf *AWD* p. 82 (80): 'I have made a very quick and flourishing attack on *To the Lighthouse*. . . .'

21. Cf *AWD* p. 85 (84), 23 Feb: 'I am blown like an old flag by my novel.' She must actually have started in early January 1926, since, expecting to finish it by the end of July, she allows seven months: cf *AWD* p. 89 (88).

22. Cf *AWD* p. 85 (84): 'I live entirely in it, and come to the surface rather obscurely . . . Of course it is largely known to me. . . .'

23. Cf *AWD* p. 88 (87): 'Yesterday I finished the first part of *To the Lighthouse*, and today began the second.'

24. Cf *AWD* p. 89 (88): 'I have finished – sketchily I admit – the second part of *To the Lighthouse* – and may, then, have it all written over by the end of July.'

25. Cf *AWD* p. 100 (99): 'I am exacerbated by the fact that I spent four days last week hammering out de Quincey, which has been lying about since June. . . .'

26. Cf *AWD* p. 99 (97): 'For the rest, Charleston, Tilton, *To the Lighthouse*, Vita, expeditions . . . such an August not come my way for years; bicycling; no settled work done, but advantage taken of air for going to the river or over the downs.'

27. Cf *AWD* p. 85 (84): 'after that battle *Jacob's Room*, that agony – all agony but the end – *Mrs Dalloway*, I am now writing as fast and freely as I have written in the whole of my life. . . .' And p. 89 (88): 'Compare this dashing fluency with *Mrs Dalloway* (save the end).'

28. Cf *AWD* p. 100 (99).

29. Cf *AWD* p. 103 (102): 'Since October 25th I have been revising and retyping (some parts three times over) and no doubt I should work at it again; but I cannot.'

30. *AWD* p. 102 (101).

31. Cf *AWD* p. 104 (103), 12 Feb 1927: 'I have to read *To the Lighthouse* tomorrow and Monday, straight through in print . . .' and 21 March, p. 106 (105): 'Dear me, how lovely some parts of the *Lighthouse* are!' She compares her impressions on 1 May, p. 106 (105): 'I was disappointed when I read it through the first time. Later I liked it.'

32. Cf *AWD* p. 104 (103): 'Roger [Fry] it is clear did not like "Time Passes".'

33. Cf *AWD* pp. 106–7 (105): 'I write however in the shadow of the damp cloud of *The Times Lit. Sup.* review. . . .'

34. Cf *AWD* 11 May and 16 May 1927, p. 107 (106).

35. Cf Lodwick Hartley, 'Of Time and Mrs Woolf', in *Sewanee Review*, XLVII (1939) 235: 'Change of tack. Instead of showing how many lives influence one character, it deals with the influence of one character on several lives.'

36. Cf *AWD* p. 81 (80).

37. Cf D. H. Lawrence, Letter to Edward Garnett, 5 June 1914. Quoted by A. Huxley in *Stories, Essays and Poems* (1938) p. 342: 'You must not look in my novel for the old stable *ego* of the character. There is another *ego*, according to whose action the individual is unrecognisable, and passes through, as it were, allotropic states which it needs a deeper sense than any we've been used to exercise, to discover are states of the same single radically unchanged element (Like as diamond and coal are the same pure single element of carbon).'

38. Cf *To the L* pp. 227–8 (219): 'like everything else this strange morning the words became symbols, wrote themselves all over the grey-green walls'.

39. Cf *To the L* part I, section 11, pp. 99–104 (95–100), particularly p. 99 (95): 'To be silent; to be alone. All the being and the doing, expansive, glittering, vocal, evaporated; and one shrunk, with a sense of solemnity, to being oneself, a wedge-shaped core of darkness, something invisible to others.'

40. Cf *To the L* pp. 244–5 (235–6), 249 (240), 278–9 (269–70), 296–7 (288), 309–10 (299–300).

41. Leonard Woolf has suggested that the analysis of the painter's processes in Lily Briscoe is based on Vanessa Stephen, who married Clive Bell.

42. Cf *AWD* pp. 120–1 (118–19).

43. *AWD* p. 107 (106).

44. Cf *AWD* p. 138 (135).

45. In *The Voyage Out* and *Night and Day*.

46. *AWD* p. 106 (105).

47. 'Leslie Stephen' see pp. 50–5 of this volume.

48. Noel Annan, *Leslie Stephen* (London, 1951; Boston, 1952). See extracts, pp. 36–50, in this volume.

49. It was following the death of her mother that Virginia Woolf had her first nervous breakdown and tried to commit suicide. Cf Irma Rantavaara, *Virginia Woolf and Bloomsbury* (1953) p. 106.

50. *To the L* p. 303 (294).

51. Cf Mary Electa Kelsey, 'Virginia Woolf and the She-condition', in *Sewanee Review* (Oct–Dec 1931) esp. pp. 433 and 442.

52. [Editor's note.] Cf M. Guiguet's book from which the present essay is taken, *Virginia Woolf and Her Works*, pp. 66–70.

53. Ruth Gruber, *Virginia Woolf: a study* (Leipzig, 1935) p. 100. Quoted by Rantavaara, p. 148.

54. *AWD* pp. 68–9 (67).

55. Cf *AWD* p. 99 (97).

56. Cf *AWD* pp. 110 (108), 113–14 (112).

57. Cf *AWD* p. 103 (102), 23 Jan 1927.

58. Cf V. Sackville-West in *Horizon*, III (May 1941) 318–24, and *AWD* p. 133 (131): 'I went to Burgundy with Vita . . . on 26th September when I went to France.'

59. *To the L* p. 295 (286). The phrase occurs in Lily Briscoe's interior monologue and is both personal and reminiscent of Mrs Ramsay's words; it echoes Mrs Ramsay's thought, p. 162 (157): 'one of those unclassified affections of which there are so many'.

60. Cf *The Voyage Out* (1929) p. 370 (302).

61. Cf Bernard Blackstone, *Virginia Woolf: a commentary* (1949) pp. 100 and 113.

62. *AWD* p. 98 (96–7).

63. Cf *AWD* p. 107 (105): 'I am anxious about "Time Passes".'

64. Cf AWD p. 104 (103): 'Roger it is clear did not like "Time Passes".'

65. Cf A. Bennett in the *Evening Standard*, 23 June 1927: 'The middle part does not succeed. It is a short cut, but a short cut that does not get you anywhere. . . . I doubt the very difficult business of conveying the idea of the passage of a very considerable amount of time can be completed by means of a device . . . (it) has to be conveyed gradually without any direct insistence – in the manner of life itself.'

66. *AWD* p. 100 (98).

67. In 1951 eleven editions of *To the Lighthouse* as against seven of *Mrs Dalloway* and *Jacob's Room* and six of *The Voyage Out*.

68. Cf Conrad Aiken, 'The Novel as Work of Art', in *Dial*, LXXXIII (July 1927) (see pp. 76–80 of this volume); Orlo Williams, ['*To the Lighthouse*'], in *Monthly Criterion*, VI (July 1927) 74–8; D. M. Hoare, *Some Studies in the Modern Novel* (1938) p. 61; Robert Peel, 'Virginia Woolf', in *Criterion*, XIII (Oct 1933) 91; Martin Turnell, 'Virginia Woolf', in *Horizon*, VI (July 1942) 53–4. Among critics generally favourable to Virginia Woolf, E. M. Forster (*Virginia Woolf*, 1941, p. 14), David Daiches (*Virginia Woolf*, 1942, pp. 95–6 (pp. 102–3 of this volume); and I. Rantavaara (*Virginia Woolf and Bloomsbury*, 1953, p. 116) assert their preference for *To the Lighthouse*.

SELECT BIBLIOGRAPHY

See, also, the various books and essays discussed in the Introduction.

BOOKS

Joan Bennett, *Virginia Woolf: her art as a novelist,* rev. ed. (Cambridge University Press, 1964).
   Good, and conveniently short. Originally published 1945.

Bernard Blackstone, *Virginia Woolf: a commentary* (Hogarth, 1949; Harcourt, Brace, 1949).
   For comments on this valuable study, see the Introduction.

Bernard Blackstone, *Virginia Woolf* ('Writers and Their Work': no. 33), rev. ed. (Longmans, Green, 1956).
   A pamphlet.

David Daiches, *Virginia Woolf,* rev. ed. (New Directions, 1963).
   Originally published 1942, and very influential on subsequent studies of Virginia Woolf.

E. M. Forster, *Virginia Woolf* (Cambridge University Press, 1942; Harcourt, Brace, 1942).
   This brief volume gains added interest through Forster's own stature, as well as through his friendship with Virginia Woolf.

Jean Guiguet, *Virginia Woolf and Her Works,* trans. Jean Stewart (Hogarth, 1965; Harcourt, Brace, 1965).
   Originally published 1962 as *Virginia Woolf et son œuvre: l'art et la quête du réel.* The most exhaustive book on Virginia Woolf (and at times the most exhausting). Not to be ignored. Contains an extensive bibliography.

James Hafley, *The Glass Roof: Virginia Woolf as Novelist* (University of California Press, 1954).
   Stresses Virginia Woolf's alleged 'Bergsonism'.

B. J. Kirkpatrick, *A Bibliography of Virginia Woolf* (Rupert Hart-Davis, 1957; rev. ed. 1967).

A very useful list of the primary works.

A. D. Moody, *Virginia Woolf* (Oliver & Boyd, 1963; Grove, 1963).

A good, brief book, with a largely philosophical emphasis.

ESSAYS

M. C. Bradbrook, 'Notes on the Style of Mrs Woolf', in *Scrutiny*, I (May 1932) 33–8.

A seminal attack. See the comments in the Introduction.

Ruby Cohn, 'Art in *To the Lighthouse*', in *Modern Fiction Studies*, VIII (Summer 1962) 127–36.

An illuminating essay, especially interesting on the relationship between Mr Ramsay landing at the Lighthouse and Lily finishing her picture.

S. H. Derbyshire, 'An Analysis of Mrs Woolf's *To the Lighthouse*', in *College English*, III (Jan 1942) 353–60.

Valuable, although its symbolic reading of the novel seems a bit too pat and systematic.

William Empson, 'Virginia Woolf', in *Scrutinies Vol. II*, ed. Edgell Rickword (Wishart, 1931) pp. 203–16.

Begins by concentrating on particular passages from *To the Lighthouse*, to see what they reveal about Mrs Woolf's art.

Ralph Freedman, *The Lyrical Novel: studies in Herman Hesse, André Gide, and Virginia Woolf* (Princeton University Press, 1963) pp. 226–43.

Concentrates on the interplay between the images of the window and the Lighthouse, and what these motifs reveal about the marriage of Mr and Mrs Ramsay.

Shahnaz Hashmi, 'Indirect Style in *To the Lighthouse*', in *Indian Journal of English Studies*, II (1961) 112–20.

Virginia Woolf as an 'expressionist'.

Arnold Kettle, 'Mr Bennett and Mrs Woolf', in *An Introduction to the English Novel*, II *Henry James to the Present* (Hutchinson's University Library, 1953) pp. 100–10.

Basically, or ultimately, an attack – and at the same time a
defence of Bennett, Wells, and Galsworthy.

Keith M. May, 'The Symbol of "Painting" in Virginia Woolf's
   To the Lighthouse', in *Review of English Literature*, VIII
   (April 1967) 91–8.

John Hawley Roberts, ' "Vision and Design" in Virginia Woolf',
   In *PMLA* LXI (Sept 1946) 835–47.

On aesthetic problems and Mrs Woolf's relationship to the
aestheticians of Bloomsbury.

Philip Toynbee, 'Virginia Woolf: a study of three experimental
   novels', in *Horizon*, XIV (Nov 1946) 290–304.

A fine examination of Virginia Woolf's place in modern
British literature.

ADDENDA TO 1978 REPRINT

N. Nicolson and J. Trautmann (eds), *The Letters of Virginia
   Woolf*, to be published in six volumes (Hogarth Press;
   Harcourt Brace Jovanovich); vol. I, 1975; vol. II, 1976;
   vol. III, 1977.

A.O. Bell (ed.), *The Diary of Virginia Woolf*; in preparation
   (Hogarth Press; Harcourt Brace Jovanovich).

Q. Bell, *Virginia Woolf: A Biography* (1972: Hogarth Press;
   Harcourt Brace Jovanovich).

J. Lehmann, *Virginia Woolf and Her World* (1975: Thames
   and Hudson; Harcourt Brace Jovanovich).

J. Schulkind (ed.), *Moments of Being: Unpublished Autobiographical Writings* (1976: Sussex University Press;
   Harcourt Brace Jovanovich).

NOTES ON CONTRIBUTORS

CONRAD AIKEN (1889-1973), famous American poet and novelist. His poetry won the Pulitzer Prize (for *Selected Poems,* 1929), the National Book Award (for *Collected Poems,* 1953), and the Bollingen Prize (for *A Letter from Li Po, and Other Poems,* 1955).

NOËL GILROY ANNAN, Provost of University College, London. His *Leslie Stephen: his thought and character in relation to his time* (1952), from which our excerpts are taken, was awarded the James Tait Black Memorial Prize for 1951.

ERICH AUERBACH (1892–1957) left Nazi Germany and became a professor at the Turkish State University in Istanbul, where he wrote *Mimesis: Dargestellte Wirklichkeit in der abendländischen Literatur* (1946). Later became Sterling professor of romance philology at Yale University.

MORRIS BEJA, Professor of English at Ohio State University, and the author of *Epiphany in the Modern Novel* (1971), one chapter of which is a greatly expanded version of the essay in this volume. Editor of *Psychological Fiction* (1971), and of the Casebook on *James Joyce: 'Dubliners' and 'A Portrait of the Artist as a Young Man'* (1973).

JOSEPH BLOTNER, Professor of English at the University of Michigan, and author of *Faulkner: A Biography* (1974).

DAVID DAICHES, Professor of English, University of Sussex (1961–77), he previously taught at Cornell and Cambridge.

His studies of modern literature, include *The Novel and the Modern World* (1939; rev. 1960), *Poetry and the Modern World* (1940), and *The Present Age in British Literature* (1958).

NORMAN FRIEDMAN, Professor of English at Queens College, the City University of New York, and the author of *E. E. Cummings: the art of his poetry* (1960).

JEAN GUIGUET, Université de Nice. In addition to writing the book on Virginia Woolf from which the essay in this volume has been taken, M. Guiguet has also edited a volume of Mrs Woolf's essays on *Contemporary Writers* (1965).

JAMES HAFLEY, Professor of English at St John's University, Jamaica, New York.

SHARON KAEHELE and HOWARD GERMAN have collaborated on several articles in scholarly and literary journals.

F. W. MAITLAND (1850–1906), Leslie Stephen's friend. A prominent historian of the English legal system.

WILLIAM TROY (1903–61) was a lecturer at the New School for Research, New York, and a prominent critic. His *Selected Essays* have been edited by Stanley Edgar Hyman (1967).

LEONARD WOOLF (1880–1969) editor, publisher, author; married Virginia Stephen 1912. The author of a novel, *The Village in the Jungle* (1913), and many volumes on politics and government, including *Principia Politica: a study of communal psychology* (1953).

INDEX

Aiken, Conrad 17, 76–80, 168 n, 245 n
Annan, Noël 14, 36–50, 238
'Art of Biography, The' 14
Athena 132 n
Auerbach, Erich 23–4, 105–32, 168 n
Austen, Jane 66, 76, 77, 79; *Mansfield Park* 77; *Pride and Prejudice* 77

Bacchus 176
Balzac, Honoré de 116
BANKES, WILLIAM 15, 30, 98, 105, 107–8, 109, 110, 112, 113–17, 120–2, 146, 152–3, 160, 161, 172, 174, 176, 203, 207, 209 n
Beach, Joseph Warren 168 n
Beja, Morris 11–31, 210–30
Bell, Clive 63, 220–1, 244 n
Bell, Vanessa (*née* Stephen) 16, 63, 65, 237, 244 n
Benét, William R. 187 n
Bennett, Arnold 18, 64, 66–8, 85, 240, 245 n; *The Old Wives' Tale* 67
Bennett, Joan 23, 135, 168 n
Bergson, Henri 25, 85, 135, 137, 138, 148 n, 220
Between the Acts 229; Miss La Trobe 229; Mrs Swithin 229
Blackstone, Bernard 23, 168 n, 171, 187 n, 240, 245 n

Blotner, Joseph L. 22, 25, 28, 169–88
Bradbrook, F. W. 20
Bradbrook, M. C. 20, 64
Brewster, Dorothy 140, 148 n
Brill, A. A. 188 n
BRISCOE, LILY 13, 14, 21, 25, 30, 59, 60, 62, 75, 77, 79, 89, 90, 91, 94–102, 105, 109, 110, 112, 130, 134–5, 137, 141–5, 147, 148 n, 149–50, 152–4, 161–7, 172, 174–175, 180–3, 188 n, 189, 199, 200–8, 209 n, 223, 224–7, 229, 234–7, 239, 245 n
Brontë, Emily 27
Brooks, Van Wyck 39
Buck, Pearl 131
Bulfinch, Thomas 171
Burgum, Edwin B. 187 n
Burne-Jones, Sir Edward Coley 36
Burrell, Angus 140, 148 n

Cahoon, Herbert 230 n
Carlyle, Thomas 44
CARMICHAEL, MR 40, 59, 94, 95, 99, 141, 166, 172, 174, 203, 204, 209 n, 224–7, 234
Case, Janet 60
Cervantes, Miguel de 23
Chambers, R. L. 23, 148 n, 168 n
Chastaing, Maxime 24
Chekov, Anton, *see* Tchekov
Christ 171

Cicero 175, 187n

Coleridge, Samuel Taylor 206, 215

Common Reader, The 56, 60, 232

Conrad, Joseph 27, 67, 71, 230; *Lord Jim* 230n; *The Nigger of the Narcissus* 230n; *Youth* 71

Cowper, William 199

Cronos 173, 175

Daiches, David 22, 24, 90–104, 135, 148n, 167n, 245n

Dante 124; *The Divine Comedy* 124

Delattre, Floris 22, 24

Demeter 169, 172, 175–84, 187n, 188n

De Quincey, Thomas 233, 243n

Derbyshire, S. H. 167n

Dickens, Charles 116

Dionysus 175

Dostoevsky, Fyodor 28, 188n; *The Brothers Karamazov* 188n

DOYLE, MINTA 95, 134, 162, 163, 176, 204

Doyle, Nathan H. 188n

Duckworth, Herbert 37

Eliot, George 86

Eliot, T. S. 20; *The Waste Land* 20

Elton, Charles 191

Fielding, Henry 66

Fisher, H. A. L. 47

Flaubert, Gustave 28, 124, 129; *Bouvard et Pécuchet* 124; *Madame Bovary* 124

Ford, Boris 21n

Forster, E. M. 22, 27, 49, 56, 60, 145, 148n, 182, 188n, 225, 245n; *Howards End* 145, 225; *A Passage to India* 60, 182; *Virginia Woolf* 22, 148n, 245n;

Where Angels Fear to Tread 145

Frazer, Sir James George 170, 171, 180, 187n; *The Golden Bough* 171, 187n

Freud, Sigmund 28ff, 170, 184–186, 188n, 209n

Friedman, Norman 21, 25, 27

Fry, Roger 220, 230n, 240, 243n

Gaea 173

Galsworthy, John 18, 66–8

Garnett, Constance 188n

Garnett, Edward 244n

German, Howard 27, 189–209

Goethe, Johann Wolfgang von 116, 125; *Faust* 125

Graham, John 136

Grimm, Jacob Ludwig Carl and Wilhelm Carl 194; 'The Fisherman and His Wife' 158–9, 177–8, 194

Gruber, Ruth 22, 239, 245n

Guiguet, Jean 17n, 27, 231–45

Hades 172, 178–81

Hafley, James 21, 25, 133–48, 208n

Hamilton, Edith 179, 187n

Hamsun, Knut 124

Hardy, Thomas 48, 49, 55, 67, 71; *The Mayor of Casterbridge* 71; 'The Schreckhorn (With Thoughts of Leslie Stephen)' 49, 55

Hartley, Lodwick 244n

Haunted House and Other Short Stories, A 210–12

Heine, Heinrich 81

Henley, William Ernest 47

Hermes 179

Hoare, Dorothy M. 167n, 245n

Hoffman, Charles G. 168n

Holroyd, Michael 16n, 18

Holtby, Winifred 12, 22, 168n

Homer 23, 120–2, 131–2 n, 169;
   The Odyssey 120–2, 131–2 n
Hudson, W. H. 67; *Far Away and
   Long Ago* 67; *Green Mansions*
   67; *The Purple Land* 67
Hughes, Thomas 36
Hull, R. F. C. 187 n
Hunt, Holman 37
Huxley, Aldous 28, 244 n
Huysmans, Joris-Karl 117; *A
   rebours* 117
Hyman, Stanley Edgar 17 n

Isherwood, Christopher 28

Jacob's Room 15, 59, 61, 62, 63, 76,
   78, 142, 147, 211, 212, 213, 227,
   233–4, 243 n, 245 n; Betty Flan-
   ders 142; Jacob Flanders 142
James, Henry 75, 86, 87
Jeremiah 81
Jocasta 184
Johnstone, J. K. 24, 209 n
Jowett, Benjamin 46
Joyce, James 16, 20, 27, 28, 70–1,
   76, 78, 119, 124, 129, 135, 210,
   212, 224; *Finnegans Wake* 135;
   *A Portrait of the Artist as a
   Young Man* 70–1; *Stephen
   Hero* 210, 224, 230 n; *Ulysses*
   16, 20, 70, 78, 124, 129
Jung, Carl Gustav 170, 177, 183,
   186, 187 n, 188 n

Kaehele, Sharon 27, 189–209
Keller, Gottfried 116
Kelsey, Mary Electa 244 n
Kerényi, C. 176, 187 n, 188 n
Keynes, John Maynard 59
Kohler, Dayton 167 n
Kore 169, 170, 176–7, 181–3,
   188 n
Koteliansky, A. B. 147 n
Kronenberger, Louis 16

'Lady in the Looking-Glass: A
   Reflection, The' 211–12; Isa-
   bella, 211–12
Las Vergnas, R. 241
Lawrence, D. H. 27, 236, 244 n
Leavis, F. R. 11–12, 17, 19–20
Leavis, Q. D. 20, 136–7, 148 n
'Leslie Stephen' 50–5, 238
Letters 13
Lighthouse 21–2, 29, 95–7, 135–6,
   149, 154–6, 164–5, 186–7, 189–
   197, 199, 200, 208 n, 209 n, 221,
   223, 234
Lockridge, Ross 168 n
'Lord Jim' 230 n
Lowell, James Russell 39–40, 55

MACALISTER 104, 161, 201
MacCarthy, Desmond 47
MCNAB, MRS 104 n, 141, 153, 182,
   197–9
Maeterlinck, Maurice 100; *Interior*
   100
Maitland, Frederic William 14,
   35–6, 47, 148 n
Manchester, Edward W. 168 n
Mann, Thomas 124; *Budden-
   brooks* 124
Mansfield, Katherine 78, 79
MARIE 106–7, 111, 114, 115, 117,
   119, 123
Mauron, Charles 220–1
Meredith, George 13, 40, 47, 55,
   73, 116; *The Egoist* 13, 40
Mérimée, Prosper 131
Milton, John 51
'Modern Fiction' 15, 66–73
Moment and Other Essays, The 230
'Moment: Summer's Night, The'
   230 n
'Moments of Being: "Slater's Pins
   Have No Points" ' 210–11;
   Julia Craye 210–11; Fanny
   Wilmot 211

'Moments of Vision' 212, 230n
Monday or Tuesday 213
Monroe, N. Elizabeth 168n
Moody, A. D. 17n, 18–19, 26
Moore, G. E. 209n, 220–1
Morrell, Lady Ottoline 63
'Mr Bennett and Mrs Brown' 78, 85
Mrs Dalloway 15, 16, 17, 22–3, 27, 56, 58, 59, 60, 61, 62, 63, 73, 76, 78, 87, 89, 90, 93, 101, 103, 133–4, 136, 145, 147, 199, 212, 213–19, 225, 227, 228, 231–7, 239, 242n, 243n, 245n; Clarissa Dalloway 16, 77, 87, 89, 101, 136, 145, 214–19, 229, 232, 234–7, 239, 242n; Elizabeth Dalloway 214, 217, 239; Richard Dalloway 216, 217, 240; Miss Kilman 239; Sally Seton 216, 218, 219, 239; Lucrezia Smith 214; Septimus Warren Smith 101, 214, 217, 218–19, 236; Peter Walsh 87, 214, 216–19, 242n
Muir, Edwin 60, 168n

Neptune 176
'New Biography, The' 14
Newbolt, Sir Henry John 48
Newton, Deborah 167n
Night and Day 42, 57, 212, 228, 233, 236, 237, 244n; Katharine Hilbery 228; Mrs Hilbery 42, 237

Oedipus 169, 170, 184, 186
On Being Ill 163, 168n
'On Not Knowing Greek' 170
Orlando 24, 63, 178, 216, 221–2, 288, 230n, 239–40
Ouranos 173
Overcarsh, F. L. 25, 135–6, 167n, 187n

Pater, Clara 59, 210
PAUNCEFORTE 141, 148n
Pedersen, Glenn 26, 28n, 209n
Peel, Robert 19, 245n
Persephone 169, 172, 178–80, 183–4, 186, 187n
Pinkerton, Percy E. 188n
Pippett, Aileen 12
Pound, Ezra 20; *Hugh Selwyn Mauberley* 20
Prinsep, Thoby 36
Proust, Marcel 64, 85, 86, 118, 124–5, 141, 145, 212, 216; *Albertine disparue* 148n; *Sodome et Gomorrhe* 145

Rabelais, François 23
Racine, Jean 125; *Phédre* 125
RAMSAY, ANDREW 13, 90, 105, 106, 110, 111, 141, 149, 182, 197, 198, 203
RAMSAY, CAM 30, 40, 134–5, 141, 144, 149, 165, 166, 182, 183, 185–7, 193, 199–202, 205, 224–5, 235
RAMSAY, JAMES 21, 25, 29, 40, 74, 91–2, 97, 100, 102, 105–13, 115, 117, 119–20, 134–5, 141, 144, 149, 153–4, 157–8, 164–7, 173–4, 178, 183, 184–7, 190–1, 193–4, 199–201, 207, 222–5, 234–5
RAMSAY, JASPER 106
RAMSAY, MR 12ff, 21, 25, 26, 27, 28ff, 40ff, 59, 65, 74, 75, 90–102, 104n, 105, 108, 109, 111, 134–44, 148n, 149–50, 152–5, 159–62, 164–7, 172–5, 177–8, 182, 183–7, 189–201, 204, 205–8, 220, 222–7, 234–40
RAMSAY, MRS 12, 13, 25, 26, 28ff, 42, 74, 75, 77, 79, 80, 88, 89, 90–102, 105–23, 129–30, 134–146, 148n, 151–5, 157–60, 162–163, 169, 171–87, 188n, 189–208,

209 n, 218, 220, 221–7, 234–7,
239–40, 245 n
RAMSAY, NANCY   11, 151
RAMSAY, PRUE   90, 141, 181, 182,
188 n, 197, 207
RAMSAY, ROSE   106
Rantavaara, Irma   24, 28 n, 29,
244 n, 245 n
RAYLEY, PAUL   95, 134, 162, 163,
176, 240
Rhea   169, 172, 175, 179–81
Richardson, Dorothy   76, 78;
Pilgrimage   78
Ritchie, Anne Isabella   40, 51
Roberts, John Hawley   23, 167 n,
168 n, 171, 187 n
Romains, Jules   76, 78;   The
Death of a Nobody   78
Room of One's Own, A   169, 189,
206, 209 n, 215, 229–30
Russell, H. K.   135, 148 n, 168 n

Sackville-West, Victoria   59, 63,
239, 243 n, 245 n
Sands, Ethel   211
Sanna, Vittoria   24
Savage, D. S.   167 n
Schaefer, Josephine   26, 28 n
Schiller, Friedrich   188 n
Schubert, Franz Peter   81
Scott, Sir Walter   48, 153, 159;
Marmion   48
Shakespeare, William   125, 139,
159;   Hamlet   125;   Sonnet
(No. 98)   159
Shaw, George Bernard   48;   Can-
dida   48
Slocum, John J.   230 n
Sophocles   184
SORLEY   107
Spencer, Theodore   230 n
Stendhal   23, 56
Stephen, Adrian   43
Stephen, Fitzjames   48, 53

Stephen, Julia (née Jackson, later
Duckworth)   12, 13, 35–8, 41–2,
55, 63, 64–5, 148 n, 237–8, 244 n
Stephen, Karin   148 n
Stephen, Sir Leslie   12 ff, 35–55,
63, 64–5, 80, 136–7, 148 n, 237–8,
243 n
Stephen, Minny   36, 41
Sterne, Laurence   27, 71, 73;
Tristram Shandy   71
Strachey, James   13 n
Strachey, Lytton   13, 16, 18, 137
'Summing Up, A'   213
Swift, Jonathan   56, 57

TANSLEY, CHARLES   21, 28, 95,
100–1, 109, 139, 152–3, 172, 174,
191, 198, 202, 203, 207, 234
Tchekov, Anton   72, 79;   'Gusev'
72
Thackeray, William Makepeace
71;   Pendennis   71
Thakur, N. C.   13 n, 26
Three Guineas   169
Times Literary Supplement   review
of   To the Lighthouse   16, 62,
73–6, 244 n
Tindall, William York   11, 28 n,
168 n, 208 n
'Together and Apart'   213
Tolstoi, Count Leo   133, 147 n
Toynbee, Philip   23, 27–8
Trevelyan, R. C.   57
Troy, William   17, 18, 19, 22, 85–9,
168 n
Turgenev, Ivan   46;   Bazarov   46
Turnell, Martin   245 n

'Unwritten Novel, An'   213

Victoria, Queen   48, 53, 174
Voyage Out, The   42, 87, 134, 212,
216, 237, 240, 244 n, 245 n;
Helen Ambrose   42, 237, 240;

Ridley Ambrose 237; Terence
Hewet 136; Rachel Vinrace
216, 240

Watts, George Frederic 36, 48
Waves, The 17, 24, 64, 86–7, 212,
228–9, 230 n, 240, 241; Bernard
86–7, 212, 228–9; Neville 87;
Percival 87
Welby, T. Earle 16
Wells, H. G. 18, 64, 66–8, 85
West, Rebecca 86
Williams, Orlo 245 n
Wilson, James Southall 168 n
Woolf, Leonard 12, 13 n, 15, 16,
27, 28 n, 61–2, 65, 187 n, 220,
230 n, 244 n

Woolner, Thomas 37
Wordsworth, William 51
Writer's Diary, A 12, 15, 20 n, 21,
24, 56–65, 148 n, 170, 172–3, 177,
181, 187 n, 210–13, 226, 228,
230 n, 231–4, 237, 239–40, 242–
245 n

Years, The 80, 215, 229; Eleanor
Pargiter 229
Yeats, William Butler 11, 22;
'Sailing to Byzantium' 11, 22

Zeus 169, 171, 173, 175, 179
Zola, Émile 117